TIME CAPSULE/1944

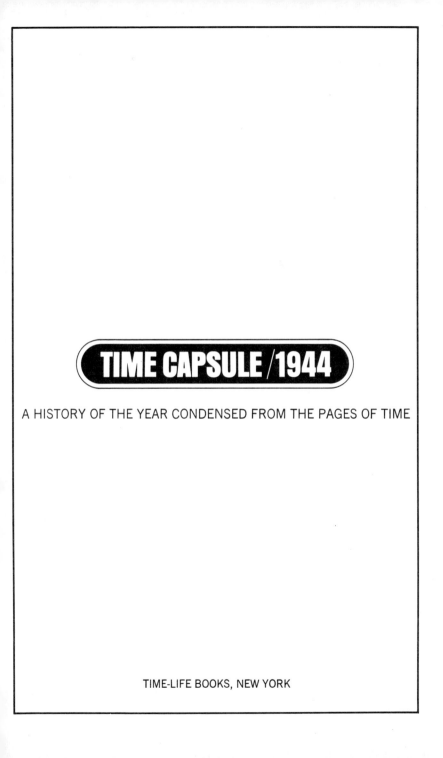

TIME CAPSULE /1944

A HISTORY OF THE YEAR CONDENSED FROM THE PAGES OF TIME

TIME-LIFE BOOKS, NEW YORK

TIME / **1944**

EDITORS *Henry R. Luce, Manfred Gottfried*
MANAGING EDITOR *T. S. Matthews*
SENIOR EDITORS *Roy Alexander, Whittaker Chambers,
Wilder Hobson, Hubert Kay, Sidney Olson,
John Osborne, Content Peckham, Dana Tasker,
Charles Wertenbaker*
ASSOCIATE EDITORS *James Agee, Louise Wells Baker,
Robert W. Boyd Jr., Robert Cantwell, Robert T. Elson,
Otto Fuerbringer, Emeline Nolan,
Duncan Norton-Taylor, Joseph Purtell, Williston Rich,
Winthrop Sargeant, Robert Sherrod, Walter Stockly,
Leon Svirsky, John Walker*

EDITOR *Maitland A. Edey*
EXECUTIVE EDITOR *Jerry Korn*
TEXT DIRECTOR *Martin Mann*
ART DIRECTOR *Sheldon Cotler*
CHIEF OF RESEARCH *Beatrice T. Dobie*

SERIES EDITOR *John Dille*
ASSISTANT EDITOR *Carl Solberg*
ASSISTANT *John Stanton*
RESEARCHER *Louise Samuels*
ASSISTANT ART DIRECTOR *Arnold Holeywell*
ASSISTANT DESIGNER *John Woods*
COPYREADER *Rosemarie Conefrey*

PUBLISHER *Rhett Austell*

COVER ILLUSTRATION *Lou Lomonaco*

EVENTS OF THE YEAR

Editors' Note

The decisive battles of World War II occurred in 1944. As the year began, U.S. troops were poised in England for the invasion of Europe. In the Pacific, ships, planes and men were cutting away at the outer island defenses of Japan. Because the war overshadowed all other events of the year, news about it crops up throughout this volume. Detailed accounts of the battles themselves and the military aspects of the war are contained in a separate World Battlefronts section, beginning on page 69. The political effects of the war are described in the Foreign News section, page 127.

Life went on at home, too—Mel Ott of the New York Giants set a new big-league record for runs scored; comedian Jimmy Durante had one of his best seasons in 21 years of show business; a nonsense song called "Mairzy Doats" was sweeping the country; and President Franklin D. Roosevelt was elected to an unprecedented fourth term. Accounts of this last event are found both in The Presidency section, starting on page 9, and in a separate section devoted to Politics, which begins on page 35.

■

TIME CAPSULE/1944 is one of a series of volumes, each adapted and condensed from a year's contents of TIME, the Weekly Newsmagazine. The words, except for a few connecting passages, are those of the magazine itself, and therefore reflect the flavor, the attitudes and the state of knowledge of the day—sometimes innocent, sometimes opinionated, sometimes prescient. The book is divided, like the magazine, into departments, and is organized so that each department forms a chronological chapter for the entire year. The dates in the margin are the issue dates of the magazine.

$$\boxed{\text{U.S. AT WAR}}$$

The Presidency

As 1944 began, the nation was becoming increasingly concerned with the state of Franklin Roosevelt's health, and there was much speculation over whether he would run for a fourth term. He had begun to lose his touch with Congress—in which, for the first time since he became President, the Democrats had less than a majority in the House of Representatives. To offset this political handicap, however, the Allies were making excellent progress in the war, both in Europe and the Pacific. If the President did decide to run again, he would obviously count heavily on his role as Commander in Chief of the Armed Forces to maintain his public prestige and insure his re-election.

JAN. 3 **GRANDPA'S CHRISTMAS:** The eleventh Christmas since Franklin Roosevelt was first elected President was also the first he had spent at Hyde Park since 1932. Then he had four grandchildren. By last week, five marriages and three divorces later, he had 14 grandchildren, and the seven who were on hand to spend Christmas with him made the 20 bric-a-brac-filled rooms of the Hyde Park mansion seem precariously crowded.

Grandpa Roosevelt—his hair considerably whiter than in 1932 and, as he remarked to a photographer, thinning just short of baldness—presided at gift-unwrapping in the library, carved the turkey at dinner and read aloud, as always, Dickens' *Christmas Carol.* Of the reading, Grandma Roosevelt reported in her column that "he cuts the whole story, of course, but he is so expert at reading it now, he can hold even the small children's attention for a little while."

DEATH OF A LABEL: To a stay-late guest at a White House press conference Franklin Roosevelt confided that he wished reporters wouldn't use that term New Deal. There is no need of a New Deal now, said the President. He hoped somebody would think up a catchy way to sloganize "win the war."

Franklin Roosevelt had closed his speech and opened an era at Chicago in 1932 with his famed line: "I pledge you— I pledge myself—to a new deal for the American people."

But that mauve decade had died long ago. The voters and the Congress and the President himself had been busily killing the New Deal for years. Now, when only the name was left, the President suddenly obliterated even that—the name of his biggest contribution to U.S. political history.

ONLY 348 DAYS UNTIL . . . : U.S. citizens were reminded for JAN. 24 the umpteenth time of the incredible energy and resolution which set Eleanor Roosevelt apart from ordinary women: the First Lady reported in her column of Jan. 12 that she had been out the day before buying "some Christmas presents for the coming year."

The following statement ran in an early 1944 issue of TIME:
TO SAVE PAPER
Please share your copy of TIME with friends. This year TIME and its brother publications, LIFE, FORTUNE and THE ARCHITECTURAL FORUM, cooperating with the War Production Board, will increase their paper saving two and a half times over last year. This means that our four magazines will use 73,000,000 pounds (1,450 freight carloads) less paper in 1944 than in 1942. Obviously there cannot be enough copies for everyone.

MUM ON TERM IV: Junketing in California, Vice President FEB. 14 Henry Wallace was asked the inevitable question at a San Francisco press conference. He replied: "There is no doubt in my mind that the President will run."

This was pretty official on TERM IV; its acknowledgment could come from only one higher source. That source, as usual, was mum.

MILITARY SECRET: Last week, throughout the historic period MARCH 6 of grinding friction between the President and Congress, the

U.S. knew only that the President was "out of the city." He often rests for days at a time at Hyde Park. He may or may not have been there last week. For much of the time the U.S. doesn't know where the President is.

MARCH 13 **ALWAYS ROOSEVELT:** Outside the crimson-hung windows streamed a heavy rain. Inside the crystal-and-gilt East Room streamed 200 friends, relatives and distinguished guests. Since March 4, 1933, when he was first inaugurated, the President has observed each anniversary with religious services. Usually he has gone to St. John's Episcopal Church, just across Lafayette Square. Last week St. John's came to the East Room. A mixed choir sang an anthem *("Get not far from us, O God; cast us not away in time of stress").* The President's old friend and Groton schoolmaster, the Rev. Dr. Endicott Peabody, 86, led three other ministers in asking divine help for "Thy servant, Franklin" and to "save us from all false choices." The President's face was grave.

That night, at an informal dinner given by White House correspondents, the President threw back his head and guffawed at Comedian Bob Hope's pointed prattle: "I've always voted for Roosevelt as President. My father always voted for Roosevelt as President."

APRIL 10 **MILD CASE:** Out at Naval Hospital in Bethesda, Md., they X-rayed Franklin Roosevelt's chest. It was a mild case of bronchitis, going into its third week. To reporters, the President pooh-poohed his illness, continued to smoke from his long cigaret holder, continued to cough softly but persistently.

ASSISTANT PRESIDENT: To the Clinic staff, even to his brisk, dark-haired Nurse Mary Conway, the patient was just another one of the 100,000 who come to Mayo's each year. But to Franklin Roosevelt, anxiously reading the wired reports, the man in Room 301 was much more important.

Harry Hopkins, 53, was back at Mayo's for the third time in seven years, for his second major stomach operation.

When Harry Hopkins, who comes closest to being the real Assistant President of the U.S., is not at work, the President has more visitors, more decisions to make, more troubles. Hopkins, besides being the one real Roosevelt confidant,

holds a dazzling combination of official posts. Ill but indefatigable, he works in snatches over long hours, drops for
occasional catnaps in odd places. His co-workers—who are
almost always hero-worshipers—credit him with a whop-
ping memory and a steel-trap mind.

Officially, Harry Hopkins is the President's special assistant, chairman of the Munitions Assignments Board, the top
U.S.-British Unit which, with the Combined Chiefs of Staff,
allocates all United Nations war equipment. Unofficially,
Harry Hopkins often serves as the President's eyes, ears, hands,
feet, brains. His bony shoulders are piled high with the war's
weightiest military secrets. He shuns human contacts outside
his job. By nature outspoken and gregarious, he frankly tells
reporters why he avoids them: he knows too much and he
loves to talk.

If Hopkins now needs several months to recover, the President will have lost the valuable services of his closest friend at
a time when he needs him most.

FALA'S BIRTHDAY: The best-known U.S. dog had a birthday APRIL 17
last week. Franklin Roosevelt's Fala, his eyes hidden under a
mass of black hair, received photographers on the south lawn
of the White House, sniffed nonchalantly at a cake with white
frosting and four candles. For supper he had an extra bone.

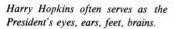

Harry Hopkins often serves as the　　*Fala, the President's Scottie, gets an*
President's eyes, ears, feet, brains.　　*extra bone on his fourth birthday.*

MAY 15 **BACK FROM THE BARONY:** The mystery was over, and the rumors—which had had him everywhere from the Mayo Clinic to London—were disproved. On doctor's orders Franklin Roosevelt had treated himself to the most thoroughgoing rest of his eleven years in the White House.

For four long weeks he had slept twelve hours every night in the indolent air of Hobcaw Barony, Bernard Baruch's 23,000-acre South Carolina plantation, 60 miles north of Charleston. He had sunned himself on the pier that juts out into the brackish waters of Winyah Bay. He had cast for bass in plantation ponds, gone crabbing from the pier, fished the Black and Waccamaw Rivers on a 54-ft. Coast Guard patrol boat. Under a canopy of blimps and patrol planes, he had trolled for bluefish and bonito 15 miles out in the Atlantic. He was almost caught at sea in a thunder-storm kicked up by a tornado that killed 38 people farther west.

Other days he went driving through the plantation's pines and cypresses, looking at jonquils and dogwoods in full bloom. Sometimes he "just sat" on the white-columned front porch of Hobcaw, a stately 21-room house built by Baruch twelve years ago on the 226-year-old plantation.

MAY 22 **SUDDENLY OLD:** The reporters were as curious about the President's health as about his opinions. No less than 173 of them jammed the oval White House study for their first look at Franklin Roosevelt since his return from the South.

They saw a healthy tan on the familiar face. The lines around his eyes seemed to have disappeared. He no longer drummed the arm of his green leather chair with nervous fingers. But the face was thinner. The top of the head was unequivocally bald. Suddenly, seeing him now after a month's absence, newsmen who have been seeing him once or twice a week for eleven years were struck by the realization that Franklin Roosevelt at 62 is an old man.

JUNE 12 **"TYRANTS' WAR":** Last week the President found yet another name for the war. Dissatisfied with his earlier appellation of "The War of Survival," he now adopted a suggestion sent in by a 68-year-old invalid of Murfreesboro, Tenn., that the war be known as "The Tyrants' War." But most people would probably go on calling it World War II.

"I DO NOT WANT TO RUN": "If the convention should nominate JULY 24 me for the Presidency, I shall accept. If the people elect me, I will serve.

"If the people command me to continue in this office and in this war I have as little right to withdraw as the soldier has to leave his post in the line.

"For myself I do not want to run. By next spring, I shall have been President and Commander in Chief of the armed forces for twelve years. . . . All that is within me cries out to go back to my home on the Hudson River.

"Reluctantly, but as a good soldier, I repeat that I will accept and serve in this office, if I am so ordered by the Commander in Chief of us all—the sovereign people of the United States."

So wrote Franklin Roosevelt in a letter to Democratic Chairman Robert Hannegan last week.

No one was surprised over this news. All Democrats knew that, as far as their party was concerned, Franklin Roosevelt was the indispensable 1944 candidate.

The Term IV strategy was now fairly plain. The President, occupied with the problems of the whole teeming world, would seem to be too busy to engage in the "usual partisan" politics. Further, he would appear more & more in his self-emphasized role as Commander in Chief. Both attitudes were aimed at making Republican campaigning seem partisan and maliciously domestic.

CONFERENCE IN QUEBEC: The train stood on a siding at SEPT. 18 Halifax, N.S. In the observation car sat a pudgy little man in a visored naval cap, a cheroot in his mouth, his horn-rimmed glasses focused on a newspaper. Outside, a huge crowd swirled and pushed, straining against police lines. The crowd, dressed in its Sunday best, burst into song: first, *Roll Out the Barrel;* then *There'll Always Be an England.* Finally, the pudgy man, not relinquishing his cheroot, shuffled to the rear platform, acknowledged the crowd's cheers, and asked for *Tipperary.* The crowd gave it to him, while Winston Churchill beat time.

The P.M. had arrived in Canada for his eighth wartime conference with Franklin Roosevelt. He had crossed on a transport crammed with furloughed G.I.s. The singing ended

President Roosevelt greets Prime Minister Churchill in Quebec. One has lost weight, one has lost color, but in the war "victory is everywhere."

with *God Save the King* and the train pulled out. Next day it ground to a stop on a siding at Wolfe's Cove, at Quebec. Franklin Roosevelt was there, sitting in an open car, his eyes shaded by a big Panama. The sky was cloudless, a paler blue than the blue St. Lawrence hard by.

"Hello, I'm glad to see you," he called. "Eleanor is here. Did you have a nice trip?"

Said the P.M., picking up the small talk: "We had three beautiful days." Added the ex-First Lord of the Admiralty: "But I was frightfully sick."

"I've lost some weight," said Franklin Roosevelt.

"I've lost some color," replied Winston Churchill.

Mrs. Churchill spied Eleanor Roosevelt, in a flame-colored dress, with matching hat. "Hello, there," she said, and they began a brisk conversation. Fala scurried about, sniffing the shoes of the famous.

Turning to reporters, Winston Churchill exclaimed: "Victory is everywhere."

SEPT. 25 **QUEBEC RESULTS:** The second Quebec Conference, concluded last week after six days of discussion, fell into two main divisions.

AREA NO. 1 was the Pacific. Chief difficulty of the conference, said the two beaming principals, as they lectured the

Mrs. Eleanor Roosevelt plays with Fala during the Quebec conference. The renowned Scottie enjoys sniffing the shoes of the famous. Page 15.

press on the sundeck of Quebec's Citadel, was how to find enough work for all hands in the Pacific. Winston Churchill had come to Quebec alarmed at the U.S. Navy's rambunctious theory that it could finish the Pacific war by itself. Said he: "You shan't have all those good things to yourselves. You must share." Final results at Quebec seemed to promise just this.

The conference, on the word of Franklin Roosevelt, did not discuss the selection of one, overall Pacific commander. The Pacific theater is too vast, said the President, for one human being to grasp. Thus the routes, and the commanders, presumably remain as they are:

¶ The drive through Burma to Singapore, under Admiral Lord Louis Mountbatten.

¶ The drive to the Philippines, under General MacArthur.

¶ The "floating command" aimed at China and the Jap homeland, under Admiral Nimitz.

AREA NO. 2 of the Quebec discussions was on the fate of postwar Germany. Here the two principals kept mum. But it was obvious that a plan for the management of postwar Germany had received much attention. Foreign Secretary Anthony Eden flew through heavy weather to bring a brief case full of British proposals.

But beyond the technical details of occupation, the question of Germany's fate was largely political. Russia, unrepresented at Quebec, must be considered. Reports from London said that Russia was disturbed over an Anglo-American "frontier" in Occupied Germany.

RETURN: Harry Hopkins, still gaunt from long illness, was finally back on his old six-day work week at the White House. Each day last week his familiar slouched figure could be seen entering the East Wing at 9 a.m. Shut off, even from telephone calls and intimate friends, he worked until 7 p.m., and sometimes far into the evening.

He was still a mystery man to the U.S. Only a few understood that the deep bond between the Squire of Hyde Park and the Iowa harnessmaker's son was based on Hopkins' absolute personal loyalty to the man he idolizes. After eleven years of the kaleidoscopic changes of the New Deal, Harry Hopkins was still the man Franklin Roosevelt most trusts.

OCT. 16 **"RECKLESS WORDS":** Some 50 guests, including Fala, crowded into the little red-carpeted, basement Oval Room where Franklin Roosevelt has made many a radio fireside chat during the past eleven years. At 10 p.m. the President, apparently chipper despite his continuing head cold, then began his second political speech of the 1944 campaign.

He voiced a statesmanlike hope that all Americans, "regardless of party," would register and vote this year. And, for the second time in a fortnight, he accused GOPsters of trying to make it hard for U.S. servicemen to vote: "There are politicians and others who quite openly worked to restrict the use of the ballot in this election, hoping selfishly for a small vote."

Then, figuratively, he took off his Commander in Chief hat and put on the old campaign hat he really loves. Tom Dewey had charged that the Administration planned to keep the boys in uniform because the New Deal is "afraid of the peace." "It seems a pity," said the President, "that reckless words, based on unauthoritative sources, should be used to mislead and weaken morale."

Finally Candidate Roosevelt came to a main piece of business in his speech—an attempt to give a brisk brushoff to Earl Browder, the top U.S. Communist, and his enthusiastic

Communist support for Term IV, without alienating any of the needed votes: "I have never sought and I do not welcome the support of any person or group committed to Communism or Fascism, or any other foreign ideology which would undermine the American system of government."

"HE'S PERFECTLY O.K.": "Let's not be squeamish . . ." OCT. 23 began the arch-Republican New York *Sun* in a front-page editorial one day last week. "It is convention, not the Constitution which forbids open comment on the possibility that a President may be succeeded by his Vice President. Six Presidents have died in office." By this week the rabidly anti-Roosevelt New York *Daily News,* which is seldom squeamish about anything, was bravely facing the facts that Tom Dewey is 42 and Franklin Roosevelt is 62.

The *Sun* and the *News* were saying out loud what many a citizen has wondered about: is the President too old or tired to live out Term IV? Plainly Franklin Roosevelt's health was a political issue.

It was obvious to the White House last week that a report to the U.S. people was needed. Vice Admiral Ross T. McIntire, White House physician, spoke up.

Dr. McIntire, an ophthalmologist and otolaryngologist whose specialty is sinus (Franklin Roosevelt's most nagging health problem), is a balding, relaxed Oregonian whose rosy face is younger than his 55 years. Every morning around 8:30 he parks his five-year-old Lincoln convertible in front of the White House, strolls into the Presidential bedroom, insinuates himself into the daily bedside bull session. Each afternoon, he checks up at the White House again. Admiral McIntire told a reporter:

Franklin Roosevelt is "eight or nine pounds under his best weight. Frankly, I wish he'd put on a few pounds.

"He hasn't been in the pool since before going to Quebec. But he's going to start in the pool again now. He is a powerful swimmer and that gives him a good workout. The buoyancy of the water enables him to walk and he gets exercise there that he can't get any other way.

"Nothing wrong organically with him at all. He's perfectly O.K. He does a terrific day's work. But he stands up under it amazingly. The stories that he is in bad health are understandable enough around election time, but they are not true."

NOV. 20 **THE CHAMP COMES HOME:** At daybreak, rain drummed on the windowpanes of Washington, D.C. But the city awakened with a stir of excitement like a college town on the morning the football team comes home with the championship. Two days after being elected to Term IV, Franklin Roosevelt was coming back to the White House from Hyde Park. At 7:30 a.m. crowds were standing in the grey morning outside the Union Station. By 8:28, when the President's special train pulled in, there were 30,000 people on the wet plaza before the station, and a third of a million more along the two miles to the White House.

The big, black automobile with bulletproof windows moved up beside the train, with the President's grandson, five-year-old Johnnie Boettiger, wriggling excitedly beside the driver. Franklin Roosevelt appeared on the rear platform at 9 o'clock, and the Metropolitan Police Band launched brassily into ruffles, flourishes and the resounding *Hail to the Chief.* Franklin Roosevelt, bundled in a grey raincoat, ordered the automobile's top put down before he settled in beside Harry Truman and Henry Wallace.

The President had slept late at Hyde Park the day before, had dictated letters, and then lazed through the afternoon, relaxed after the tense final weeks of the campaign. Messages of congratulation had poured in all day from all over the world. But now, as his car rolled into the plaza, he heard and saw something more satisfying than telegrams—the sudden sound of cheering, the sight of thousands of umbrellas shining in the rain.

Radio men placed microphones on a board across the President's lap. He chuckled as he talked: "I hope some of the scribes in the papers won't intimate that I expect to make Washington my permanent residence." He talked extemporaneously for three minutes, with the rain beginning to drip from the brim of his grey campaign hat. "This is a very wonderful welcome home, a welcome I shall always remember."

The line of motorcycles and automobiles swept in through

the White House gates at 9:30 in a steady downpour. Inside the Executive Mansion the President shed his dripping coat and hat and immediately went to his office for a press conference. The conference began with a burst of laughter. Franklin Roosevelt had just informed the men in the front row that he had no news—and they had replied, "Thank God."

Then the President, leaning back in his baggy tweeds, agreed to disclose his private pre-election guess on the division of electoral votes. He searched in a drawer for an envelope he had sealed before election day. Paper in hand, he guessed that he had been a little too conservative. He had given himself 335 votes, Governor Dewey 196. (Final vote: 432 to 99.) The short conference ended with another roar of laughter after the Baltimore *Sun*'s Paul Ward threw a quick curve:

"Mr. President, may I be the first to ask you if you will run in 1948?"

The Congress

FIRST ISSUE: The 1944 Presidential campaign battle began FEB. 7 bitterly in Congress last week. In a truculent message, President Roosevelt accused the Senate of attempting to perpetrate a "fraud on the soldiers and sailors and marines" and "on the American people."

The President's message applied to the Soldiers' Voting bill passed by the Senate last December and approved by the House Elections Committee last fortnight. Under this bill, which leaves the whole matter of soldier voting to the states, the President charged that "the vast majority" of the 11,000,000 men & women in the armed services would be deprived of the vote in 1944. House Republicans booed the charge of fraud.

Balding, humorless Bob Taft, ordinarily dry and legal in manner, leaped up with red face and flailing arms. He called the President's message a "direct insult" to Congress and charged that the President is planning to line up soldiers for a Fourth Term.

The question of how the armed services shall vote had unquestionably become the first issue of the 1944 Presidential campaign. President Roosevelt's message was not designed to persuade Congress but to put it on a spot. He clearly succeeded.

FEB. 14 **WILL SOLDIERS VOTE?:** John Rankin, Mississippi Democrat, stood up in the House to denounce the Administration-backed soldiers' vote bill:

"Now who is behind this bill? Who is the chief sponsor of it? The chief publicist is *PM,* the uptown edition of the Communist *Daily Worker* that is being financed by the tax-escaping fortune of Marshall Field III, and the chief broadcaster for it is Walter Winchell—alias no telling what."

Prompted Michigan's Republican Clare Hoffman: "Who is he?"

Replied John Rankin: "The little kike I was telling you about the other day, who called this body the "House of Reprehensibles."

This was a new low in demagoguery, even for John Rankin, but in the entire House no one rose to protest.

Everybody knew where Rankin stood, which was four-square against a federal ballot for soldiers, eight-square against the Administration, and, of course, 16-square in favor of the poll-tax, white supremacy and Southern woman-hood.

The House, enraged by Franklin Roosevelt's taunts had its mind made up to smite the President. Now, as Republican Leader Joe Martin saw that he had the votes, a roll call was ordered, and the House howled down an Administration-backed Worley bill to provide federal ballots for soldiers, 224-to-168. Then it passed the Eastland-Rankin state-ballot measure, 328-to-69.

MARCH 6 **THE MASTER BEDROOM:** To Alben Barkley the scene was familiar: the high-ceilinged room, and the big man propped up in the plain mahogany bed, his tremendous shoulders bulging his pajama coat. In seven years as majority leader of the U.S. Senate, Kentucky's Barkley had talked with President Roosevelt literally hundreds of times, at all hours and in many places, including the President's bedroom.

The President's regular Monday conference with the Democratic leaders of Congress is usually held in his big oval office in the Executive wing of the White House. But last week Mr. Roosevelt held the conference in his bedroom. The other leaders—Vice President Wallace, Speaker Rayburn, House Majority Leader John McCormack—were already there when Alben Barkley walked in.

The President was jovial. He announced cheerfully he had decided to veto the new tax bill. He proceeded to read excerpts from his veto message. A three-against-one argument promptly boiled up. While Wallace sat silent, Barkley, Rayburn and McCormack vigorously tried to persuade the President to change his mind. A veto, they argued, would simply mean throwing away more than two billion dollars in revenue. Why not let this bill become law without his signature?

The argument remained polite. The President remained adamant. Leader Barkley summed up. He knew the bill was far from perfect. But this bill was the work and the will of Congress. If the President persisted in his veto, he, Barkley, would have to stand up on the floor of the Senate and defend his position. Mr. Roosevelt remarked that this was understandable. The conference broke up in strained good humor.

Next day the President sent the veto message to the Capitol. It was the first time in history that a U.S. President had vetoed a general revenue bill. Leader Barkley read his copy three times, incredulous, shocked, then angry. The temperate words which the President had read aloud the day before were still there. But peppered among them now were other bitter, taunting, contemptuous words which stung the majority leader like slaps in the face: "unwise," "inept," "indefensible special privileges to favored groups," "dangerous precedents for the future," "disappoint and fail the American taxpayers." Taxpayers' confusion, asserted the President, was not the Treasury's fault but "squarely the fault of the Congress of the United States."

Meanest slap of all was a neat turn of phrase of the kind in which Franklin Roosevelt delights: "It is not a tax bill, but a tax relief bill providing relief not for the needy but for the greedy."

Shaken to the soles of his solid brogues, Leader Barkley quickly checked a dozen other Democratic Senators, found every one livid with rage. Alben Barkley kept a tight grip on himself and held his peace. After adjournment at 2:15 p.m., he went to his office and began to think.

By 11 p.m. Alben Barkley knew what he had to do and next morning, when he sat down to dictate in his office, the words came rumbling out so fast that his pretty red-haired secretary, Loraine Winfrey, could hardly get them down. When he strode up the center aisle of the Senate to his front-row seat at noon, there were only seven freshly typewritten sheets in his hand. Back in his office, Miss Winfrey was typing frantically at the rest.

Every eye on the floor and in the packed galleries was fixed on Leader Barkley as, his greying hair freshly cut and wetted down, his portly frame neatly draped in brown, he rose to deliver his historic speech. Adjusting his incomplete manuscript on a little reading stand, he took a deep breath, hitched at his belt, put on his heavy-rimmed spectacles, fixed his eyes firmly on Vice President Wallace for a moment and began to speak. His heavy voice was clear, his tone deadly earnest.

Thereupon long-suffering Alben Barkley proceeded to rip Franklin Roosevelt's veto message to shreds & tatters. The President's "needy-greedy" crack, he cried, "is a calculated and deliberate assault upon the legislative integrity of every member of the Congress of the United States. As for me, I do not intend to take this unjustifiable assault lying down."

Leader Barkley's voice was low and several times near breaking as he recalled his 31 years in Congress. "For twelve years," he said, "I have carried to the best of my ability the flag of Franklin D. Roosevelt. I dare say that for the last seven years of tenure as majority leader, I have carried that flag over rougher territory than was ever traversed by any previous majority leader. I have called a conference of the Democratic majority for 10:30 o'clock tomorrow morning at which time my resignation will be tendered."

Alben Barkley had dropped his political blockbuster. He added a final blast: "If the Congress of the United States has any self-respect yet left, it will override the veto of the President and enact this tax bill into law, his objections to the contrary notwithstanding."

As the majority leader finished and sat down, there was a

moment of unbroken hush. Then a round of clapping on the floor was quickly drowned by a thunder of applause from the galleries. It was the greatest ovation in the memory of living Senators. Leader Barkley declared: "Now I am content. My cup runneth over. I have never felt calmer in my life."

Perhaps only three people in the world—Winston Churchill, Joseph Stalin and Eleanor Roosevelt—could have denounced Franklin Roosevelt with more sensational effect. With lightning speed, the master politician acted. He wrote a telegram to "Dear Alben." It was a beautiful letter. The President protested that he had never intended to attack "the integrity of yourself and other members of Congress." He declared that at the Monday conference "I did not realize how very strongly you felt about that basic decision." Key paragraph, a political master stroke brilliantly designed to turn prospective rebuff into apparent triumph, was one urging Barkley not to persist in his intention to resign, hoping that if he did his colleagues would not accept, "but if they do, I sincerely hope they will immediately and unanimously re-elect you."

Since the U.S. at large did not know that this procedure was already all set, the President regained some prestige next day, for the Democratic conference did precisely that. At first, Leader-Elect Barkley hung back. He wanted a few days to "think it over" lest the public should interpret his prompt acceptance as knuckling under. But no one was fooled. Alben Barkley was no longer the President's errand boy.

That afternoon the House made the rebellion flat and final, overriding the President's veto with a sweeping 299 votes to 95. Next day the Senate set the seal to the historic week by an even worse crushing vote 72 to 14. Long ago distrust between the Elective and Legislative branches of the U.S. government had become a breach; now the breach reached crisis.

G.I. BILL OF RIGHTS: To the time-honored list of things which U.S. politicians may be counted upon to denounce relentlessly—the house-fly, the common cold, the man-eating shark —Missouri's Bennett Champ Clark hit on something last fortnight which politicians almost as unanimously favor. He introduced a veterans' benefits bill, jointly sponsored by 80 other Senators. APRIL 3

Last week, amid plaints by the remaining 15 Senators that they had not had a chance to sign it in advance, the Senate passed the bill unanimously. The House is expected to follow suit this week.

The bill came from the American Legion. It was nicknamed the "G.I. Bill of Rights," as it combined in a single measure most of the proposals for helping veterans that have been made in Congress. Prime provisions:

¶ Schooling for at least one year, and up to four; in elementary, business, high or higher schools; with allowances of $500 a year for tuition, plus $50 a month for subsistence and an extra $25 for one or more dependents.

¶ Loans up to $1,000 for buying homes, farms, farm equipment or business properties, with no interest the first year, and only 3% thereafter.

¶ Special job-finding services.

¶ Unemployment benefits up to 52 weeks at $15 a week, plus an extra $5 for one dependent, $8 for two, $10 for three.

¶ $500,000,000 for new veterans' hospitals.

¶ The Veterans' Administration, which would manage these benefits, would now become a primary war agency, with priorities second only to those of the War and Navy Departments in obtaining personnel, equipment and supplies.

Chairman Walter F. George of the Senate Finance Committee guesstimated the bill's cost at $3,500,000,000. But the economy-minded Senator and his Committee were not aghast at this sum. While the bill is "admittedly more extensive and generous" than any in history, said they, "we view it as true economy, the best money that can be spent for the future welfare of the nation. The men and women who compose our armed forces . . . not only now hold the destiny of this Republic firmly in their hands, they will so hold it for a generation to come." [Over the next two decades, nearly seven million veterans had received some $66 billion in loans for homes, and over ten million veterans had received nearly $20 billion to pay for their education and training.]

HIS HONOR SPEAKS: A jug-eared little U.S. Senator filled the tank of his sleek, grey Cadillac and drove 1,000 miles to address the Legislature of his own State. Home to campaign —for 1946—was Mississippi's red-necktied Theodore Gilmore ("The Man") Bilbo, who boasts, at 66, that ladies still find him fascinating ("I don't expect to reach my prime until I'm 75").

Before he had finished his long anti-Negro harangue, some of Mississippi's listening Senators, Representatives and assorted littlewigs had propped their feet on legislative desks, were deep in the pages of the Jackson *Daily News*. But Fustianeer Bilbo ranted on. Stepping gingerly as Agag through the bad eggs of his logic, he somehow managed to: 1) praise Franklin Roosevelt, 2) damn Eleanor Roosevelt, 3) boom Term IV, 4) denounce New Deal bureaucracy, 5) predict bloody postwar race riots, 6) deny that U.S. Negroes have any right to vote. Typical Bilboisms:

"We people of the South must draw the color line tighter & tighter."

"The white man is the custodian of the gospel of Jesus Christ."

"We will tell our Negro-loving Yankee friends to go straight to hell."

Senator Robert Taft charges that FDR is lining up the soldier vote. Page 20.

Mississippi's Senator Bilbo: "We tell our Negro-loving friends to go to hell."

The Man's words distressed some in Jackson, Miss., but they gave a stomach-ache to the good citizens of Washington, D.C. As Chairman of the Senate District Committee, The Man is mayor of the nation's capital. For a quarter of a century, disfranchised residents of Washington have agitated for a vote. Now Mayor Bilbo explained why he is determined that they shall not have it: "Negroes already compose 30 to 40% of the population of the capital city. The alleys would outvote the avenues."

MAY 8 **VERY PERSONAL:** Like Franklin Roosevelt and Cordell Hull, Senator Kenneth Douglas McKellar considers Columnist Drew Pearson a liar. Last week on the Senate floor the feuding, 75-year-old Tennessean said so, 23 times, in a speech covering three and a half pages of the *Congressional Record.*

In one of his columns, Washington Merry-Go-Rounder Pearson rehashed some old stories about McKellar's choleric temper and his insatiable hunger for patronage. That afternoon the bulb-nosed Senator took advantage of a large audience, proceeded to bellow for over an hour what he chose to title "Personal Statement about a Lying Human Skunk." Excerpts: "Pearson is just an ignorant liar, a pusillanimous liar, a peewee liar, even if he is a paid liar. When a man is a natural-born liar, a liar during his manhood and all the time, a congenital liar, a liar by profession, a liar for a living, a liar in the attempt to amuse, or to be as he thinks smart, a liar in the daytime, and a liar in the nighttime, it is remarkable how he can lie."

At tirade's end the puffing Senator had admitted that three of his immediate family are on the Federal payroll, that he is still sponsoring an amendment which would give Senate spoilsmen control of all Federal jobs paying more than $4,500 a year, and proved that he has a terrible temper. He had specifically denied only one Pearson charge: "I never pulled a knife on any Senator."

SEPT. 11 **DOGGIE STORY:** Minnesota's kewpie-shaped Harold Knutson, 63, one of the most incorrigible rumormongers in Congress, was at it again last week.

Mr. Knutson told his colleagues about "the rumor that Fala, that little Scotty dog, had been inadvertently left behind at the Aleutians on the President's return trip, and that they did not discover the absence of the little doggie until the party reached Seattle, and that it is rumored a destroyer was sent a thousand miles to fetch him."

Majority Leader John McCormack hastened to get the White House answer. Next day he took the floor:

Mr. McCormack: "I talked with Admiral Leahy this morning—and I think all the American people will accept Admiral Leahy's word. I can quote him: 'The story about the dog is made out of whole cloth. The dog was never lost.' "

The Nation

TAXI!: In Sacramento, Calif., for two days last week, only five JAN. 3 taxicabs remained in service to handle emergency calls. All five cabs stayed clear of hotels; one even hid in a downtown alley. The other 115 Sacramento cabs had used the last gallon of their quarterly gas ration.

During the 40 necessary trips that drivers of the emergency cabs dared make, they were stopped by at least a dozen people who pleaded that they were practically dying on the street. By mid-week the five cabs were gas-dry.

HE ARMED THE REPUBLIC: The man who, more than any other, could be said to have armed the Republic was George Catlett Marshall, Chief of Staff.

The American people do not, as a general rule, like or trust the military. But they like and trust George Marshall. This is no more paradoxical than the fact that General Marshall hates war. Hired by the U.S. people to do a job, he will be as good, as ruthless, as tough, as this job requires. There his ambitions stop. "He has only one interest," said one of his intimates, "to win this damned war as quick as he can, with the fewest lives lost and money expended, and get the hell down to Leesburg, Va., and enjoy life." He shuns all avoidable publicity, he is a man of great personal reserve, but the U.S. people have learned why they trust General Marshall more than they have trusted any military man since George Washington: he is a *civis Americanus*.

The job he assumed on the day Germany invaded Poland was to transform a worse-than-disarmed U.S. into the world's most effective military power—and in time. He started with an army of about 200,000 in 1939 and, against the background of the Alice-in-Wonderlandish Congress of the '30s, shaped it into what it is today.

He laid out a program of training and a schedule of equipment that are unmatched anywhere. Once the U.S. entered the war, more than anyone else he insisted on, and gradually achieved, unity of command in all Allied forces in every theater of war. He refused to be panicked by nervous demands of theater commanders into sending out green and half-equipped troops; and in this he endured through the most extreme pressures. He early recognized the importance of air power and pushed his airmen into bigger and ever bigger programs. He started to break the traditionally supercilious War Department enmity toward innovations of equipment. New ordnance gets Marshall's immediate attention.

Above all, a strategy had to be shaped. Marshall's mind, which works with an earthbound simplicity that is the precise opposite of Hitler's "intuition," cut through all the cross currents in this planetary war. The pattern that emerged was simple and inescapable: first, while checking the Japanese advance, to clean Hitler out of Africa, then push him up on the Continent, and finally hit him with everything at once, from all possible directions. The story of General Marshall's achievements was best told in the masterly report to the nation he released last September. It contained also the story of General Marshall: his saga of U.S. growth toward victory, written in mature prose, is without a single "I."

JAN. 17 **STOP SAVING TUBES:** Come March 1, toothpaste buyers need no longer turn in old tubes. The War Production Board hastened to explain that tubes made during 1943 are low in tin and worthless for salvage. If anyone is still saving prewar toothpaste tubes, WPB would still like to have them.

MARCH 27 **THE COST OF WAR:** The U.S. spent money for war faster than ever in February, reported the War Production Board. The outlay each day: $312,300,000. Average daily cost to every U.S. citizen over 19: $3.37—or a total of $1,230 each per year. Spent on the war since June 1940: $168,600,000,000.

MAY 1 **"CRACKPOTS":** The green-walled courtroom in Washington's Federal District Court building was small (40 x 38 ft.)

for the largest sedition trial in U.S. history. The everpresent question before the court was big: can a democracy defend itself legally?

Each of the 28 men and two women on trial last week faced ten years in prison, a $10,000 fine. The charge: the 30 had conspired to overthrow the U.S. Government in favor of a Nazi dictatorship, and had tried to demoralize the armed forces. The probable defense: the accused were merely enjoying their constitutional right to free speech when they expressed such sentiments as:

¶ "The Japanese attack upon Pearl Harbor was deliberately invited by the public officials of the U.S."

¶ "The Government of the U.S. and Congress are controlled by Communists, International Jews and plutocrats."

¶ "The cause of the Axis powers is the cause of justice and morality and any act of war against them is unjust and immoral."

The accused were a strangely assorted crew. Handsome Joe McWilliams, the soapbox Führer who used to berate the Jews and laud Hitler on Manhattan street corners, got top billing in the indictment ("United States of America *v.* Joseph E. McWilliams, *et al*"). Quiet, swart Lawrence Dennis, U.S. fascism's No. 1 intellectual, sat glumly near benign-faced James True, organizer of America First, Inc., and inventor of

Mrs. "T.N.T." Washburn. On trial for sedition, she demonstrates her allegiance to Hitler's cause with a stiff-armed Nazi salute.

the "kike-killer" (Pat. No. 2,026,077), a short rounded club made in two sizes (one for ladies). Chicago's Mrs. Elizabeth *(The Red Network)* Dilling, leader of the "Mothers' Crusade" which once sprawled noisily in the hall of the Senate office building, looked coldly at her co-defendant, peppery Mrs. Lois de Lafayette ("T.N.T.") Washburn, who favored delighted photographers with a stiff-armed Nazi salute.

On behalf of their clients, who have shown little enthusiasm for democratic ways, the 22 lawyers energetically demanded every final democratic safe-guard. All week long the legalists bobbed up & down, objecting, concurring, complaining. They applied for a writ of mandamus to have the whole thing dropped.

Most of the U.S. press called for a fair trial, but no nonsense. But the isolationist Chicago *Tribune,* favorite organ of most of the defendants, wrote indulgently of the "crackpots" who were the victims of a New Deal "smear campaign." [The trial went on for seven and a half months. The trial judge died before completion of it and no re-trial was held. The indictment was later dismissed.]

MAY 22 **MEMORIES OF BROOKLYN:** For men in the Mediterranean theater, where fighting has been bitter and reflection sharp, the War Department lately conducted an essay contest on "Why I Fight." Last week twelve Army judges, after pondering 300 entries, picked the winners. All three were from New York City—two from Brooklyn. First prize went to Corp. Jack J. Zurofsky, 28, of Brooklyn, now recovering from combat wounds. Excerpt:

"I fight because of my memories—the laughter and play of my childhood, the ball games I was in, the better ones I watched, my mother telling me why my father and she came to America, my high-school graduation, the first time I saw a cow, the first year we could afford a vacation, hikes in the fall, weenie and marshmallow roasts, the first time I voted, my first date and the slap in the face I got instead of the kiss I attempted, the El going down, streets being widened to let the sun in, new tenements replacing the old slums, the crowd applauding the time I came through with the hit that won us the Borough championship—the memories, which, if people like me do not fight, our children will never have."

MIDSUMMER MOOD: In Ed Massey's barbershop at 3306 JULY 17
Main Street, Kansas City, a big muscular man eased himself
out of a barber's chair. He had just had "the works." Time
was when the big man, a steamfitter by trade, would have
thought it mad folly to come to Ed Massey's for anything
but a haircut. But last week his pay envelope held $140, and
he now frankly enjoyed these little male luxuries: haircut,
shave, shampoo, scalp massage and shoe shine—everything
except a manicure. The big man picked up the paper and read
aloud: RED SPEED STUNS NAZIS, YANKS STRIKE IN FRANCE.

"Well, boys," the big man said, "I guess it's all over now
but the shouting. I wouldn't be surprised to see those Heinies
fold up tomorrow."

"Yep," said the man in the second chair, "I got a $10 bet
that this little show will be over by Labor Day."

In varying forms, this scene was repeated all over the U.S.
last week. The signs were not only in the headlines. Whole
communities sniffed the new optimism and reasoned that this
would be the last summer for at least the European war.

In some ways it seemed almost like a prewar summer. After
two and a half years of war the hardest things to get were
kleenex, Camel cigarets, and shirts from the laundry.

Of the 14 novels on the New York *Times*'s best-seller list,
only two had a war setting; of the 16 nonfiction titles, only
four concerned the war. The top song hit was a bouncy novelty
for children, *Swingin' on a Star.*

THE WAY HOME: Across the land last week, for six warm days AUG. 7
& nights, a troop train rumbled. It was an old train, with no
fancy name. To the engineers and switchmen, it was No.
7452-C. The men on board dubbed it the "Home Again Special," and wrote the new name in chalk on the sides of the old
Pullman cars.

The men aboard were 370 members of the 1st Marine Division—survivors of Tulagi, conquerors of Guadalcanal; the
men who mowed down the Japs like hay at Bloody Ridge, the
invaders of Cape Gloucester, the rain-drenched fighters of
Talasea, the men who took Hill 660 when they should have
been annihilated halfway up; the unnamed defenders of
Nameless Hill, the survivors of Coffin Corner.

These men on the troop train, already famed in communi-

Home on furlough, Marines ride a troop train across the U.S. They fought at Guadalcanal; now they pay extra for their second beer.

qués and the war's best-sellers (*Guadalcanal Diary, Battle for the Solomons,* etc.) were heading home for a 30-day furlough after 27 months of battle.

The heroes peeled off their natty field greens and settled down in their khakis on the scratchy green seats, scared and lonely, wondering how home would be now that it was suddenly so close. "I'm a little worried about how I'll look to them, about how much I've changed."

The train clacked on slowly, through the desert and up the mountains. At Tucumcari, there was time for a beer at the station hotel: on the first round it cost a quarter; by the second the price shot to 40¢. Said the red-haired sergeant from Rochester, not complaining, but just noticing: "Somebody's making money, and it isn't us."

At Philadelphia, there was a string of taxicabs, at Jersey City, just the ferry to Manhattan. The marines silently looked at the New York skyline. Lieut. Camille Tamucci, the tough guy in charge, who had been dreaming of mounds of spaghetti, began brooding about his stomach. "It's all tied in knots," he said.

SEPT. 4 **A BURST OF JOY:** A blizzard of confetti, ticker tape and torn newspapers fell dizzily through the afternoon sun into Manhattan's Rockefeller Plaza. The crowd wept happily. They

Opera star Lily Pons sings the "Marseillaise" when Paris is freed.

Hildegarde sings "I'll Be Seeing You" —and clearly means in Paris.

cheered all speakers impartially; they laughed, jumped up & down, fluttered the Tricolor and the Cross of Lorraine. The Metropolitan Opera's tiny Lily Pons, in her U.S.O. overseas uniform, stood up with clenched fists and sang the *Marseillaise*. The crowd that heard her was motley but united on one thing: cheers for Paris. Paris was free.

It did not matter much that an over-zealous press last week flashed the news prematurely by some 48 hours. The U.S. had been tensely waiting the good word too long to care. Even Washington, whose normal reaction to a victory is a stern lecture on overoptimism, caught the mood. Correct old Cordell Hull unbended to sum up: "Heartening."

All the U.S. felt it. Radio dance orchestras announced as many tunes as possible by French titles. Manhattan's Hildegarde, a songstress who worked in Paris cafés in the '30s went on plugging the sentimental melody which she had helped to make No. 1 on the Hit Parade: *I'll Be Seeing You* (in "all the old familiar places"—of Paris the lyrics imply). In Hollywood, husky-voiced Tallulah Bankhead, who had vowed not to take a drink until complete Allied victory, was rumored to have fallen off the wagon.

THE TWO RULES: Armless and legless young soldiers, learning OCT. 2 to use artificial limbs at Washington's Walter Reed Hospital, dread going into the streets. One soldier told the New York *Times,* "We meet three kinds of people. Some are intelligent enough not to stare and ask questions. Some are well meaning and want to do something, but they always say the wrong thing. And then there are the long-nosed gossips who ask us fool questions and try to pry." The veterans asked the U.S. to help them back into a normal existence by observing two rules: 1) don't stare; 2) don't ask questions.

DEC. 25 **AND THEN THERE WERE NONE:** The nation's druggists, grocers, confectioners and tobacconists had turned amiable liars. There was hardly a U.S. store anywhere last week without the sign NO CIGARETS. Yet under the counters, at least part of the time, the cigarets were there, saved for the old customers.

The merest shred of comfort came from S. Clay Williams, board chairman of potent R. J. Reynolds Tobacco Co. To a Senate investigating committee, he confessed that even he had to walk more than a mile for a Camel.

Politics

JAN. 31 **MAN OF THE WEST:** Big, blond, blue-eyed Earl Warren, California's 30th governor and favorite son for the Republican Presidential nomination, seems to radiate goodness and warmth. Impressed by his relaxed good nature, his evident simplicity, the eager "yes, yes" and "uh-huh, uh-huh" with which he indicates earnest interest in everything they have to say, his visitors see him not merely as a perfect political candidate, but as the forerunner in U.S. politics of a new era of friendly men to succeed the recent era of angry men—the Burt Wheelers, the Huey Longs and the Harold Ickeses.

Examination of Earl Warren's 25-year record in public office fails to reveal much promise that he is a potential giant in U.S. history. The Warren utterances and speeches have never risen above the level of safe, dull political prose. He has rarely tried anything which had not been tried before. A calm man of Swedish descent, slow to anger, he has stuck close to the middle of the road. But the record does reveal an able, hardworking, personally attractive public servant who, with the westering sun of California behind him, is casting a longer and longer shadow across the land.

At the meeting of Republican committeemen in Chicago last fortnight, Earl Warren's was the name most mentioned for second place on the Presidential ticket. As leader of a 50-vote delegation, the governor of the great, growing and no longer so screwy State of California is sure to be a power at the G.O.P. convention.

VANDENBERG ON MacARTHUR: Senator Arthur Vandenberg FEB. 14 of Michigan last week told *Collier's* readers "Why I Am for MacArthur." He wrote:

MacArthur "is granite in the face of duty, a composite of all our necessities. Mr. Roosevelt intends to run primarily as our commander in chief. Should we not offer the people a better commander in chief?"

HICKENLOOPER: In the June primaries Iowa's dapper, young FEB. 21 (47), first-term Governor will go for the seat of resigning Democrat Guy Gillette. He makes a political asset of his fascinating name: Bourke Blakemore Hickenlooper. Against the better judgment of his advisers, Governor Hickenlooper campaigned in 1938 by telling a joke on himself. A drugstore clerk refused to charge 10¢ worth of asafetida to the Hickenlooper account. "Take it for nothing," said the clerk, "I wouldn't write both asafetida and Hickenlooper for a dime."

Wendell L. Willkie, a one-time utilities executive and an aggressive, articulate spokesman for the liberal wing of the Republican Party, was defeated in his 1940 Presidential campaign against Franklin Roosevelt. He then traveled around the world as a bipartisan ambassador of goodwill for President Roosevelt, and returned to write a best-selling book called One World, *which was an eloquent plea for internationalism. As a result of these activities, Willkie was out of favor with important segments of the Republican Party. In 1944 he waged a futile campaign to capture the Republican nomination for the Presidency.*

WILLKIE'S TRAIN: Wendell Willkie began in earnest the long, uphill fight to win once more the GOPresidential nomination. His special car, so ancient a Pullman that the Union Pacific refused to hitch it to the super-streamlined *City of San Francisco,* rumbled west behind the *Overland Limited.*

Wendell Willkie. A "poison" candidate shakes 2,000 hands in 40 minutes.

"Jimmie" Davis. Music lovers pick him as Louisiana's governor. Page 38.

This was no feverish campaign special. There were no mammoth prearranged parades or bunting-draped cities. Like the other passengers, Willkie took his meals in the diner, spent most of his spare hours at his favorite pastime—talking and arguing with a few friends.

But in Boise, the 300 tickets for the Willkie luncheon sold in 20 minutes; in Seattle, Willkie shook 2,000 hands in 40 minutes. Party workers flocked to see and hear the candidate who, only the week before, was supposed to be poison.

FEB. 28 **SWIFT SHIFT:** This week Americans could learn how fabulously a U.S. opinion about internationalism had shifted in three swift years.

Less than three years ago the FORTUNE Survey found a bare 13% of Americans in favor of U.S. participation in any kind of international organization. In the current survey in the March issue that figure has surged up to a decisive 68%.

TRIUMPHANT MINSTREL: Music lovers chose the Governor MARCH 13 of Louisiana last week. The choice was a blow—1) to the remnants of the Huey Long machine, 2) for music.

The victor was tall, twangy, easygoing James H. ("Jimmie") Davis, 43, a fancy dressing hillbilly tenor and composer of such eminent sockeroos as *You Are My Sunshine, Nobody's Darlin' but Mine,* and *It Makes No Difference Now.* Tenor Davis, supported by Governor Sam Houston ("Sweet-Smellin' Sam") Jones, gave the Longsters a terrible walloping —he won by a 37,000 vote majority.

Jimmie Davis campaigned mostly by plugging his own sad ballads, moving around the state with his five-man hillbilly band, usually talking less than ten minutes before he went into his act. He sang and moved on, and the Bayou citizens remembered the music and something about low taxes.

WILLKIE BOWS OUT: The news trickled in in driblets: a radio APRIL 17 flash, an A.P. bulletin, a telephone call from Wisconsin, where Wendell Willkie had entered his name in the Presidential primary. Right from the first it was bad, incredibly, disastrously bad. When the reports from only 50 out of more than 3,000 precincts were in, Wendell Willkie said: "Well, that looks like it. We said it would be all or nothing, and it looks like nothing."

Huddled with the newsmen in the bedroom, he asked them again & again: "What does it mean?" Was the nation more isolationist than he had thought? Had the Wisconsin voters repudiated his principles? Or him personally? He decided it was partly both. But he had no regrets. "I'm glad I made the fight," he said. "I'd do the same thing if I had it to do over again." At midnight he went off to bed.

Next morning he appeared in the hotel lobby looking composed and reconciled. He had made up his mind to go through with that day's schedule.

The party sped on to Omaha. This was the last stop on the spectacular road which Wendell Willkie had traveled since the winter of 1939-40 when a few friends began to suggest that the big utilities president run for the Presidency. The crowd sang; a band played several tunes, including a tactless *I'm Going Back to Indiana.* Mr. and Mrs. Willkie came in 25 minutes late, stiff and determined.

"I wish," he said, "that under the peculiar circumstances of this evening I could speak to you just from my heart. But if I did I would perhaps express too much emotion. It would be perhaps too great a castigation of certain individuals and of what I consider one of the curses of American politics, the combinations of little cliques of mean and subversive elements." Then he launched into his prepared address:

"What Is America's Foreign Policy?" was one of his strongest and ablest attacks on the Roosevelt Administration. When he had finished it, he said: "Now, my fellow Americans, I have something quite personal I want to say." In a flat silence he read his statement.

The conclusion was inescapable. The taut Omaha audience heard it as Willkie reached the climax of his statement: "It is obvious now that I cannot be nominated. I therefore am asking my friends to desist from any activity toward that end and not to present my name to the convention."

Embarrassed, the audience applauded uneasily. There were handshakes all around, sympathetic words of "Sorry," and "Good fight," and "Can't understand it." When it was over at 1:30 a.m., dog-tired ex-Candidate Willkie boarded a train to return to New York and his law practice.

APRIL 24 **THE MacARTHUR CANDIDACY:** In the free-spoken, never-adjourned town meeting which the vast American democracy tries to resemble, one subject that had long been on people's minds had never, until last week, been put squarely on the agenda. That was the Presidential candidacy of General Douglas MacArthur.

There could be no doubt that hundreds of thousands of plain people thought highly of him. But generally, despite an occasional serious utterance such as the open advocacy of Senator Arthur Vandenberg, most of the press and radio kept dead-pan to the attitude that MacArthur-for-President was not a proper subject for discussion.

Last week all that was suddenly changed. A Republican freshman, Congressman Albert Lewis Miller of Kimball, Neb., suddenly remembered that he had exchanged letters with General MacArthur—and released them to the press. The Correspondence:

"Dear General: There is a tremendous groundswell in

this country against the New Deal. They have crucified themselves on the cross of too many unnecessary rules and regulations.

"You should permit the people of the country to draft you for President. I am convinced you will carry every state in the union.

"I am certain that unless this New Deal can be stopped this time our American way of life is forever doomed. You owe it to civilization and the children yet unborn to accept the nomination. You will be our next President."

General MacArthur replied, evidently much struck by the Congressman's grasp of everything:

"Dear Congressman Miller: I do not anticipate in any way your flattering predictions, but I do unreservedly agree with the complete wisdom and statesmanship of your comments."

Flattered and warmed, Congressman Miller wrote the General again, denouncing the New Deal even more roughly:

"If this system of left-wingers and New Dealism is continued another four years, I am certain that this monarchy which is being established in America will destroy the rights of the common people."

General MacArthur again replied eloquently:

"I appreciate very much your scholarly letter. Your description of conditions in the United States is a sobering one indeed and is calculated to arouse the thoughtful consideration of every true patriot.

"We must not inadvertently slip into the same condition internally as the one which we fight externally. Like Abraham Lincoln, I am a firm believer in the people, and, if given the truth, they can be depended upon to meet any national crises. The great point is to bring before them the real facts.

"Out here we are doing what we can with what we have. I will be glad, however, when more substantial forces are placed at my disposition."

The letters made hubbub. Then, this week General MacArthur emphatically explained. The letters had never been intended for publication.

Said General MacArthur: "Perusal of the letters will show any fair-minded person that they were neither politically inspired nor intended to convey blanket approval of the Congressman's views."

As to the Presidency, General MacArthur said: "I can only say, as I have said before, I have not sought the office, nor do I seek it."

MAY 8 **"NOR WOULD I ACCEPT IT"**: General Douglas MacArthur put a firm end to all the talk. He said:

"I have had brought to my attention a widespread public opinion that it is detrimental to our war effort to have an officer in high position on active service at the front considered for nomination for the office of President. I have on several occasions announced I was not a candidate for the position. To make my position unequivocal, I do not covet it, nor would I accept it."

JULY 3 **TOM DEWEY TAKES OVER**: It was Dewey in a walkaway. Without lifting a finger, without once giving to the men from Maine to Oregon the sign they asked for, Governor Thomas E. Dewey became Candidate Dewey, G.O.P. nominee for the Presidency of the U.S.

The opposition to Dewey collapsed in the face of one question: how can you argue with the people? With Dewey so clearly in front in all public soundings, to reject him for some other candidate might suggest a picture of sinister men in smoke-filled rooms, defying the will of the people.

THE NEXT PRESIDENT?: Like most small-town boys, Thomas Edmund Dewey began picking up spending money in his early teens—delivering papers, clerking in the drugstore, hiring out as a farm hand in the summers.

At the University of Michigan he pulled down As in history, economics and rhetoric without any midnight oil, but he was much more excited by the discovery that he had the best baritone voice on the campus. The first victory of his life came easily in the Michigan State Singing Contest (in the nationals, he placed third). At graduation he was torn between music and law. He plunged into both. But, forced to sing at an important concert when he had a sore throat, he decided once & for all that he could not let his future depend on such a fragile thing as his vocal chords.

Thomas E. Dewey. He pulled A's in history and rhetoric at college, rolled into New York's state house on rubber tires, and now seeks a Washington address.

After Columbia Law School, Tom Dewey went into a substantial law firm. Within three years he became an officer of New York City's Young Republican Club, had been spotted as a comer by U.S. District Attorney George Zerdin Medalie. Just 29, Thomas Dewey became Chief Assistant to District Attorney Medalie and the administrative head of the largest prosecuting office in the federal Government, with 60 lawyers under him. Appointed Special Prosecutor, and elected District Attorney for New York County, by 1938 Thomas Dewey had made the name racket-buster synonymous with his own.

As a prosecutor Thomas Dewey: 1) sent Prohibition Racketeer "Legs" Diamond to Atlanta for four years—Legs's first conviction; 2) smashed a loan-shark ring; 3) gave the order to arrest "Dutch" Schultz, Harlem's policy-racket tsar; 4) broke the luck of "Lucky" Luciano, worst racketeer in New York racket history, by a sentence of 30 to 50 years; 5) as Special Prosecutor, made the sensational record of 72 convictions out of 73 cases tried.

Many Partymen had little stomach for this always successful, always self-contained newcomer. But Thomas Dewey could get votes, and votes salve political wounds. He took over New York's Governorship in 1942 with a rubber-tired steam roller.

At 42, Thomas Dewey could be the youngest President in U.S. history. [The youngest President was Theodore Roosevelt, who was nearly 43 when he took office at the death of President McKinley. The youngest President elected in his own right was John F. Kennedy, 43.]

JULY 10   **FOR THE FOURTH TIME:** In 40 minutes of ponderous eulogy Senator Alben Barkley formally nominated Franklin Roosevelt for a fourth term at the Democratic National Convention in Chicago. Instantly the aisles were crowded with marchers, hundreds of delegates ably abetted by the leather-lunged 27th Ward-heelers who stooge for Chicago's Mayor Ed Kelly. Placards which they had been holding face down as they sat were now waved high: "Roosevelt and Victory"; "Roosevelt and Lasting Peace." The organ and a brassy band blanketed the loud-speakers with furious music.

That night Franklin Roosevelt sat before a microphone in his private railroad car on the West Coast. His voice blared into the convention hall from giant four-way amplifiers in the rafters of the stadium. As they listened, most of the delegates kept their eyes on the empty speaker's stand, where klieg lights were still focused. The effect was eerie.

Franklin Roosevelt's acceptance set firmly the line of the Term IV campaign:

"I shall not campaign, in the usual sense, for the office. In these days of tragic sorrow, I do not consider it fitting. And besides, in these days of global warfare, I shall however, feel free to correct any misrepresentations.

"The people of the United States will decide this fall whether they wish to turn over this 1944 job, this world-wide job, to inexperienced or immature hands, to those who opposed lend-lease and international cooperation, or whether they wish to leave it to those who saw the danger from abroad, and met it head-on."

JULY 31   **HOW THE BOSSES DID IT:** Harry Truman, the grey little junior Senator from Missouri, was nominated for the Vice Presidency twice. The second time was last week, by a majority of the 1,176 delegates to the 29th Democratic Convention. The first time was at a meeting in the White House, the week before.

At that White House meeting were present the Democratic National Chairman, strapping Bob Hannegan, Chicago's Boss and Mayor, Ed Kelly, and four others. The visitors had political business with the President; they wanted to name over the various Vice Presidential possibilities: Henry Wallace, Truman, "Assistant President" Jimmy Byrnes, Supreme Court Justice William O. Douglas, Senator Alben Barkley. The President indicated, in each case, that it would be a pleasure to run with the man named. But everyone thought he detected a slightly firmer emphasis on the word "pleasure" as Harry Truman's name was trotted out.

The Truman boom was under way, managed carefully by Hannegan, Frank Walker, and Bosses Ed Kelly and Ed Flynn of New York. Harry Truman insisted that he did not want the job. For one thing, unlike all the other candidates in Chicago, he did not believe that the President really had chosen him. A story got around that he broke down in his hotel room and cried, telling friends that the Vice Presidential responsibilities were beyond him.

The bosses went to work. His collar open, his shirt sweat-soaked, Bob Hannegan dickered all Wednesday afternoon in his Blackstone suite. Better than anyone else, he knew that a majority of the 1,176 delegates were both: 1) anti-Wallace, and 2) at sea, waiting for a signal from the lighthouse. Hannegan then let it be known that he had telephoned the President, and that the President wanted Truman.

Kentucky's massive, paunchy Alben Barkley was so outraged at this report (he, too, had been given a friendly Roosevelt back-pat) that he called back all advance copies of his address nominating Franklin Roosevelt for Term IV, and threatened not to make the speech at all. Cried "Dear Alben": "I certainly don't know which shell the pea is under."

By now the strategy was clear. The bosses would nominate all possible favorite sons, confuse and wear down the delegates, then try to push through Truman, or a compromise. The Wallace camp was holding firm, determined to switch to no one.

Henry Wallace, battling for his political life, got the most honest ovation of the convention, three minutes of real cheering. Later that same day, the name of Henry Wallace set the galleries afire. From every corner of the Stadium came the chant: "We want Wallace!" At this point the Wallace nomination might have been roared through. Balding Chairman Sam Jackson, try as he might, could not stop the chanting and the noise. Finally, he called for adjournment. The entire Stadium rocked with a chorus of "No!" But Sam Jackson purred smoothly: "The ayes have it."

By next day, everything was organized. All tickets to the Stadium were checked not once, by ushers, but twice, by Ed Kelly's blue-shirted cops. Clusters of tieless war workers, carrying clusters of Wallace placards, were turned away. They just did not seem to have the right kind of tickets.

The bosses were very busy. Their work was done in the air-conditioned "Private Room H," reached by a dark corridor underneath the speaker's stand. Harry Truman stayed there for three hours, handshaking the delegates as the bosses brought them in. Inside, someone was always on the telephone, and whispered snatches of conversation floated to the door. One of the most impressive lines, used with small-town delegates, was the whisper: "I think they have the President on the wire."

The first ballot turned out to be a trial run. Wallace led all the way, Truman relied heavily on the big delegations. The result: Wallace, $429\frac{1}{2}$; Truman, $319\frac{1}{2}$. The 13 favorite sons, with $393\frac{1}{2}$ votes, held the balance of power.

Ballot II was a thrilling battle until the break came. At the quartermark, Wallace led, 148 votes to Truman's 125, with seven key states "passing" (waiting to see which way to jump). Then Ed Flynn brought in $74\frac{1}{2}$ New York votes, and Truman went ahead for the first time. The score: Truman 246; Wallace 187. Then Favorite Son Bob Kerr, Governor of Oklahoma, withdrew his name: 22 more votes for Truman.

At the halfway mark the count stood Truman, 342; Wallace, 286. But the Wallacemen were fighting; the count narrowed; suddenly it was neck-&-neck: Truman, 400; Wallace, 395.

With Truman holding a narrow lead, $477\frac{1}{2}$-to-$472\frac{1}{2}$, the bosses could wait no longer. Alabama's Bankhead withdrew his name, threw 22 votes to Truman. South Carolina switched all 18 votes to Truman. The galleries howled and screamed. The real rush had begun. State chairmen frantically waved their banners for recognition. The Wallace total shrank swiftly.

By now the fickle crowd was on its feet, cheering every Truman gain, as the last, faint chants of "We want Wallace" came from the upper tiers. Then West Virginia, whose Governor Matt Neely had held firm for Wallace, broke down. It added 13 votes for Truman, enough to put him over.

Suddenly, all the hundreds of Wallace placards vanished. The three huge white Wallace balloons, which had hung over the convention all day, were let go; they floated swiftly to the dim rafters overhead, there to bump softly above the smoke, the lights, and the cheers.

Once again, the bosses had won.

Harry S. Truman. He is nominated twice for Vice President.　　*John W. Bricker. "Truman? I never can remember that name."*

A NAME TO REMEMBER: Republican Vice Presidential candidate John Bricker made the first comment of the Dewey-Bricker team on the Democratic Convention. Said he, scratching his brow: "Truman—that's his name, isn't it? I never can remember that name."

AFRAID OF PEACE?: Like an able prosecutor, Tom Dewey SEPT. 18 took his case before the U.S. jury: "This is a campaign against an Administration which was conceived in defeatism, which failed for eight straight years to restore our domestic economy, which has been the most wasteful, extravagant and incompetent Administration in the history of the nation, and worst of all, which has lost faith in the American people."

SEPT. 25 **PRECISION:** With almost metronomic precision, the Dewey train clacked West. It arrived late only once (Des Moines); if it was ahead of time, it loitered in the yards so as to arrive in town on the very pin point of schedule. The advance of the train was prepared for with the crispest American efficiency. This at first bored, then interested, then absorbed the 63 newsmen on the train.

At every stop, six copies of all local papers were brought aboard for the candidate. At each important stop, the routine was exactly the same: a brief speech to the station crowd, a 25-car motorcade to the leading hotel, a half-hour press conference, followed by closed conferences with local GOP-sters, farmers, businessmen and—as the train went farther west—cattlemen, wool growers, lumbermen. Each of these conferences lasted exactly half an hour—no more, no less.

In each city, Tom Dewey followed exactly the same procedure. If a speech was to be made, the local committee was told in advance just how high the lectern must be. The best method for a Dewey entrance was finally worked out: he waited in the wings until the introductory speaker intoned his name, then walked briskly forward.

Tom Dewey was meticulously groomed, changing suits daily—brown, blue, grey pin-striped, always single-breasted. Always, when he alighted, the grey Homburg was in his hand. Never did he seem flustered.

Not even Dewey's most ardent admirers pretended that he ever showed a superabundance of warmth, or relaxed in back-slapping informality. His deportment was precise and correct, at times even chill. But the GOPsters invariably were pleased that they did not have a candidate for whom they had to apologize (like Landon) or whose lusty statements kept them in hot water (like Willkie).

OCT. 2 **THE OLD MAGIC:** In the Presidential Room of Washington's Statler Hotel were gathered the elite of the International Brotherhood of Teamsters, Chauffeurs, Warehousemen and Helpers of America, and the elite of the city's political society.

They were met together to eat roast chicken, Virginia ham, peas, potato croquettes, salad, ice cream and coffee, to drink California sauterne and, more important, to get an answer to the biggest of the Democrats' political questions: has The Old Master still got it?

The Old Master looked considerably thinner but very fit. He ate heartily, drank only half of his glass of California sauterne, and sat thoughtfully oversmoking through the banquet. For the benefit of the Teamsters, the band played *Don't Change Horses in the Middle of the Stream,* while Franklin Roosevelt made penciled notes on his manuscript. Then it was time to go on the air, before the millions of citizens who were also asking: Has he still got it?

The Old Master still had it. Franklin Roosevelt was at his best. He was like a veteran virtuoso playing a piece he has loved for years, who fingers his way through it with a delicate fire, a perfection of timing and tone, and an assurance that no young player, no matter how gifted, can equal. The President was playing what he loves to play—politics.

He started smoothly with a reference to the "mess that was dumped into our laps in 1933," and then got down to cases. His first attack was on those Republicans, who, he said, "suddenly discover" every four years, just before Election Day, that they love labor—after having attacked labor for three years and six months.

He paused in the attack just long enough to defend his Administration's preparations for war. His defense: the isolationist record of the Republicans in Congress who opposed Lend-Lease and other preparedness measures.

The President, in all his 33-minute address, by his actor's timing, by the voice that purrs softly and then strikes hard, by the frank ham-acting, kept his audience with him every minute that he was on the offensive.

The President kept his tone mainly light and good-humored, even in some of his most savage digs. But at one point his voice dropped into solemnity and he said: "These Republican leaders have not been content with attacks on me, or on my wife, or on my sons—no, not content with that —they now include my little dog Fala." The audience roared; even the stoniest of Republican faces around U.S. radios cracked into a smile.

OCT. 9 **SERENADE FOR HARRY:** Democratic Vice Presidential Nominee Harry Truman was serenaded at a Kansas City political dinner:

> *We sing our praise of Vice President*
> *Truman, parley-vous,*
> *The man who's loved all over the world*
> *By me and you.*
> *Vice President by acclamation,*
> *An American credit to our nation—*
> *Hinkey dinkey parley-vous!*

Harry Truman, who rose to the U.S. Senate under the sponsorship of Kansas City's old Pendergast machine, responded with a bit of his political philosophy. "I'm a Jackson County organization Democrat and I'm proud of it," he said. "That's the way I got to be a county judge, a senator and candidate for vice president." Then he added: "A statesman is only a dead politician. I never want to be a statesman."

HOLLYWOOD v. HOLLYWOOD: The political guns, big & little, were now zeroed on the plain U.S. citizen. In this battle, Hollywood fought glamor with glamor. The Hollywood-for-Dewey Committee had nice legs, a pretty wit and good lungs: Ginger Rogers, Hedda Hopper, Rosalind Russell, Cecil B. de Mille, Anne Baxter, Leo Carrillo and Adolphe Menjou. So did the Hollywood Committee of New Dealers: Rita Hayworth, Olivia de Havilland, Katharine Hepburn, Orson Welles, Harpo Marx, Lana Turner, Walter Huston, Fanny Brice.

OCT. 16 **"WITH ALL MY HEART":** *"I accept the nomination of the Republican Party for President of the United States."*
> —Wendell Willkie, Aug. 17, 1940

This week Wendell Willkie died. The news came as an actual shock; if there had been a seismograph to measure such things, it would have recorded that the shock was felt by human beings clear around the world. All over the U.S. the people said the same things to each other: simple words of half-angry disbelief, of loss, or sorrow. That was a man, said the people.

Wendell Willkie's sudden death, at 52, somehow made it suddenly apparent how valuable were the things he stood for: courage, integrity, deep belief in democracy, deep faith in humanity, a passionate dedication to the ideal of freedom.

Every American who was aware of the world in 1940 could recall as if it were yesterday the big, intense Indianan as he rolled through the country in the fabulous Willkie train, the most wonderful political caravan that has traveled the U.S. in this generation.

There in their minds he stands, the big, stubborn-faced Midlander, 6 ft. 1 in., 220 lbs., a joshing look around his big firm mouth, the dark brown hair beginning to tumble over his forehead; the rich, growling voice slurring over the words: "Fellow Amurricans!"

The men who came to Philadelphia to nominate a candidate to run against Term III came there under a growing pressure of public opinion that moved like an irresistible flood. The professional politicians never fully realized what happened to them. Nothing in their lives, nothing in American political history could have prepared them for the almost religious passion that forced the Willkie candidacy over every barrier that political tricks could devise, overwhelming all precedents under the mighty chant of the galleries, a chant that echoed all over America. "We Want Willkie!"

The crowd that moved in on Elwood, Ind. from all the states and towns around to hear his acceptance speech on Aug. 17 was unquestionably the greatest crowd in U.S. political history. It was uncountable; no stadium could have held it; the estimates ranged as high as 500,000.

Then began the "crusade," when the big man roared over & over: "Only the strong can be free and only the productive can be strong." Wendell Willkie exhorted his fellow citizens as perhaps they have never been exhorted before. Arms spread wide in a gesture of appeal, his tangled hair awry, he drove through the streets of scores on scores of towns, appealing hoarsely to the people to understand, to help him in his crusade against the New Deal.

Defeated as a Presidential candidate, Willkie became the leader of the "loyal opposition," and it was as such that he became world-famed as a man of good will.

He taught the U.S. about the world. His book, *One*

World, became one of the greatest best-sellers on record (over 1,000,000 copies). But his political prestige within his own party sank; the Republicans turned to Thomas E. Dewey as the man likeliest to beat Term IV.

This week Willkie suffered a heart attack, in Rushville, Ind. He got off the train in Manhattan, pale and ill. Soon after, he entered Manhattan's Lenox Hill hospital, on Sept. 6, for a physical checkup. His big heart was no longer strong; he had coronary thrombosis. But he made some progress; the doctors grew cautiously optimistic. Friends readied a house in Florida, where he could fly for a long rest.

Then suddenly, he caught a streptococcic throat infection; his fever soared to 104°. Big in the white cotton hospital gown, he stirred restlessly in his bed. He was feeling better. Penicillin injections had destroyed the germs and brought his temperature to 102, then down toward normal. In a few days, he hoped, he would go home.

Then the sharp pain came back; fighting the infection had brought on the second heart attack. But the heart he had pledged to the people was still strong enough. He weathered the crisis, but lay back exhausted, his thick dark hair tangled on the pillow. At midnight he fell asleep, and the transparent folds of an oxygen tent were draped about his head to help his breathing.

An hour later he awoke. The nurse came in, and the doctor. The nurse swabbed his raw throat. The doctor asked him how he felt. "How can I talk," he joked, "with all this stuff in my mouth?" "Maybe you'd like a Scotch and water —for a stimulant," the doctor said. "You could use one." "Okay, if you make it warm," the big man said. His voice, as always, was hoarse, and it had a far-away sound.

A short hour later, the third attack came and this time it was more than his heart could stand.

At 2:20 a.m. on a Sunday morning, Wendell Willkie died, a look of worry on his still-boyish face. His wife, standing at the bedside, wavered as she watched his life flicker out. His former secretary, Lamoyne Jones, walked out of the room, tears in his eyes, to the newsmen waiting in the lobby below. An hour before, he had brought out words of hope. Now his hands were raised in a gesture of surrender. "It's all over," he said. "He went very fast."

THE HAPPY WARRIOR: New York in August seemed oppressively hot to him. In the old days there had been little open garden patches in mid-Manhattan, but now the skyscrapers shut out the harbor breeze. The old "governor" was 70; finally he went to the hospital, for a "rest." But autumn came and he did not go home. Suddenly he was gravely ill. He prayed in his conscious moments, and one night the Most Rev. J. Francis A. McIntyre, auxiliary bishop of New York, administered the last sacrament. He rallied; but four days later, Death, as it must to all men, came to Alfred Emanuel Smith.

Millions of Americans, who had almost forgotten Al Smith the politician, remembered him as a symbol of a wonderful era—the years of the never-ending bull market, of the hip flask, of F. Scott Fitzgerald and the Dempsey fights. Al Smith's hoarse and genial East Side voice, his chewed cigar, his violent pajamas and his rasping expletive, "Baloney!" belonged to the fabulous '20s as much as *It Ain't Gonna Rain No Mo'*. He was against the Volstead Act; and in the '20s the U.S. almost elected him its President.

But Al Smith was devoutly religious, a family man who never went into nightclubs. The jazz age never won him away from songs like the *Mulligan Guards*. He toiled stubbornly for social reform. His life story had the old Horatio Alger plot. He was a poor East Side boy with an Irish gift for politics and people, who made good against tremendous odds.

He was elected governor of New York in 1918. By now he was a shrewd, blunt, humorous campaigner, with an unequaled knowledge of the state's affairs. He was also a great legislative technician with an uncanny ability to rasp out simple, pointed explanations of complicated governmental problems. He battled for slum clearance, set up children's courts, got additional millions for teachers' salaries. He wanted people to enjoy themselves—he took the ban off Sunday baseball.

His fame spread outside the state, and by the 1924 Democratic Convention he had begun his great losing battle for the White House. Franklin Roosevelt put his name in nomination for President, and gave him the nickname that stuck for the rest of his life—"The Happy Warrior." It was not Al Smith's year. He was a Catholic and a Wet, and the Southerners and the Drys were against him. But by 1928 a Democratic boom for Al Smith swept the country. When the convention met at Houston, Tex., the opposition forces of 1924 had swung behind him.

Al Smith, the first U.S. Catholic to run for President as the nominee of a major party, went out to stump the nation. He was met by one of the most virulent whispering campaigns in U.S. history. Thousands muttered that he was building a tunnel to connect the White House with the Vatican.

The Happy Warrior fought back. But the shrewd, hoarse eloquence, the administrative abilities that he had, and the support of all liberals, were not enough—the Great Engineer was elected. But now Smith had the fever. He became convinced that next time he would make it. When his old friend Franklin D. Roosevelt won the 1932 nomination, Al Smith felt betrayed.

He campaigned for Roosevelt in 1932, but by 1936 he could no longer contain his bitterness. He invented the term "alphabet soup" to describe the plethora of New Deal agencies, spoke for Alf Landon, and warned the U.S. sarcastically that "You can't lick Santa Claus." Then he quit politics. His last years were quiet but busy. He became president of the Empire State Building, a director of a half-dozen corporations. His wife died last spring. After that Al Smith grew old quickly.

On the day of his funeral, New York's Fifth Avenue lay empty and silent, cleared of all traffic. The crowds stood bareheaded and motionless; there was hardly a sound as the funeral procession started on its long way to the place beside his wife, under a simple headstone in a Queens cemetery. He would not be forgotten; to millions of Americans, as long as they lived, the jingling strains of *The Sidewalks of New York* would bring back the memory of The Happy Warrior of the Fabulous '20s.

OCT. 23 **"CARD GAMES?":** Harry Truman arrived in New Orleans and started campaigning before a roomful of servicemen's wives, each of whom had a baby in her arms. Confronted with a practical politician's dilemma—to kiss or not to kiss— he escaped neatly by explaining that he had a cold. Back in his hotel room he added another reason, "I might have dropped one."

When a newsman asked him if he played cards, Truman endeavored to please old ladies and poker fiends alike. "Card games?", the candidate mused. "The only game I know anything about is that game—let me see—I don't know what the name is, but you put one card face down on the table, and four face up, and you bet." Then Truman headed for California.

GONNA LIVE TO 93: The train pulling Harry Truman's special OCT. 30 car ground to a stop at flat, dusty Uvalde, Tex. As vestibule doors banged in the silence of the sunny afternoon, a little old man with a bright pink face came hurrying up to the train. It was ex-Vice President "Cactus Jack" Garner, the copilot whom Franklin Roosevelt had dropped in 1940.

John Garner, now 75, was wearing a worn work shirt, buttoned at the throat, a pair of dingy pants. His hands were stained black. He leaned forward slightly, favoring his left ear, talking fast. "Got my hands like this hulling pecans yesterday. Today I've been in the cornfield since early morning. I wish we had time to strike a blow for Liberty, Harry."

"We have got time, Jack," Truman said. "You come right back here in my car. We've got some good bourbon whiskey." The nominee led the way.

When he was seated inside the car the old man slapped his leg. "Yes, sir," he said, "this is fine." "Put a little branch water in there, son," he told the grizzled porter. "Yes, sir, Harry, I never felt better in my life. I'll be 76 next month and I'm gonna live to 93. I get to bed early—and I still drink whiskey. Couldn't live to 93 if I didn't." He tossed off a hefty drink. "Well, Harry, this train is fixing to pull out." He got up, glanced carefully at the bottom of his glass, said goodbye and started for the door.

He stood, looking up, as the train began to roll away. Then he walked off, stopping once to strike a kitchen match expertly on the seat of his trousers and relight the frayed stump of his Mexican cigar. [When Garner died in 1967, two weeks before his 99th birthday, he had given up whiskey on advice of his doctors.]

NOV. 13 **THE WINNER:** From the green-curtained voting booth came a clank of gears as the main control lever jerked irritably back & forth. Then a voice, familiar to all of the U.S. and to most of the world, spoke distinctly from behind the curtains: "The goddamned thing won't work."

A solicitous election official hastened forward with advice. The lever clanked again, caught correctly this time. Franklin Delano Roosevelt, 62, self-styled tree grower of New York State, voter No. 251 of Hyde Park village, had exercised his right as a U.S. citizen.

In voting booths throughout the nation, some 40,000,000 other U.S. citizens were exercising the same right. Before midnight, the verdict was clear: Franklin Roosevelt, the first U.S. President to serve three terms in the White House, had rolled up a huge popular vote—and a landslide electoral vote —to give him his fourth term.

Labor

JAN. 3 **STRONG ARM:** The big news of the week—and one of the biggest pieces of news in all 1943—was that President Roosevelt got tough. At last he stood fast against Labor's demands; at last he solidly backed up the anti-inflation Little Steel formula [an attempt to link wage increases to increases in the cost of living].

The President, in seizing the $28,000,000,000 railroad industry, served sharp notice on the millions in union labor's legions that the formula must hold; that the concessions to John Lewis [increased payments made to coal miners in 1943] were the last sizable concessions that would be made. This was direct notice to the C.I.O. and Phil Murray's 600,000 Steel Workers—of whom 170,000 were out on strike this week. The new Roosevelt technique worked perfectly: Phil Murray called the Steel Workers back to the mills.

The President had given the 20 railroad unions the same terms—anything within reason, but the line must be held. He had warned the 1,450,000 railroaders to call off their strike by Dec. 27. Three of the 20 unions balked. Said Mr. Roosevelt: "I cannot wait until the last moment." That night the President gave Secretary of War Stimson complete power over every one of the 233,670 miles of railroad track in the U.S., from the one-mile long Valley Railroad in McKean County, Penna. to the $2,000,000,000 Pennsy (24,928 miles). The Secretary may even take over subways, tunnels and streetcar lines, if need be.

Behind the velvet-glove technique of offering concessions, within the formula, was Franklin Roosevelt's iron hand—and the iron hand was the news.

RAILROAD TAKEOVER: A major and a lieutenant colonel, JAN. 10 armed with a mimeograph of the Presidential order directing the Army to seize all U.S. railroads, walked into Union Pacific's towering Omaha headquarters building at 8 o'clock one morning last week. They took an elevator to the 12th-floor executive offices, began knocking at doors. At last they came to the office of tough little Vice President G.F. Ashby. He grinned and guessed: "You've come to take us over, have you?"

He led them in to see big President Bill Jeffers. Everybody shook hands. Said Jeffers: "Anything you want, just let us know." They moved in with an armful of orders. As an afterthought, Jeffers' assistant provided the officers with an advertising folder, containing a map of the Union Pacific's rail network for them to study.

Thus last week the Army began "operating" all U.S. railroads. Trains ran as usual. Companies collected and kept fares. Seven major railroad heads became uniformed colonels overnight—then continued at their desks.

The President's bold seizure stopped a strike, but did not solve the unrest of the railworkers. Fifteen of the rail unions that gave in were still as angry as the three that held out. They were almost more angry about method than money. The Brotherhoods are the orderly conservatives of U.S. unionism, with a long tradition of protocol in wage negotiations. Their pleas for a wage boost had been shunted about for more than a year. They had spent 45 years building their framework of bargaining, only to have Franklin Roosevelt personally take over their troubles a day before they were to argue their case before the long-established National Mediation Board. To the three holdout unions this was "changing the rules in the middle of the game."

JAN. 31 **RETIRED COLONELS:** The Administration had wobbled its way through one crisis: the railroads. Away from the Army, back to industry went management of the roads, after 22 days of Government operation. The seven top rail executives who had donned Army colonels' uniforms took them off again, put them away in closets, to be taken out only for parades and grandchildren. For three weeks' active duty, they were entitled to about $360 in Army pay (besides their regular salaries). But most of them had spent $250 or more on well-tailored uniforms.

The workers fared better. The 15 big non-operating unions (1,100,000 members) got 9- to 11¢-an hour raises, though they had been willing to take 8¢.

Once more the Administration had honored the letter of Little Steel, while doing violence to its spirit. Once more the Government had covered its retreat by seizing property and thus giving the appearance of decision. But the workers lost nothing by Government operation, and won their wage demands.

One of the sensations of 1944 was the seizure by the U.S. Army of the Chicago headquarters of Montgomery Ward & Co. The issue was that the firm's president, Sewell Avery, had refused to obey an order from the War Labor Board to extend an expired labor contract with the C.I.O. union until an election could be held to determine whether the C.I.O. controlled a majority of the workers.

MAY 8 **SEIZURE!:** Serene and calm, Sewell Lee Avery sat down in the green leather chair in his paneled office, and waited. Day before, he had sent a telegram challenging the authority of the President of the U.S. to seize the Chicago plant of Montgomery Ward & Co., the $295,000,000 mail-order house of which Mr. Avery is the absolute, unchallenged boss. Mr. Avery had not long to wait.

The U.S. Government arrived, in the person of an old-family Chicagoan, Under Secretary of Commerce Wayne Chatfield Taylor—a rich man's son, product of Yale, and by no means a wild-eyed New Dealer. Sewell Avery rose from his chair, his thin lips parting in an amiable smile, and courteously, gravely asked the U.S. Government to step in. The door closed.

Out of his brief case Wayne Taylor drew a certified copy of the Presidential order directing the Secretary of Commerce to take over operation of Montgomery Ward & Co. "for the successful prosecution of the war."

An hour later Wayne Taylor emerged, informed newsmen that Sewell Avery had bluntly refused to turn over his plant. He left to telephone Commerce Secretary Jesse Jones in Washington, returned with a U.S. deputy marshal and eight gun-toting deputies. Facing the armed squadron, Sewell Avery politely told the marshal that he would not surrender. Then a call went out to Camp Skokie Valley, just north of Chicago.

Shortly after 6 p.m. three olive-drab Army trucks rolled up to Montgomery Ward's main entrance. Out jumped a 44-man unit of battle helmeted Military Police under command of Lieut. Ludwig Pincura. Bayonets glinted in the afternoon sun. Followed by four enlisted men, Lieut. Pincura began his bloodless invasion. On the eighth floor the five pairs of Army brogans moved noiselessly through the deep-carpeted executive offices.

Sewell Avery smiled. After a moment's embarrassed silence, Lieut. Pincura said: "Under authority vested in me by the President of the United States I am taking over this plant."

Asked Sewell Avery: "Does that mean I have to leave?"

"Yes," said the commander of the Army of Occupation.

"No," said Sewell Avery, answering his own question.

Sewell Avery, a tall, thin man with long thin hands, glanced calmly at his watch. "Well," he said, "time to go home anyway." He left by a rear door, ducking reporters, jumped into his waiting black Cadillac and drove to his Lake Shore Drive apartment.

Next morning Sewell Avery was not in his office. At his desk sat Wayne Taylor; at Wayne Taylor's right sat lank, birdlike Attorney General Francis Biddle, who had flown in from Washington at 4 a.m., rushed to Ward's after an hour's sleep. His eyes were red-rimmed; his jaw set.

Said the Attorney General, in his best Philadelphia Main

Sewell Avery of Montgomery Ward & Co. looks every inch an Oriental potentate as two soldiers carry him bodily from his office.

Line accent: "When Mr. Avery came in this morning I asked him if he would cooperate and turn over books to our bookkeepers. He refused to do this. I asked him to call a staff meeting and explain what our purpose was. Mr. Avery said he would not cooperate in any way. We told Mr. Avery he would have to leave. Mr. Avery refused."

Francis Biddle looked nervously about the room, then quietly dropped his bombshell: "Mr. Taylor therefore directed Major Weber to conduct Mr. Avery out of the plant. Mr. Avery refused and had to be carried out."

Newsmen nearest the door scurried out of the room to telephones. Those who stayed badgered the Attorney General with questions:

"Did they actually carry him out?"

Replied Mr. Biddle: "He was actually picked up and carried out of this chair occupied by Mr. Taylor."

"How did he react?"

Francis Biddle seemed to welcome this question. He smiled: "Well, I'll tell you something. He got pretty mad. The blood came to his face and he said to me, 'You New Dealer!' "

The actual ejection of the $100,000-a-year board chairman of Montgomery Ward was carried out by Sergeant Jacob L. Lepak of Milwaukee and Private Cecil A. Dies of Memphis. The two soldiers picked 170-lb. Sewell Avery up by his arms and thighs, carried him to the elevator. Mr. Avery refused to walk in; the soldiers picked him up again. On the main floor he again refused to budge. The soldiers hoisted him up, carried him past a handful of startled clerks in the lobby, and down the main steps. His grey hair unruffled, his blue suit coat buttoned, his hands folded benignly across his stomach, his eyes half-closed, Avery looked every inch an Oriental potentate being borne by slaves.

Photographers who had waited outside jammed plates into their cameras, snapped the most startling U.S. newspicture since a press agent set a midget on J. P. Morgan's lap in 1933. One Ward executive suggested putting the picture on the cover of Ward's next catalogue, with a caption "We take orders from everybody."

THE NEW FORCE: The most important politician at the Democratic convention in Chicago this week is, very probably, a   JULY 24

In a poster put out by the C.I.O.'s Political Action Committee, FDR is the friend of farmers, laborers, children and all races.

labor leader. The labor leader is Sidney Hillman, 57, of Manhattan, for 30 years the president of the rich and powerful Amalgamated Clothing Workers. Hillman's importance derives from the biggest new fact in U.S. politics: the C.I.O.'s Political Action Committee, of which he is chairman.

The tone and approach of P.A.C. is apparent in the very first sentence of its *Political Primer for All Americans* (2,000,-000 copies have already been distributed). Says the *Primer:* "Politics is the science of how who gets what, when and why."

The *Primer* continues: "To the average American, politicians are crooks. The truth is that politicians are no more corrupt than the people who elect them. The people corrupt the politicians. Let's quit blaming the politicians and face the responsibility of full citizenship. Let's become politicians ourselves."

Foreign Relations

By the summer of 1944, the battle against the Axis was proceeding so well that delegates from the Allied powers were already meeting in an effort to formulate an international organization that would help to maintain world peace and stability after the war ended. The organization that emerged from these deliberations was the United Nations.

AUG. 28 **AT DUMBARTON OAKS:** The World Security Conference began this week at stately Dumbarton Oaks, a magnificent 16-acre estate set like a jewel in Washington's Georgetown. The 39 delegates, none in a plug hat, strolled down the old pebble walks, through formal gardens, across arched bridges over the carp pond. Promptly at 10:30 a.m. they filed into the pink brick Georgian mansion, past the Byzantine and mediaeval *objets d'art,* into the high-ceilinged music room. There they arranged themselves around a huge U-shaped table covered with the inevitable blotter pads.

Surrounded by polychromes and ancient cathedral benches, Secretary of State Cordell Hull put on his beribboned pince-nez, rapped sharply for order and, in his best intricate diplomatic language, called on the conferees for cooperation.

The purpose of the conference is to prepare memoranda on the possible creation of a world organization to preserve the peace. The Big Three have already exchanged memos on this. The present conference will be a further exchange. After it ends, the delegates will report their findings to their governments, after which, with all the preliminaries out of the way, the participating nations will get down to real business —with the war in Europe even nearer an end.

HULL AND DULLES: The man who might be the next U.S. SEPT. 4 Secretary of State conferred with Cordell Hull last week, two hours a day for three days.

After the third session, tall, ruddy John Foster Dulles, 56, foreign-affairs adviser to Candidate Thomas E. Dewey, reported to the U.S. press. On crutches (he had an infected foot), he swung out of Mr. Hull's office, across the black & white marble checkerboard hall of the State Department, into the diplomats' waiting room. Said he:

"We have done something which is perhaps unique in American politics." The Manhattan Republican and the Tennessee Democrat had agreed—in a general way—on the machinery of a potential international peace organization,

John Foster Dulles, adviser to Dewey, may be the next Secretary of State.

Secretary of State Cordell Hull: "I'm sick and I know it." Page 64.

and were ready to take that much of foreign policy out of the 1944 campaign.

The big fact was that the Democratic and Republican candidates are agreed that the U.S. shall participate in a new League of Nations, and all the U.S. could take heart that the discussion had been conducted so far on a high and non-political level.

GAY EVENING OUT: As host to the 39 diplomats at Dumbarton Oaks (ten Russians, eleven Britons, 18 Americans), hearty, handsome Under Secretary of State Edward R. Stettinius felt the impulse to introduce a little fun-&-games into the delegates' off-hours.

Big Ed (known as "Junior" in Washington) had been much struck with the President's breezily informal address to the conferees, in which Mr. Roosevelt cheerfully pointed out that getting along was all a matter of getting together and of liking each other. The very next day Ed Stettinius began heartily backslapping the British and Russians, and would call loudly, "Alec!" and "Andrei!" to the British chief, Sir Alexander Cadogan, 59, and the Russian chief, Andrei Gromyko, 39. Sir Alexander, an urbane, reserved British Foreign Office Specialist, winced slightly; Ambassador Gromyko gave a scarcely perceptible shrug. But both bore up bravely under this American jollity, and by week's end even seemed to be used to it.

Then big Ed had an inspiration: why not take the whole kit-&-kaboodle to New York for a typical American businessman's weekend in Manhattan? This proposal was received with mixed feelings. (Said a State Department official, "It is too frivolous!") But many delegates were keen to go, and pretty soon Host Stettinius had most of them aboard a plane, off for the big city. Naturally the secrecy was intensified—perhaps no Russian wanted Joseph Stalin to hear too many lush details of bouncing about in nightclubs.

Soon the press had found the delegates—first at the Waldorf-Astoria, then at Radio City Music Hall (the Rockettes and Katharine Hepburn in *Dragon Seed*), and finally, at Billy Rose's Diamond Horseshoe, where the world planners took ringside seats for the midnight floor show.

Next morning the news broke—and some of the delegates,

literally groaning about the inquisitive freedom of the U.S. press, ate very light breakfasts. After that the motorcycle escorts and U.S. Army cars vanished; the delegates went about two-by-two in taxis, desperately dodging reporters. They managed to get in an excursion boat ride in New York harbor; some went to the theater. Sunday afternoon they flew back to Washington to face again the problems of the world's peace.

"WELL BEGUN": In a 5,000-word joint communiqué, the OCT. 16 Big Four this week told what Dumbarton Oaks accomplished.

¶ The new world order will be named The United Nations.
¶ France "in due course" will become one of a Big Five entitled to permanent seats on the eleven-man Security Council.
¶ The Assembly, to which all nations will belong, will have less power than expected. It may debate broad problems but should not "on its own initiation make recommendations" on any tough problem up before the Security Council.
¶ The United Nations should have armadas of "national air force contingents immediately available" to send against an aggressor.

MR. HULL RESIGNS: On his 73rd birthday, last Oct. 2, the DEC. 4 Administration's No. 1 Cabinet officer showed up as usual at his office, but he complained: "I'm sick and I know it." Next day he stayed home. For the past five weeks, with an occasional bedside visit from Franklin Roosevelt, good, grey Cordell Hull has lain abed in the Naval Hospital at Bethesda, Md., under observation and treatment for a throat ailment and exhaustion. This week, reluctantly and on his doctor's advice, Cordell Hull resigned as Secretary of State.

His letter of resignation eloquently told his deep disappointment. "It is a supreme tragedy to me personally," he wrote to Franklin Roosevelt. It was clear that he felt his departure a simple duty to the nation.

Franklin Roosevelt replied in kind. The resignation, he wrote, "has hit me between wind and water." To Franklin Roosevelt, Cordell Hull is "Father of the United Nations," and he hoped that Cordell Hull would be able to preside when the first triumphant United Nations assembly is held.

The man who had directed U.S. foreign affairs for twelve years—longer by four years than any other man—will continue, the President said, to be a sort of White House adviser.

In many ways, Cordell Hull's place was unique. Among his diplomatic victories he could list such achievements as the reciprocal trade agreements, the Good Neighbor policy, the 1943 Moscow Declaration and the Dumbarton Oaks agreement. The Hull failures have also been impressive. In success or failure, Mr. Hull usually preserved his native dignity. That dignity did not desert him (though it called to its aid some white-hot Tennessee cuss words) when Pearl Harbor caught him politely conferring with two grinning Japanese diplomats. It kept him at least outwardly calm when New Deal left-wingers shrilly accused him of appeasing Pétain, Darlan, Franco and Badoglio.

But in 51 years of public life—as Tennessee legislator, backwoods jurist, U.S. Congressman, Democratic National Committee Chairman, U.S. Senator, and Secretary of State—Cordell Hull acquired a wide reputation for a single trait. Most U.S. citizens, both admirers and detractors, were convinced that Cordell Hull was a pretty tough old party who fought hard for the things he believed in.

The scramble for Hull's job was short, eager and one-sided. At his noon press conference, Franklin Roosevelt had no news about a successor. Three hours later he nominated and sent to the Senate the name of platinum-topped Edward R. ("Junior") Stettinius Jr., 44, acting Secretary of State. But few doubted that under his regime the real Secretary of State would continue to be Franklin Roosevelt.

Food

APRIL 3 **THE GOOD YEARS:** Across the jagged Badlands, over the rolling plains of stubble wheat, and even in Watford City (pop. 1,087), there were still solid patches of snow. But the miracle had happened. Throughout North Dakota, the big thaw had come. The hard-bitten men who farm the northern tip of the onetime poverty-stricken U.S. "dust bowl" had survived a decade of dust, drought, WPA, grasshoppers, mortgages.

Now, after a three-year spell of war and golden weather, they could afford a little fun in town.

At the City Bar's wide wooden counter, MacKenzie County farmers, their jeans heavy with cash, drank up 40 cases of beer a day. At Christensen's hardware store they stripped the shelves nearly bare. They played poker, guzzled, loafed, had Doc Winter put gold in their teeth.

During the '30s, North Dakota lost almost everything but its weathered denims and its prized "elbow room." Last year the state came back as one of the nation's biggest breadbaskets: first in spring and durum wheat production, first in barley, second in certified seed potatoes. North Dakota farms (average 1940 census value: $8,742) brought in an average 1943 income of $7,817.

Lean grizzled old Lawyer W. S. ("Bud") Taylor sat back from making out income tax returns (at $3 each) and pulled on his pipe. "These boys are really rolling in dough this year. When the Lord gets around to raining on this land, it'll raise anything."

E IS FOR EGG: When the Government called for more agricultural produce, the 389,469,000 patriotic U.S. hens squawked but then settled down loyally to do their stuff.   JUNE 26

Long before last week the result was embarrassingly scrambled. Every U.S. hen, in effect, easily won an E for egg production. Cackling happily, the hens then went on to such a fabulous overproduction that the whole U.S. was practically walking on eggs. The War Food Administration, which had been franctically storing eggs everywhere but in their desks, was thoroughly alarmed. In May the happy hens set a new production record of 6,704,000,000 eggs. In 1,400 freight cars on Midwestern sidings last week were stacked 25,000,000 dozen eggs, getting more dubious by the day.

By week's end egg processors had taken more than half the 1,400 freight cars off WFA's hands. When it gets rid of the rest, WFA says the crisis will be past. By then the seasonal egg slump will have begun, and WFA hopes the hens will observe it.

THE GREAT HARVEST: This was going to be the biggest wheat crop in U.S. history. Nature had been good, the sun and the   JULY 10 skies kind, the land fruitful. The next great problem was manpower. Could the U.S. harvest the biggest wheat crop it had ever grown, when most of its men were off to the war or war plants? This question was being answered—childpower and womanpower and old-manpower were reaping the great harvest.

The next great problem was to haul the harvest. Could the railroads do it? Usually the Santa Fe, largest U.S. wheat carrier, spots 10,000 wheat cars at key junction points for the harvest. But last week the Santa Fe, which owns 35,000 boxcars, could spare only 889. All other cars were carrying high-priority freight up & down the nation.

In this year of plenty, with so much wheat and so many transport troubles, thousands of bushels will remain piled high in the fields after the harvest, or be stored in empty village buildings. But the wheat will still be good, and the nation will need it.

Disaster

JULY 17   **SIX MINUTES:** The smoking little flame wavered higher up the side of the cavernous tent in the big lot at Hartford, Conn. The thousands of women and their children, and the scattering of coatless men massed in the bleachers, sat quietly, second after second, watching the high-wire performers of Ringling Brothers and Barnum & Bailey's Greatest Show On Earth. They breathed the circus smells of peanuts and tigers in the hot afternoon air, and listened to the thumping circus music. Some of them watched the harmless-looking little fire crawling up the canvas.

Then the flame suddenly spurted upward with nightmare swiftness, and billowed silently across the whole top of the tent near the main entrance. The bleachers suddenly rumbled under thousands of feet; folding chairs clattered and banged.

The crowd struggled to reach the ground, flowed wildly toward the exits, clotted into groups which pushed and elbowed with silent, furious concentration in the furnace-like heat. Men & women in the high bleacher seats began dropping children to the ground, then jumped themselves.

Then great blazing patches of canvas fell. Women screamed as their hair and dresses caught fire. Then a tent pole toppled soundlessly, trailed by burning canvas. People were still struggling down from their seats.

Three minutes had passed.

There still was brassy music. The band, on its feet at the unburned end of the tent, jerkily pumped out *The Stars and Stripes Forever,* as a "Disaster march," the traditional circus warning to performers outside the tent to rally round for trouble. The aerialists slid down their ropes, began tumbling acrobatically toward safety.

A mass of the crowd headed toward the performers' exits near the band. Hundreds of them jammed up against the barred runway through which the last leopards from the animal acts were still slinking toward outside cages. As the people struggled here, some scrambling over, some lifting small children, some trampling wildly, the fire raced toward them along the collapsing canvas high overhead. The heavy tent poles fell quickly, one after another. As the last toppled, all the blazing canvas came down on the crowd. There was a brief, screaming struggle beneath it.

The sooty bandsmen, now safe outside, began to play again. Six minutes had passed.

By nightfall, Hartford knew how badly it had been hurt. In the worst circus disaster in U.S. history, 128 bodies lay on army cots, neatly set out on the drill floor of the grey, stone State Guard Armory, and others were arriving. More than half the bodies there, and more than half the swathed, drugged forms in the crowded hospitals were children.

At week's end the death toll had mounted to 169. Hartford was a city of funerals. Every hearse, every livery car was in constant use; undertakers toiled night & day, and some funeral parlors were holding services at 15-minute intervals.

The State's Attorney and the chief of State Police asked the questions which were on thousands of other lips. Why did the tent burn with that celluloid fierceness? Circus men said the 19-ton big top had been sprayed with a water-proofing solution last April. It had not been inspected before the show by the Hartford fire marshal. Five officials and employes of the circus were arrested on technical charges of manslaughter.

WORLD BATTLEFRONTS

The year saw the turning of the tide for the Allied forces everywhere. In the Pacific, U.S. ships dealt a series of crippling blows to the Japanese fleet, and soldiers and Marines started leapfrogging from one Japanese-held island to another to force the enemy out of his conquered domain. The Germans, who in the preceding five years had overrun Poland, Denmark, Norway, France, the Low Countries, the Balkans, North Africa and much of Russia, were also on the defensive. They had been forced out of Africa by U.S. and British troops. Soviet armies had launched massive counterattacks against Nazi-held territory and were gathering momentum all along the front. But the most crucial battle of all, the liberation of Europe, was about to begin.

Battle of Europe

JAN. 3 **WIELDERS OF THE WEAPON:** Invasion was coming. The timetable was set, the weapon almost forged. The London press reported millions of U.S. soldiers pouring into Britain ("strap-hanging across the Atlantic," one newspaper called it). Now the men to command the attack on the German heartland were chosen. The division of command gave sobering impressions: in the hard, costly attack from the west, U.S. troops will bear a major burden.

General Dwight David Eisenhower will direct the main assault from Britain. On the supple, affable shoulders of the 53-year-old American will fall the toughest job of military coordination since Marshal Ferdinand Foch took supreme command over 1918's Western Front.

"Ike" Eisenhower had to defend his conduct of the Italian campaign last week. But Messrs. Roosevelt & Churchill had their reasons for assigning him to the west. He is the only commander with experience in large-scale coordination of British and American forces. He is particularly respected by the British; Winston Churchill has called him "one of the finest men I ever knew." He has more schooling than any other commander in the management of amphibious operations (French North Africa, Sicily, southern Italy).

90 TONS A MINUTE: Sixty thousand men & women labored FEB. 28 through a cold winter's day in Britain last week. Seven thousand R.A.F. men listened to briefings. Then from airdromes all over England, 1,000 monster Lancasters and Halifaxes sped for Berlin.

Berlin's antiaircraft cannon hammered with fury and 43 of the four-engined bombers were downed. But within the space of half an hour 2,800 tons of explosives plummeted into the torn city—90 tons a minute. As the armada headed home, smoke from the fires of Germany's capital rose 20,000 feet in the air. It was the war's heaviest raid on bleeding Berlin or anywhere else.

CHAPLAIN'S REPORT: At a U.S. heavy-bomber base in Eng- APRIL 3 land, Chaplain Major Randolph L. Gregory, onetime Washington Baptist pastor, confirmed an oddly rough and reverent tale: One of the pilots at the station, a man of genuine piety and strict devotion to business, found his bomber butting into a buzz saw of Focke-Wulf 190s over Europe. Over the intercom to his gunners he started repeating the Lord's Prayer: "Our Father which art in heaven—Get that --- -- ------ coming in at 2 o'clock—Hallowed be Thy name—Blast that ------- at 12 o'clock."

The prayer and the Focke-Wulfs ran out simultaneously.

DEBASING THE KUDOS?: "Blimey, wotta army!" exclaimed a wizened British corporal, just back from the Middle East, as he looked at bemedaled U.S. soldiers in London's streets, "Every bloomin' one of 'em an 'ero."

In the European Theater of Operations the U.S. Army has bestowed 89,477 medals—82,280 of them in the Eighth Air Force. Altogether, in all theaters, the U.S. Army has passed out approximately 175,000 medals in World War II. In contrast to the lavish U.S. handout of tinsel and ribbon, the British Army, which has been more than two years longer in the war, has given only 10,896 medals; the British Navy, 6,570; the R.A.F., 9,685.

Nowadays, U.S. troops in England even kid one another about their medals. (A standing wisecrack: "He got that medal for preventing rape; he changed his mind.") But the U.S. is not the only reputable army with a lot on its chest. Russian officials joyfully announced last week that over 2,000,000 decorations had been bestowed on Soviet heroes.

MAY 22 **NO STONE UNTURNED:** German troops poised along the Atlantic Wall got a peremptory order to kill their 300,000 tame rabbits, bred during the past year as an escape from boredom and garrison rations. Reason for the slaughter: invasion bombs and shells might turn the cottontails loose, set them to setting off the artfully contrived mine fields and booby traps designed for Allied soldiers.

MAY 1 **DOUGHBOY'S GENERAL!:** On a mild April Monday, as he had done each week of spring, General Omar Bradley, senior commander of U.S. ground forces in the United Kingdom, left his London headquarters to visit his troops in the field. Promptly at 8:15, having breakfasted on Lend-Lease powdered eggs, he stepped out of the officers' mess and into a waiting Cadillac. Occasionally he studied a notebook, checking over the names of the officers he was to meet, down to the commanders of battalions and companies.

Suddenly he looked up, drawled to his aide: "There's a couple of pheasant—in that field over there." His aide, peering at the brownish specks 300 yards away, could recall that his boss was a famous hunter, one of the Army's finest riflemen and skeet shooters.

General Bradley looked the part of an outdoorsman. His G.I. trousers were stuffed into high paratroop boots. Under his old, stained trench coat he wore an issue combat jacket. His shirt, tie and field cap with its three stars were all issue. His tall (just over six feet), lanky, comfortably sprawling figure was anything but dashing. But his dark grey eyes, flashing from under heavy black brows in a homely, bony face ranged wide, missed nothing.

General Omar Bradley. At West Point   *General Dwight Eisenhower. In the*
he graduated 44th in a class of 164.   *same class, he ranked 61st.*

Bradley is a classic infantryman, fit and athletic, patient and persistent, fascinated and skilled with weapons. As a cadet at West Point, he graduated No. 44 in the class of 164 men; Eisenhower, who roomed across the hall, was 61. Serious, shy Omar had only 19 demerits for his course, stood sixth in conduct; brilliant, gregarious Ike had 100, stood 125th.

WHATEVER HIS FAULTS: Like an angry sun from behind storm clouds, Lieut. General George S. Patton Jr. popped out of obscurity last week. Not much had been heard of him since he was relieved of his Seventh Army command in Sicily. [In the fall of 1943, General Patton was severely criticized in the U.S. for slapping two hospitalized soldiers whom he accused of malingering. General Eisenhower rebuked Patton but kept him in command of the Seventh Army. In March 1944, Patton was sent to Britain to take command of the newly formed Third Army.]

Grim in his three-starred helmet, beribboned battle jacket, mirror-shined cavalry boots and butter-bean pants, "Old Blood & Guts" was in England reviewing troops, and it was announced that he would command a U.S. ground army.

In such a role he would be subordinate to his junior, Omar Nelson Bradley, who is also tough but never brutal. General

Bradley served under Georgie Patton in Sicily.

Apart from the soldier-slapping the fact remains that for some soldiers Patton is a fierce inspiration. General Eisenhower, with too few battle-seasoned top commanders, obviously does not feel he can get along without the two-gun General, and does not intend to.

MAY 15 **KIND & KOLOSSAL:** The Channel was kinder now. The crosscurrents and races of this turbulent moat are never still, but the long winter storms were over. The fresh wind still snatched spindrift from the whitecaps in the narrows opposite Dover. But in the bays and river mouths, along the flat sand beaches and the rocky cliffs, around the peninsulas, along the marshes and the dikes the invasion season had begun.

No fools, the Germans have had four years to weave natural defenses into the most *kolossal* lines Nazi brains and slave labor could devise for just these areas. Underwater mine fields, underwater obstacles, land mines, wire entanglements, tank obstacles, concrete bunkers, stationary and mobile weapons with lines of fire cleared, interlaced and accurately ranged—all these are to be expected.

BETTER FARTHER SOUTH: High on a ladder in the British Admiralty's war room stood a WREN (British WAVE), sticking pins in a map which marked the progress of a North Atlantic convoy. A British sea lord stalked in, glanced upward at the map. Said he:

"Captain, that WREN up there will either have to wear pants or we will have to move the convoy to the South Atlantic."

MAY 29 **IKE'S APPETITE:** One noontime last week General Eisenhower inspected huge, noisy "Willow Run," the mass-production officers' mess in London's swank Grosvenor House. Refusing a table in the alcove reserved for rank, General "Ike" joined a line of junior officers at the cafeteria. In due course he collected pork, potatoes, spinach and salad.

Presently the Supreme Commander swigged the last drop of coffee and pushed back his half-eaten meal. He had broken his own rule. A tactful escort murmured about the mess regulation on food economy, which is enforced by slips inscribed:

"Eat all you take on your plate or explain by endorsement here-on."

Said General Ike: "Doggone if I'm risking a reprimand." He polished his plate. Later he went on to inspect the kitchens.

The serving woman, who had noted his four stars and given him a double helping of everything, marveled: "Lumme, what an appetite! Like a paratroop second lieutenant."

Battle of France

JUNE 6, 1944: The commander of a U.S. base in England said JUNE 12 to his airmen: "May I have your attention, please? This is what we have been waiting for. This is invasion morning." His young men went out to their planes, and up into the Channel dawn. On invasion day sunrise came at 5:47 a.m. and high tide at 10:33 a.m.; the landings on the beaches were made between 6 and 8:25 a.m.

The Germans were apparently caught napping. According to Admiral Sir Bertram Ramsay, Allied Naval Commander, the Allies had expected to lose 10% of their landing craft. Instead they got through virtually intact. Closely timed bombardment by warships and planes put enough coast defense guns out of action to make landings possible in most places without heavy casualties. By landing on a 90-mile stretch of Normandy, the Allies placed two major ports, Cherbourg and Le Havre, in danger. If they extended their assaults in either direction, they would gain at least one of them.

Meantime the Allies poured men, supplies, tanks and big guns on to the beaches. By the first nightfall they commanded, in one sector alone—by German admission—about ten miles of once fashionable beaches from Trouville to Villers-sur-Mer, including Deauville.

DECISION: Some 30 hours before H-hour General Eisenhower made the great decision. The moon, the tide, the carefully calculated weather forecasts were favorable. At night, while his staff got out the orders, the General walked alone on the crunching cinder path near his headquarters tent. Deep within himself he wrestled with the feeling he called "boiling over." His fingers rubbed the lucky coins he had rubbed before the invasions of North Africa and Sicily. Now began the taut moments that come to every commander after the battle order has been given, and there is no turning back.

Twenty-four hours were left to bid his battle teams a last Godspeed. In the morning "Ike" Eisenhower stood at an English quayside, chinning in his friendly Kansas way with embarking Tommies. In the afternoon he called newsmen into his trailer tent, told them of the great decision. He slouched in his chair, grinned lopsidedly, chain-smoked cigarets, wisecracked a bit, once leaped like an uncoiled spring to exclaim: "The sun is out!"

All evening his khaki staff car, marked with the four red stars, rolled across the sleeping countryside as he visited his units. He joked with one youngster about his haircut. He asked a boy who had been a Dakota farmer how much wheat he had grown per acre.

Night cloaked the countryside and the airdromes were humming with preparation when he gave his last "good luck." Then from the rooftop of an ivied English mansion he watched the cavalcade of planes roaring across the sky, toward France.

JUNE NIGHT: In the carriers the paratroops dozed, or pretended to. They were the Army's elite, the tough boys—lean, wiry men clad in green camouflaged battle dress, faces stained with cocoa and linseed oil. ("We'll have something to eat if our rations run out.")

Near midnight the first planes reached their objective. Men snapped their rip cords over static lines, waited, crouching. The command came, and they leaped. White, yellow and red parachutes blossomed in the night. Men by the thousands, weapons by the thousands floated down upon captive France.

Battleships, cruisers, destroyers stood off the coast, wrapped themselves in smoke screens and hurled steel from 640 guns. Never before, not at Tarawa or Kwajalein or Salerno, had a target been subjected to such overwhelming bombardment from air and sea.

Some 15 minutes after a rosy sun lifted over the pastures

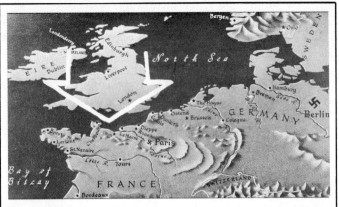

This map, which ran in the June 12 issue of TIME *describing the D-day landings, shows an arrow leading out of the invasion ports of England and pointing at the beaches of Normandy where the first Allied troops went ashore. The port city of Cherbourg, which the Allies needed for unloading supplies, was captured three weeks after D-day. The major port of Brest did not fall until September 18. Paris was liberated on August 25.*

of Normandy, khaki-clad U.S. and British troops began to pour ashore. On the way to the boats in England some of them had picked flowers, stuck them in their gun muzzles. At the boats they got the last miscellaneous tokens of the supply service care: seven sticks of chewing gum, emergency rations, insecticide powder, cigarets, a tin of canned heat, water-purification tablets, chewing tobacco, one razor blade, twelve seasickness pills, two vomit bags—which many of them used.

On the beaches the landing craft disgorged, riflemen deployed. By 10:30 in the morning bulldozers were carving out temporary airstrips. England was tied to the invasion coast at last. The Crusade was on and at day's end the boats which had landed the greatest amphibious force in history began ferrying the wounded and the dead back to England.

THE RISK: The decision to invade had been made at 4 a.m. Monday, in a charming country house somewhere in England. Around the table in the library sat a little group of men, lounging in comfortable chairs, smoking, talking quietly. JUNE 19

Eisenhower was at the head of the table. Grouped around him were the leaders of his team: his deputy, Air Chief Marshal Tedder; Admiral Sir Bertram Ramsay; General Sir Bernard Law Montgomery, the tactical air force (ground support) chief; Air Chief Marshal Leigh-Mallory; Lieut. General Walter Bedell ("Beedle") Smith, the Supreme Commander's pale, hard-working chief of staff.

Into the room came three men, the weather experts. They gave their report: what the weather was likely to do in the next few hours; probable conditions for sailors and airmen; a general forecast for the next 50 hours.

Quiet, stocky Admiral Ramsay spoke first. He gave his estimate of what the naval forces could do under those conditions. Cool, incisive Leigh-Mallory summed up the airmen's point of view. Monty said, in effect: "Well, if the Navy can get us in, and the Air can give us cover, let's go." Somebody asked the head weatherman a question. He stared intently at the table, finally said: "If I answered that I wouldn't be a meteorologist, I'd be a guesser." Everyone laughed. It was no time for guessing.

At last General Eisenhower crisply summarized the situation. He pointed out that there were many factors in favor of the operation. He spoke also of the possible fatal effects of delay, notably the problem of security, and the morale of troops already aboard ship, poised and ready. Finally he said what all were waiting to hear: "In view of all these factors, I think we had better go ahead."

The die was cast. The meeting had taken just half an hour. With one characteristically casual sentence General Eisenhower loosed the fateful lightning that will stab and flicker over Europe until Nazi Germany is down.

Similar conferences had been held twice a day for three days. On the preceding Saturday the operation had been ordered, then canceled again almost immediately, when the weather took a sudden turn for the worse. That, even the calm Tedder admitted, had been "pretty nerve-racking." But this time there would be no turning back.

SUPREME COMMANDER: The master of this titanic effort is a generally affable, obviously brainy Midwestern American. As a professional soldier he is distinctly the command-and-staff rather than the warrior type. Ike Eisenhower never took a platoon or a company into battle. He has no specific battle experience remotely comparable to that of Britain's Generals

Montgomery and Alexander, or such U.S. generals as Bradley and Patton.

A rollicking, better-than-average graduate of West Point, Ike was speedily marked down as an expert training officer, a fact which cost him his chance for combat duty in World War I. Through the peacetime interlude Eisenhower had worked hard at home and abroad—most notably as Mac-Arthur's technical adviser in the Philippines. He had acquired as solid a military background as a U.S. officer could get. He had diligently cultivated his chief virtues of smartness, judgment, a concern for fine detail and a marked ability to make people work for him.

He was definitely one of the Army's coming men; there is no reason to believe that he was particularly startled by any of the rapid promotions that in 35 months boosted him from lieutenant colonel to full general.

He is a strict disciplinarian with the troop formations under his command. He is a bear on uniform neatness, a bug on such items of military smartness as saluting. Once in Eighth Air Force headquarters he took General "Tooey" Spaatz down because West Pointer Spaatz, steeped in the Air Force ways of offhand efficiency, had banned saluting in the corridors as a damned nuisance.

D-day found Ike Eisenhower in one of his worst moods. The Supreme Commander had little to do but wait in galling idleness before the vast fleets of landing craft and gliders could put their troops ashore, and some vestige of order begin to appear out of the vast amphibious chaos. At such times the carefully controlled Eisenhower temper bends under the strain; he hates uncertainty. All he could do now was to pace around headquarters, scribble memos to himself. One of his self-memos could stand as a masterpiece of military understatement: "Now I'd like a few reports."

For this crisis in his life, Ike has kept himself in excellent physical trim. The magnitude of the gamble has not outwardly affected him. His health is robust, his sleep undisturbed. His chief recreation, in the days when he still had occasional free evenings, was a session of bridge, at which he is ruthlessly expert.

In the weeks just before D-day, he usually began his day at the stereotyped U.S. military hour of 5 a.m. He lived with his close personal friend and naval aide, Commander Harry Butcher, peacetime CBS vice president, and his orderly, Sergeant "Micky" McKeogh, onetime bellboy at New York's Plaza Hotel, in an unpretentious eight-room cottage near headquarters. Commander Butcher's role has puzzled many civilians, although veteran officers understand it well. As a general moves up in the military scale, he becomes surrounded with a loneliness not unlike that which enfolds the master of a ship at sea. No matter how close and amiable relations with his staff may be, the general is set apart, behind an invisible wall of rank and responsibility. If he is not to be completely alone on his side of the wall, he must have a special sort of confidant. This person must be a congenial friend, understanding and totally discreet, with whom the general can talk with utmost freedom. Since "Butch" is a naval officer, Ike cannot even give him promotion.

THOSE WHO FOUGHT: The Normandy poppies were pale with dust. In the fair fields where the tide had rolled, the ground was littered with the debris of battle—tanks, jeeps, rifles, ration tins, bulldozers, first-aid kits, canteens. Everywhere lay the dead—weltering in the waves along the shore, lying heaped in ditches, sprawling on the beaches. Here & there in trees hung the shattered body of a paratrooper. In field hospitals, the wounded lay.

One paratroop lieutenant survived to return and tell how the Germans "were machine-gunning us all the way down." Another officer told of seeing German tracers ripping through other men's parachutes as they descended. In one plane, a soldier laden with his 90 pounds of equipment got momentarily stuck in the door. A 20-mm. shell hit him in the belly. Fuse caps in his pockets began to go off. Part of the wounded man's load was TNT. Before this human bomb could explode, his mates behind him pushed him out. The last they saw of him, his parachute had opened and he was drifting to earth in a shroud of bursting flame.

On the beach itself were great tripods of steel rails, braced steel fences, all of them ingeniously mined. The demolition units went to work clearing paths while German shells fell among them and German machine gunners hidden in tunnels and six-foot-thick concrete pillboxes raked them.

An assault engineer said: "We had to work with water up to our necks, sometimes higher. Snipers were nipping us off. As I was working with two blokes on a tough bit of element, I suddenly found myself working alone. My two pals just gurgled and disappeared under the water."

FIRST PAYMENT: After eleven days of fighting in Normandy, JUNE 26 Lieut. General Omar Bradley announced his casualties to date: 3,283 Americans dead, 12,600 wounded.

TO CHERBOURG: Although the Allied move to envelop, capture and develop Cherbourg as a port was plainly behind schedule, the campaign was running smoothly, overcoming great handicaps. Said Bradley: "The Germans have lost their last chance to drive us into the sea." At a crossroads near Barneville not far from Cherbourg, stood five German MPs waiting to direct traffic. The traffic that came was American. Captured, the MPs conceded they were probably the most surprised men in the entire German Army of Occupation.

"FINAL STRUGGLE": The battle for Cherbourg opened on a JULY 3 clear, cool, summery day. Leaflets had warned the battered Cherbourg garrison to surrender or die. They were ignored: Nazi officers had orders to shoot any man who attempted to retreat or give up. Before the last push began, the German positions were methodically bombed for 80 minutes. The bombers' targets were close enough to the U.S. lines to make sweating doughboys hug their ditches and curse in exasperated admiration. For three days the Americans closed their ring, always moving closer, taking cover skillfully, using their superiority in air and artillery without mercy.

The Germans fought back savagely with heavy coast-defense guns, field artillery and multiple-barreled *Nebelwerfers,* whose incendiary rocket projectiles sail through the air with an unearthly noise, described by one reporter as "something like a titanic horse whinnying."

As troops pushed ahead into the city, German detachments fell back in desperate street fighting. Some of the small harbor fortifications leveled their antiaircraft guns to fire at the incoming Americans. In a few hours the German resistance had been cut into pockets, no longer under centralized control.

Just before his wireless blacked out, the Nazi commander in Cherbourg thanked his Leader: "Final struggle for Cherbourg raging. General fighting with troops. Long live the Führer and Germany."

"RACE OF GREAT FIGHTERS": The Americans had taken Cherbourg.

After three weeks of soul-testing battle, the first major objective of the Allied invasion had been won. An open wound had been gashed in the body of the German military system. In London Lord Beaverbrook's *Express,* praising the U.S. achievement, said: "Americans have proved themselves to be a race of great fighters in the very front rank of men at arms."

Lieut. Generals George Patton (left) and Omar Bradley confer with Britain's Bernard Montgomery. Bradley: "The Germans have lost their chance."

JULY 10 **MONTY:** Now that Cherbourg had fallen, Britain's General Montgomery could concentrate on breaking out from his beachhead at Caen and mounting a crashing drive into the vitals of the enemy. Eccentric, unorthodox, picturesque Monty is the military idol of his country. He has come a long way in the five years since he was a studious, all but unknown staff-college instructor, with a lieutenant colonel's crown-and-pip on his shoulders and an insufferable habit of talking down to his classes. But he was then what he is now, a completely dedicated professional soldier, with a superb sense of the big things of war, and an utter contempt for the small.

The soldiers' confidence in this pale-eyed, hawk-faced, intense man is rivaled only by Monty's fanatical confidence in himself. That driving sureness underlies all of his personality, which is subtle and contradictory, and by no means that of the bluff, simple soldier he likes to seem.

Monty regards himself as a crusader and the war as a crusade. He has chosen as his battle cry:

"Let God arise and let His enemies be scattered!"

On the other hand, in a moment of cynical disgust over army routine, Monty was heard to remark that the damned war would have to end by 1948, because all the paper in the world would be used up.

HIGH GUNS: "I'm a sa-a-ad sack!" proclaimed Lieut. Colonel Francis Gabreski. The 25-year-old pilot had just brought his Thunderbolt fighter back to its British base. His outfit had not sighted a single German plane that day. JULY 17

Previously, Gabby had shot down 27 foes in air combat, was thus tied for top U.S. scoring honors with Majors Dick Bong of Wisconsin and Bob Johnson of Oklahoma. A Pennsylvania boy himself, Gabby wanted to be high gun when he took a 30-day leave and went home to Oil City to marry his girl.

Next day, coming off an escort job near Evreux, Gabby spotted three low-flying Germans, prodded one of them into a steep, twisting climb, chased him into a cloud and out again, shot him down in flames. Thus, with 28 victims, Colonel Gabreski became—for a while, at least—top U.S. ace. [Colonel Gabreski was forced down and captured by the Germans shortly after this story appeared and spent ten months in a Nazi prison camp. At the end of World War II, with a total of $33\frac{1}{2}$ Nazi planes to his credit—$5\frac{1}{2}$ planes were destroyed on the ground—he was the U.S.' third ranking ace. The first two, Major Richard Bong (40 Japanese planes) and Major Thomas McGuire (38 Japanese planes) were later killed. Gabreski raised his total to 40 planes in the Korean war and is ranked as the U.S.'s greatest living ace.]

BRADLEY'S ROCKET: On a day in late July Lieut. General Omar Nelson Bradley briefed war correspondents and made AUG. 14

them a promise. His pledge: give him three hours of good flying weather any forenoon and he would break out of Normandy. The pent power of his U.S. forces back of Saint-Lô, like a gigantic rocket, would be loosed into the chute carved by a 2,000-plane air bombardment.

Omar Bradley got his good weather on July 25 and touched off his rocket. It swooshed through the chute, burst out of Normandy, burned a path to Avranches and the north corner of the Breton peninsula. Omar Bradley, the infantryman's general, was using the greatest U.S. striking force in World War II. In the Normandy stalemate after the capture of Cherbourg, he had used it tentatively, so G.I.s seemed to think, among the baffling hedgerows of the *bocage* country. But when the breakthrough came there was nothing tentative about it: Bradley kept plowing ahead without giving the Germans a chance to recover their balance.

AUG. 28 **"OPEN FIRE!":** In northwestern France, Sergeant Robert Beeton of Clinton, N.C. was tooling along a road in a Jeep with two buddies. Among them they had a Tommy gun, two pistols.

"We turned a bend," Beeton said later, "and there, coming down the road, was what looked like an entire company of well-armed Krauts. I stopped the Jeep and trained the Tommy gun on them.

"The German officer shouts to his men: 'Open fire!' They opened fire, all right—but on him, not on us. Then they surrendered."

SEPT. 4 **PATTON ON THE MOVE:** Lieut. General George S. Patton Jr. rapped the map with his leather riding crop, pointed with it to the next objective, a town 50 miles away. Said he to a Third Army corps commander: "Get there—any way you want to." As he had before, he was demanding the impossible of his supply officers. As before, in this miraculous month, they would get the impossible done.

By last week "Georgie" Patton's supply lines reached more than halfway across France. He was getting gasoline by parachute for his forward tanks. Exactly how far along toward Germany's borders his 35-ton daggers were by this week was something for the enemy to worry about. As a rule,

This map, from the September 4 issue of TIME, *shows the swift progress made through France by Allied troops, spearheaded (southernmost arrows) by the tanks of General George S. Patton's Third Army. On September 9, Canadian units had over-run the rocket bases near the Channel from which the Germans were bombarding London. And on September 11 troops of the U.S. First Army moved up to the Siegfried Line and became the first American units to fight inside Germany.*

they did not find out until the tanks were upon them, blazing away at their rear.

UP FROM THE SOUTH: The Allied Seventh Army ballooned out through southern France in the fastest development of a beachhead since North Africa. The ordinary rules no longer held; an army superbly equipped, trained and led exploded into the vacuum made by 1) an unexpectedly weak German defense; 2) the French Forces of the Interior.

French guerrillas popped up with everything from Italian pistols to ancient hunting rifles. Patriots swarmed to the advancing Americans like children to the Pied Piper. They came on cycles trailing little wagons, on horse-drawn carts, in wood-burning busses to which they had hitched draft animals when the engines quit. Men of all ages were armed and burning for the revenge for which they had waited for years. Any German hope of evacuating large bodies of troops from southern France was virtually ended.

SEPT. 11 **MARCH ON THE ROBOTS:** The robomb-launching coast lay ahead. As the British swung north from the Seine to the Somme, a general said to his men: "For the first time in this war we are fighting to free our homes, our wives and our children from German attacks. Every yard we advance reduces the area from which he can launch his secret weapons. Let us drive forward ruthlessly and relentlessly, taking as our motto, 'One more kilometer and one less bomb.'" [For the effect the bombs were having on Britain, see page 149.]

Battle of Germany

As the Allies continued wrapping-up operations in France, the first of General Eisenhower's units approached the final target—the soil and defenses of Nazi Germany.

SEPT. 11 **TO THE SIEGFRIED LINE:** By this week the Allies had smashed deep into the Low Countries and U.S. forces probed at the outer hedgehogs of the Siegfried Line. Battles would soon boil on German soil. The Allied landslide in France had engulfed almost everything, including the German strategy. In 78 hours last week units of General Patton's Third Army swept over the Marne near Paris, zipped through to Verdun. Within another 48 hours they were in Alsace, then they were reported stabbing into the Reich's rich industrial Saar Basin. In four days they had covered an area that, in World War I, had been fought over for four years.

SEPT. 25 **THE PAY-OFF:** Last week was pay-off time. In the Siegfried Line before Aachen, U.S. troops captured hastily trained boys, old reservists, convalescents from the Russian front.

But Germany's manpower shortage was not as serious as her military disorganization. In 48 hours, the two-ply Siegfried Line at Aachen was broken in five places. Western Germany had been successfully invaded for the first time since Napoleon.

THE MIRACLE OF SUPPLY: If the war ends soon, it will be because the Germans never dreamed that General Eisenhower could be such a madman. By last week he had landed well over 1,000,000 men on the Continent, but he still, apparently, had only one good usable port—some 500 miles behind his front—through which to supply his armies.

According to all the military textbooks, this was madness. But there was a methodical miracle in that madness. General Eisenhower's whole successful campaign hinged upon that calculated miracle. The miracle could be stated in simple, arithmetical terms: in the first 100 days after D-day, over 1,000,000 long tons of supplies (700,000 items) and 100,000 vehicles poured into France. These supplies closely followed the slashing, wheeling, speeding columns of Allied tanks and infantry via plane, truck, pipeline and railroad.

This miracle was in the American tradition, a tradition the Germans have never really understood. It was begotten of a people accustomed to great spaces, to transcontinental railways, to nationwide trucking chains, to endless roads and millions of automobiles, to mail-order houses, department stores and supermarkets; of a nation of builders and movers.

"IF ONLY . . .": Aachen was doomed, but the destruction of OCT. 23 Charlemagne's historic residence was now no more than an episode in the tense tactical drama on the western front. In the shattered city the fighting had run the range from dive-bombing of German headquarters buildings, through tank skirmishes, to the rooting out of individual Germans from cellars. The enemy fought as if the city were the cornerstone of the whole front, launched attack after futile attack upon Crucifix Hill, where the cross itself had been used as an observation post. Even after their one escape gap had been sealed, the Germans rushed through the rubble to new attacks, shouting *"Heil Hitler!"*

After three days, Americans fought their way to a vast

shelter, routed out some 3,000 begrimed, hungry, thirsty German civilians. The older women, looking back at their smashed homes as they trudged to the safety of a U.S. camp, wept. Said one, still unconverted to reality: "If the English had only given in in 1940 we would have peace now."

DEC. 11 **WHAT AMMO SHORTAGE?:** The Germans fought for the Roer River, between Aachen and Cologne, as if it were the Meuse, the Marne and the Somme of the last war all rolled into one. German radio broadcasts called it "the most terrible and ferocious battle in the history of all wars."

Hardly more than a creek in summer, the Roer was now swollen by rain. The Germans increased the flood by blowing dams and opening sluice gates, until the shallow brown water in one place spread almost a mile across the plain. They fought like wild men. Driven out of the town of Inden, they lanced back in with armor and crack infantry, blew up a bridge. Ousted again, they put down an artillery barrage in which the Yanks counted 60 shells a minute. Doughboys bitterly asked correspondents if they were the ones who had written about a Nazi "ammunition shortage."

DEC. 25 **EXPLOSION:** On a 60-mile front, from gloomy, bloodsoaked Hürtgen Forest to the eastern bulge of Luxembourg, the Germans finally smashed back.

Field Marshal Gerd von Rundstedt proclaimed to his troops: "Your great hour has struck. Strong attacking armies are advancing today against the Anglo-Americans. I do not need to say more to you. You all feel it. Everything is at stake. You bear the holy duty to achieve the superhuman for our Fatherland and our Führer."

After a short spell of bad weather which grounded Allied reconnaissance and attack planes, Rundstedt struck. Crack German armored and infantry divisions drove in behind massive artillery barrages. German paratroops landed behind the U.S. lines, tried to snarl communications. Buzz-bombs, rockets and a new, undescribed V-weapon came over the lines.

In clearer weather, the resurgent *Luftwaffe* showed a burst of offensive strength. Hundreds of German bombers and fighters supported the ground attack.

Heaviest German thrust was delivered in the heart of the

Ardennes, east of Malmédy, where they overran the U.S. forward positions entirely, advanced five miles into Belgium. [Thus began the "Battle of the Bulge" with American units cut off in Bastogne and St. Vith, but still hanging on desperately as the year ended.]

Battle of Italy

While the stage was being set for the Allied liberation of France and the invasion of Germany, some 20 Nazi divisions under Field Marshal Albert Kesselring continued to fight a stubborn battle against Allied forces in Italy. Unable to dislodge the German units dug in south of Rome, General Mark Clark of the U.S. Fifth Army decided to outflank them and executed a landing behind the German lines near the port town of Anzio. At first the tactic seemed successful. But the Germans launched a furious attack against the Anzio beachhead, and the Allies were forced to renew their pressure against the main German positions—including an almost impregnable strong point near a mountain called Cassino. The decision to bomb Mt. Cassino—and the famous monastery on its summit —was one of the most controversial of the war. The fighting on the main Italian front was bitter and brutal all winter long; the following story describes it.

BY BITS & PIECES: The stalled Fifth Army front suddenly JAN. 17 cracked into action. Through low, sleet-laden clouds attack-bombers dived on Nazi pillboxes. The Fifth's indefatigable artillery gouged the terrain. Alpine-trained U.S. and Canadian troops climbed snowy slopes where German guns lorded it over the valley floor. But the hardest assignment fell to the muddy, regular U.S. infantry. Through shell-scarred olive and fig groves on a terraced hillside, the Americans moved into San Vittore, a crescent-shaped village converted into a German fortress. For two days a bitter, bits-&-pieces battle tossed and tumbled from house to house, basement to basement. Every one of San Vittore's 200-odd buildings was wrecked. So close and confused was the melee that officers talking over field telephones had to hush their voices lest the enemy overhear.

Just after noon on the second day a 20-year-old Austrian lieutenant stumbled from a cellar, surrendered the last organized remnant of Germans, exhausted, grimy, self-dubbed *Kriegsverlängerer* (war prolongers). From other, forgotten basements crawled pale, cadaverous, smelly, lice-ridden villagers. For weeks they had lived underground on popcorn, dried beans and water; now, amid the ruins of their homes, they cackled with hysterical relief.

The Americans moved on to the next fortress-village, San Giusta, less than a mile north. There they won another house-to-house battle, then struck for Cassino, where the valley broadens, where tanks may be used advantageously, and Highway 6 begins its last 70 miles to Rome.

FAREWELL TO A TEXAN: One night last week, in the battle-scarred Italian mountains, Scripps-Howard Correspondent Ernie Pyle [see page 241] watched as the bodies of U.S. fighting men were brought down from the heights. His report:

"In this war I have known a lot of officers who were loved and respected by the soldiers under them. But never have I crossed the trail of any man as beloved as Captain Henry T. Waskow of Belton, Texas.

"Captain Waskow was a company commander in the 36th Division. He had been in this company since long before he left the States. He was very young, only in his middle 20s, but he carried in him a sincerity and gentleness that made people want to be guided by him.

"I was at the foot of the mule trail the night they brought Captain Waskow down. Dead men had been coming down the mountain all evening, lashed on to the backs of mules. Then a soldier said there were some more bodies outside. We went out into the road. Four mules stood there in the moonlight. The soldiers who led them stood there waiting.

"'This one is Captain Waskow,' one of them said quickly.

"Two men unlashed his body from the mule and lifted it off and laid it in the shadow beside the stone wall. The uncertain mules moved off to their olive groves. The men in the road seemed reluctant to leave. They stood around, and gradually I could sense them moving, one by one, close to

Captain Waskow's body. Not so much to look as to say something in finality to him and to themselves. I stood close by and I could hear.

"One soldier came and looked down, and he said out loud:

" 'God damn it!'

"That's all he said, and then he walked away.

"Another one came, and he said, 'God damn it to hell anyway!' He looked down for a few last moments and then turned and left.

"Another man came. I think he was an officer. It was hard to tell in the dim light, for everybody was grimy and dirty. The man looked down into the dead Captain's face and then spoke directly to him, as though he were alive: 'I'm sorry, old man.'

"Then a soldier came and stood beside the officer and bent over, and he too spoke to his dead Captain, not in a whisper but awfully tenderly, and he said: 'I sure am sorry, sir.'

"Then the first man squatted down, and he reached and took the Captain's hand, and he sat there for a full five minutes holding the dead hand in his own and looking intently into the dead face. And he never uttered a sound all the time he sat there.

"Finally he put the hand down. He reached up and gently straightened the points of the Captain's shirt collar, and then he sort of rearranged the tattered edges of his uniform around the wound, and then he got up and walked away down the road in the moonlight."

THIRD LANDING: The Tyrrhenian Sea lay calm. Somewhere JAN. 31 above the moonlit clouds purred Allied planes. To the east, two miles away, loomed Italy's dark shape. Landing craft churned toward Nettuno's eroded frosted beach. Tense, eager men jumped into the icy rollers, waded ashore. Thus last week began the third Allied landing in Italy. [The beachhead was later known as Anzio for the nearby resort town of that name.]

UNDER FIRE: At its deepest point last week the Anzio beach- FEB. 21 head ran about eight miles inland. The Germans had dragged up 210-mm. guns. Virtually every yard of the area was exposed to artillery fire as well as bombing. Even field hospitals (plainly marked with Red Cross emblems) were in range of the guns. Within six days three Allied hospitals were bombed or shelled, six U.S. Army nurses were killed.

FEB. 28 **THE BOMBING OF MONTE CASSINO:** The meaning of the Cassino Monastery Incident was 80 miles north—in Rome. Must the Allies bomb St. Peter's into rubble and then fight their way, chapel by chapel, through the Vatican?

In the valley below Mt. Cassino an American artillery-battery commander spoke: "I don't give a damn about the monastery. I have Catholic gunners in this battery and they've asked me for permission to fire on it, but I haven't been able to give it to them. They don't like it."

The Germans were using the famed 1,400-year-old Benedictine abbey as an artillery-observation post. This seemed well established, as hundreds of young Americans died on the slope below. The slaughter of American soldiers grew too great. After weeks of soul-searching and delay, the Allies decided to bomb and to shell the abbey. They followed a Dec. 29, 1943 order of General Dwight Eisenhower:

"We are fighting in a country rich in monuments which illustrate the growth of the civilization which is ours. We are bound to respect those monuments so far as war allows. If we have to choose between destroying a famous building and sacrificing our own men, then our men's lives count infinitely more, and the buildings must go."

On a sunlit morning last week the buildings went.

In the Liri Valley, thousands of U.S. soldiers, whose buddies had died on the slope, watched. Then, at 9:28 a.m., from beyond the snow-capped peaks, came the first wave of lordly B-17 Fortresses. From the mountain peak came great orange bursts of flame, billowing smoke. The muffled crunch of explosions grew like a roll of thunder.

Three minutes later came more Fortresses; the third wave at 9:45. Watching the precision bombing, a U.S. general cried: "That's beautiful." He seemed to want to direct the planes: "That's the way. Keep them over to the left. Oh, oh, that one's a little bit close. Oh, that's beautiful." As the next to last wave of 20 Marauders dropped a cluster smack on the abbey, an American soldier yelled: "Touchdown."

Thus the great Benedictine abbey, built 400 years ago on ground where Benedictine abbeys had stood for 1,400 years, was demolished. Only one wall section remained standing, and the next day Marauders swooped over to pick these ribs.

But the Americans got no farther forward. If there had been no Germans there before, there were now. The Nazis moved swiftly into the ruins, to defend them in the best Stalingrad fashion. Soon out of the rubble pricked scores of gun barrels.

U.S. bombs burst near the monastery on Monte Cassino. The abbey is demolished and the Germans are "outraged."

Said the German radio: "Outrage." For two days Nazi communiqués flatly stated that there had been no German soldiers within the abbey or in its immediate vicinity. Said Field Marshal Albert Kesselring: "I have only the deepest contempt for the cynical and sanctimonious mendacity with which the Anglo-Saxon Commands now attempt to make me responsible for their acts."

BETTER MOUSETRAP: All afternoon, in a village near Cassino, German soldiers walked up to the door of a battalion command post, clicked heels, saluted snappily and called out: *"Ist der Herr Hauptmann da?"* The answer was always the same: *"Ja, der Hauptmann ist hier."* Each German strode into the building—and out of the war, a prisoner.

Reason for all this was that a U.S. patrol had captured the command post. The invitation to enter was shouted by its commander Lieut. Paul M. Koerner of Pontiac, Ill. *Der Herr Hauptmann* [the German captain] was in a ravine outside, quite dead.

MARCH 13 **SEVENTEEN DAYS:** As the Fifth Army fronts in Italy hung in stalemate last week, military observers suggested that a special medal should be struck off. The candidates for the medal: the few U.S. infantrymen who got across the Rapido River, cracked their way into Cassino, then clung to a few shattered buildings for 17 days & nights.

Those days saw fighting as bitter as any in the war. Every day the artillery on both sides poured thousands of shells into the doomed town. Stone buildings were chewed apart, room by room, floor by floor. Some of the men who came out were close to madness from the strain.

On one street Sergeant Howard Finch (Sheldon, Iowa) found himself in a building with Germans in the basement below. He boldly hung out the window, signaled wildly to an approaching Sherman tank, then jumped back as the tank hurled five shells through the basement window a few feet below him.

There were rare intervals of crazy humor. Lieut. Vincent Kelley took a group into one building, killed two Germans and found a bottle of German Army issue champagne. The Germans at once counterattacked with 75 men and chased the small band of Americans away. "It couldn't have been the house they wanted," Kelley solemnly observed. "It wasn't worth a damn any more. They must have been sore about losing that champagne."

Men slept, when they slept at all, during the relatively quiet midday period. They munched packaged K-rations, slipped in to them the night before. At night patrols prowled the streets, trying to make contact with enemy forces. Challenging a dark figure in the normal way was suicide. The Americans used a code of whistled recognition signals; the Germans seemed to be using a kind of cat cry.

Sometimes patrols never returned. An American sergeant nicknamed "Knobby," with a reputation for taking prisoners, led one eleven-man patrol out to capture a house. Behind and out of sight another patrol waited for the signal to join the first. The signal never came. No shots were fired, no sound heard. Knobby and his men, all veterans of 25 months overseas, simply disappeared.

"THE GERMANS STOPPED US": Weary Allied troops APRIL 10 camped near Cassino last week, bitter in defeat. In Washington, War Secretary Stimson pronounced the epitaph on the latest Allied attack: "The simple fact is the Germans stopped us." A postmortem was written by the *Army and Navy Journal:*

"There was the decision to enter Italy by the toe of the boot. This offered ample opportunity for German defense, as we unfortunately have learned. There was the old story of too little and too late at Anzio, with the result that, although the landing was a surprise, the troops, instead of moving to cut the supply line of the German forces, began consolidation of the beachhead, where they are besieged."

The fact seems clear that in the original landing at Anzio too few troops were employed for the depth of penetration necessary to make this flanking move a success.

CURTAIN RAISER: As the German armies in France poised to MAY 22 meet the invasion about to come, the Allies launched another major offensive in Italy as the opening scene. Why had the Allies chosen to strike now in Italy? To capture Rome? To wipe out the Cassino disgrace? It was much more than that. Said General Sir Harold R.L.G. Alexander in his order of the day: "We are going to destroy the German armies in Italy."

There were undoubtedly other factors which General Alexander did not mention. So long as Nazi Field Marshal Albert Kesselring's 20-odd divisions were kept tied up in Italy, the Nazis would have to divert supplies to them which might otherwise go to the invasion coast.

The moment General Alexander chose for attacking was probably as favorable as he would ever have. Italy's severest winter in many years had melted into warm, hazy springtime. The Allies had complete naval supremacy, which enabled them to bring in thousands of tons of supplies. They had air supremacy too. Major General John ("Uncle Joe") Cannon, tactical air commander in Italy, boasted that his planes had knocked out rail communications so completely that no through trains had moved south from the Po Valley since March 24; the Germans had to rely on truck transport, chiefly at night.

Regardless of these advantages, General Alexander's polyglot troops faced the stern necessity of climbing mountains over land mines, through entrenched machine-gun fire, delivered by desperately determined troops. His best hope of destroying the German army lay in forcing Hitler's men to consume their accumulated stocks of supplies, their large store of ammunition. His infantry men narrowed their lips and started climbing.

Liberated Romans flock into the street to greet Lieut. General Mark Clark, as grinning Americans march over ground once trod by Caesars. Page 96.

JUNE 12 **THE ETERNAL CITY:** It was Trinity Sunday and, through all the last stages of the advance on Rome, U.S. and Canadian soldiers could hear the church bells summoning the faithful to Mass.

The city limits, marked by a highway sign "Roma," were just ahead. A German shell crashed into the first tank as it crossed the line into the city. It burst into flame. A machine gun began to chatter from the side. The infantry piled off and disappeared into nearby ditches and backyard bushes. It was the last German roadblock on Via Casilina.

There was a sharp, four-hour fight. Civilians, not comprehending what was going on, walked time and again through the middle of it and some were hit. One young Italian boy cycling down the road was hit in the head by a German sniper's bullet, lay dead beside his wheel while bullets cracked above him.

The tanks, followed by infantry, piled into the city. For a few hours there were sporadic skirmishes. But by sundown the last relic of that kind of fighting—a burned-out German car—lay blackened and dead almost in the shadow of Trajan's Column.

The Allied troops pressed on. They passed the Colosseum, slogged through the Piazza Venezia where Mussolini once harangued his people. They marched and motored over ground that had been trod by Caesars, by Alaric and St. Paul. But there was no time to think of history. The troops and their enemy were making it.

Mostly the troops grinned as they passed through, but one officer said: "I'll bet enough fascist party badges have been thrown into the Tiber to make the fish sick."

PURSUIT'S END: The Germans were now backing into the JULY 17 Italian mountain defenses where they expected to make a major stand. Temporarily, at least, they had slowed their pursuers to a walk. As Allied strategists saw it, the Germans would drop back another 20 miles to the fortified Gothic Line. Allied headquarters carefully prepared the public for the coming halt. Spokesmen said the Gothic Line was the strongest natural-defense line in Italy, more formidable even than the Gustav Line which held below Rome all winter.

STILL DEADLOCK: The melancholy winter sky of Italy cleared DEC. 11 briefly. Gratefully the Allies flung out their Air Force, sending 2,500 planes over German positions for the best day's work in three months. To the wet, cold, tired doughfoot slogging endlessly up Italian mountains and across Italian rivers, it was a welcome but temporary sight. The weather would soon close down again, return the infantrymen to the dreariest, most discouraging fighting in Europe.

It was slow and inconclusive on the ground. In some places the Germans attacked, won back a few mountain positions from the Fifth Army; in others the Allies attacked, won a few hundred yards from the Germans. The net result was still deadlock in months-old positions.

DEC. 18 . . . **AND ONE BOMB:** In an epitaph on a grave in Italy, U.S. doughboys read this definitive description of the career of Peggy, a British Army mule.

"In memory of Peggy who in her lifetime kicked one brigadier, two colonels, four majors, ten captains, 24 lieutenants, 42 sergeants, 60 corporals, 436 other ranks and one bomb."

Battle of Russia

As the war between Germany and Russia entered its third year, supplies began to play a critical role. German industry had been badly crippled by Allied bombing while the Russian supplies of war material had increased—partly as the result of shipments from the U.S. Aided by this advantage in equipment, the Russians had been able to launch a series of counteroffensives, including a spectacular breakthrough in the winter of 1943 that forced 22 Nazi divisions into retreat and resulted in the recapture by Soviet troops of the key city of Kiev. The next big goal for the Russians was Leningrad.

JAN. 10 **GANGRENOUS DEFEAT:** To the German burgher, this was the blackest New Year since Versailles. No oratory, no promise of retribution could conceal the calamitous defeat in the East.

Defeat was a gangrenous infection which grew and spread, and with each hour became more dangerous. Not even German Field Marshal Fritz Erich von Manstein, with all his genius for war, knew how to end the infection. All he could do now was to retreat with all speed, and hope that the pursuer would wear himself out in the steadily widening belt of devastated land.

JAN. 31 **END OF SIEGE:** At 9:20 on a misty morning the signal came. Then all of Leningrad listened breathlessly to the music of battle. Like moles the Germans had burrowed deep into the alien earth; now thousands of tons of explosives dug them out. By

German Field Marshal Von Manstein.
All he can do is retreat. Page 97.

Soviet pilot Pokryshkin, with 59 stars
on his plane, is Allied ace of aces.

the fourth day, the enemy's positions had been breached, his men put to flight.

This was a great victory: an 880-day siege had been lifted, 25,000 Germans (according to Moscow) had been killed in six days, 85 huge siege guns had been captured. Last week, after their long torture, the survivors of Leningrad could hardly believe that the siege had ended. Already there was talk of making the city beautiful again. But on many a wall a sign still warned: "Citizens, this side of the street is dangerous during shelling."

BLOSSOMS & MUD: In Bessarabia last week the air was thick APRIL 3 with the aroma of apple blossoms and Marshal Ivan Konev was there to enjoy it. Even more he could enjoy the knowledge that his was the major credit for breaking through one compartment after another of the German defenses, and forcing the Germans to retreat back where they had started 1,009 days before. To do this in mid-spring when the Ukraine is knee-deep in mud was a military masterpiece.

As much as a man could be, Konev was responsible for this miracle of a great offensive at mud-time. He produced it by keeping his men on grueling marches few other armies could survive. Konev used his tanks both to fight and to transport. His favorite tank is the adaptable T-34, with its broad treads, high belly clearance, a reinforced axle. Its German counterpart, Mark V, or Panther, often bogs down in the mud and breaks its axle. Where possible, Konev uses Studebaker trucks, for whose six wheels, four gears and sturdiness Red officers profess high regard. Artillery is hauled by tractors, men, and small, shaggy Siberian ponies, which need amazingly little food and rest. U.S. Jeeps do the rest, because the Russians have found them marvelous mud buggies.

APRIL 24 **ACHTUNG POKRYSHKIN:** Moscow's hero worshipers last week heard the latest: Major Alexander Pokryshkin had shot down his 59th enemy plane, was still, beyond challenge, the ace of all Allied aces.

Muscovites guessed the tight-knit, blond, blue-eyed ex-mechanic scored his latest triumph over Rumania, where in 1941 he began his fighting career. He was then 28 and middle-aged by U.S. or British fighter-pilot standards. Since then he has fought more than 500 air battles, has been shot down thrice. Pokryshkin has earned a chestful of medals (including the U.S. Distinguished Service Medal), a bust in his native Novosibirsk. But the highest prize comes through his earphones when he slashes into enemy formations. Then the German flight leaders identify his plane with its cluster of red stars—one for each aircraft downed—and shout *"Achtung, Achtung—Pokryshkin."*

JUNE 19 **SHUTTLE:** Fortnight ago Flying Fortresses from Italy made history by bombing Rumanian targets and then going on into Russia where they landed at bases arranged at the Teheran Conference. Last week they made more history by running off the first U.S. bombing raid from Russian soil—a heavy strike at the Rumanian Danube port of Galati.

Meanwhile the big American ground crew now stationed in the Ukraine worked at maintenance, spent its off hours learning some Russian and teaching the Russians U.S. slang. The first interchange of languages had already produced some startling results. One morning a Russian sentry greeted a U.S. colonel with a respectful: "Good morning, jerk."

SEPT. 11 **OIL TREATMENT:** In one week the Germans in Rumania lost the rich oil fields of Ploesti; Constanta, Rumania's chief port on the Black Sea; Bucharest, the "little Paris" of the Balkans. Worst of all, the Russians, now heading for a junction with Marshal Tito's forces in Yugoslavia, threatened to cut off all the remaining *Wehrmacht* divisions—estimated at 15 to 20— in the southern Balkan peninsula.

The Germans had done their best to defend Ploesti with heavy smoke screens, a formidable thicket of ack-ack, a strong fleet of fighters. They had repaired the bomb damage with their usual nimbleness, had covered vital pipelines and machinery with massive roofings of concrete. When they fled, they fired the wells and tanks and vented their fury at their lost Rumanian satellite by a savage air bombing of Bucharest. The famed Athenée Palace hotel and the university library were wrecked, the national theater burned to the ground. Seven Bucharest hospitals were hit. The Red tanks and cavalry entered Bucharest without a fight, and Moscow was careful not to call it a "capture," since Rumania was now an ally.

RED DAWN OVER WARSAW: After six weeks of build-up, So- SEPT. 25
viet Marshal Rokossovsky (of Polish descent) began to close in. The famed Russian artillery, massed on the east bank of the Vistula, began pounding the Germans point blank, 500 yards across the river.

Warsaw, which had writhed under the Nazi heel longer than any other United Nations capital (since Sept. 28, 1939), was due for liberation by the fifth anniversary of its subjugation. From sections of Warsaw which they now controlled, General Bor's underground forces of the resistance could see the Russians approaching at last. [But the Russians never came. They stopped a few miles outside Warsaw and let the rebellion exhaust itself. Their aim: to discredit the Polish government-in-exile in London, and set up a Russian-controlled régime in its stead.] The Germans were demolishing barracks, factories, public utilities and all large buildings. This destruction, added to that of past bombardments and bombings, and the fight between General Bor and the Nazis, reduced most of Warsaw to rubble.

SILENCE: The sounds of battle between Polish partisans and OCT. 16
Germans in Warsaw died out. The spokesman and leader of the partisans, the man who made himself known to the world

as General Bor, flashed a message to the Polish government in London: "Warsaw has fallen after exhausting all supplies and ammunition on the 63rd day of the struggle." Then Bor surrendered to the Germans with his garrison, his staff and his wife, who had borne a child during the uprising.

Previously, the London Poles had disclosed that Bor was Lieut. General Tadeusz Komorowski, a regular-army cavalry officer. Blue-eyed, dapper, clean-shaven, lean and tall, he was born 46 years ago, fought the Germans in the last war.

He was commanding a cavalry brigade in 1939 when Poland fell. In the summer of 1943 General Wladislaw Sikorsky appointed him chief of the Polish underground, less than 24 hours before Sikorsky was killed in an airplane crash. The Germans were said to have put 200 agents on his track, a price of $1,600,000 on his head.

Last week they canceled this price, accepted Komorowski and all his surviving partisans as prisoners of war in good standing. Obviously the Nazis hoped to profit by the political reverberations and implications of the Warsaw tragedy. The military fact was ugly enough: thousands of Poles had fought bravely and died heroically in Warsaw without advancing the Allied cause by a single mile or a single hour.

OCT. 30 **INTO EAST PRUSSIA:** For a week Berlin radio jittered with its strongest superlatives. "One of the war's bloodiest struggles," "mammoth offensive," "grand assault," "unheard-of numerical superiority," "monstrous force."

For six days Moscow was officially silent, permitted correspondents to cable that "when the news is finally released it is expected to be sensational." It was clear that three years and four months after Germany had invaded Russia, the Russians had invaded Germany. The battle for East Prussia —Germany's "bowels of iron and heart of steel"—had begun.

Battle of the Pacific

By 1944 the U.S. Navy was at full strength. It had recovered from Pearl Harbor and survived the bitter battles for Guadal-

canal in 1942, Tarawa in 1943. Now it was poised for another leap 600 miles closer to Japan—the stronghold of Kwajalein in the Marshall Islands.

"THE JESUS FACTOR": Whatever the objective of the next JAN. 31 major blow in the Pacific, one thing is certain: the Navy has no present hope of drawing the Jap Fleet into conclusive combat, of destroying it and thus ending the Pacific war. In the central Pacific, Admiral Chester Nimitz has settled down to island-hopping.

As the Navy views the situation its Pacific Fleet dares not steam straight across 5,000 miles of ocean through shoals of Japanese submarines, past the airfields in the Marshalls and the Carolines, and attempt to land an invasion force in Japan. Instead the Navy must first secure bases in its rear as it moves. For the Pacific is dotted with islands that have been made into unsinkable Jap airplane carriers and sub bases which cannot be left in the rear of an invading convoy. These bases must be 1) neutralized or 2) taken.

Out of the furnace of its battles so far, the Navy has forged a powerful weapon. To its fleet has been added strange, unheard-of craft which open their mouths like Jonah's whale to spew trucks, howitzers, Marines, Seabees, infantrymen, seagoing tanks, onto beaches. To naval warfare has been added a whole new book of "standard procedures" covering the hazardous, complicated job of ship-to-shore ferrying. The "beach master" who stands on shore directing the weird traffic assumes as much importance as the master of a ship.

But in any attack, no system or plan will ever carry through with mathematical exactitude. There will always be unforeseen reactions from the enemy, freaks of weather, sudden collapses of men in the stress of battle. Said a Navy strategist in Pearl Harbor: "We can plan up to a point. After that there is the Jesus factor—the unpredictable."

"SMARTLY DONE": From Washington Admiral Ernest J. FEB. 14 King signaled: "To all hands concerned with the Marshall Islands operation: Well and smartly done. Carry on."

The U.S. attack on the Marshall Islands had caused Navy tacticians many a sleepless night since the decision was made, last summer, to open the Central Pacific. Largest of these islands is Kwajalein. It is two and a half miles long, a third of a mile wide. The Navy learned at Tarawa that 3,000 tons of bombs and shells (more weight than ever hit Berlin in a single raid) was not enough to knock out the Japs' coconut-log, steel and concrete fortifications. The Navy also learned that four hours of pounding was not enough and that frontal assault was costly in manpower. So before the troops were ready to land at Kwajalein the island and its outer defenses had really had it: some 15,000 tons of bombs and shells—a total without precedent in history.

Then it was time for the foot soldiers to go in. This time the Army troops landed first on a small islet on Kwajalein's flank, dragging their artillery through the water with them. The pillbox-to-pillbox struggle ended after four bitter days. Then, surprised and delighted, Admiral Richmond Kelly ("Terrible") Turner could speculate: "Maybe we had too many men (30,000) and too many ships (2,000,000 tons—greater than the entire prewar Navy) for this job." But he was glad he had force on his side: "I prefer to do things that way. It was many lives saved for us."

BUSINESS JAPANESE: On the way to Kwajalein, troops of the 7th Division followed the old tourist custom of learning a few basic phrases for dickering with the picturesque inhabitants. What they learned (in phonetic phrases):

"Drop your rifle!" (JOO-o-stay-RO!)

"Come out of that hole!" (so-NO-ah-NA-ka-ra-det-ay-KOY!)

"Put up your hands!" (TAY-o-ah-gay-RO!)

FEB. 28 **RETURN VISIT:** Few white men had ever seen Truk, one of the world's great naval outposts. The Japs clamped a lid on it years ago when they began developing it as the key to their South Pacific empire-to-be. Last week, in a swift and massive surprise attack by a great U.S. task force, the veil was rent. For two days, swarms of Naval aviators saw Truk, again & again. And Truk took a savage, historic pounding.

U.S. planes destroyed 127 enemy aircraft in combat and 74 on the ground, shot up 50 more so badly they never took the air. It was a classic job of air attack. U.S. bombers sank 19

Jap ships: two light cruisers, three destroyers, one ammunition ship, one seaplane tender, two oilers, two gunboats, eight cargo ships.

Said the Navy communiqué: "The Pacific fleet has returned in Truk the visit made by the Japanese fleet on Dec. 7, 1941, and effected the partial settlement of the debt."

ACE RACE: In the U.S. air ace race out in front last week was APRIL 24 a blond, crinkle-eyed, corn-fed youngster from Poplar, Wis. Over Hollandia, New Guinea, the Army Air Forces' stocky, 23-year-old Richard Ira Bong had smashed Captain Eddie Rickenbacker's 26-year-old record by knocking down his 26th and 27th Jap aircraft.

Douglas MacArthur proclaimed Dick Bong the top U.S. man of the air. In New York, Eddie Rickenbacker announced that he was making good his promise to the first over-26 fighter in the Australian Theater—a case of Scotch.

The superintendent of the Iowa Anti-Saloon League urged Eddie Rickenbacker "to consider the far-reaching implications of your press endorsement of whiskey for American flyers." Douglas MacArthur said he did not consider "liquor or spiritous wines as appropriate recognition for Bong's deeds."

This baffled Rickenbacker, who told newsmen MacArthur

U.S. Air Ace Dick Bong, crinkle-eyed and corn-fed, displays an oversize picture of his fiancee, Marge Vattendahl, on the fuselage of his P-38 fighter.

had matched his offer 16 months ago with the promise of a case of champagne. But it probably made no difference to Bong—he is a teetotaler anyhow.

One of a Wisconsin farmer's brood of eight, he is well disciplined, modest, has little to say either about his life in little Poplar (pop. 462)—where he sang in the church choir—or his fabulous exploits in the air. Other pilots rate him as daring, imaginative, a dead shot.

This week fellow airmen saw Dick Bong pottering about his P-38, *Marge,* surveying the oversize photograph of his girl. Marge Vattendahl is a senior at Superior (Wis.) State Teachers' College, met Dick last November when he was home on leave. When he went back to action, her picture and name went on his famed Lockheed. [Dick Bong went on to account for a total of 40 enemy aircraft and was the U.S.'s top World War II ace. He married Marjorie Vattendahl in February 1945 after his return home. Six months later he was killed testing a jet fighter in California.]

MAY 1 **SPEED LIMIT:** At a Solomons base, the U.S. Navy issued a stern order: commanders of naval vessels, particularly PT boats, must not exceed 25 knots through the inlet. Reason: the wake at high speeds (as delighted small-boat skippers had discovered) washed the Army privies off their stilts, dropped the structures and their occupants into the water. Also forbidden: painting pictures of privies on small-boat bridges, with scores marked underneath.

JUNE 26 **THE BEGINNING:** A Japanese nightmare burst into harsh and thunderous reality. The mainland was attacked. The U.S.'s new and secret B-29 Superfortress bombers came up out of China last week and bombed a vital industrial target in the Empire's heartland—the Imperial Iron & Steel Works at Yawata: "Japan's Pittsburgh."

Unlike the carrier-based Doolittle raid of two years ago, this was not to be a single strike at Japan. The long-range planes flew some 2,000 miles from bases that had been painfully carved out of the field of western China by nearly 500,000 coolies. The attack was the first mounted by the new, world-ranging U.S. Twentieth Army Air Force. But it would not be the last, and Japan knew it.

For this and for future raids, the worst problem for the B-29's now is supply. All bombs, gas and technical equipment must be flown in over the "Hump," across the mountains from India. Planes bringing in gas use several times the amount of their payload, just to get it there.

After the capture of Kwajalein, U.S. forces in the Pacific made another 400-mile leap-frog to attack Eniwetok and an even more ambitious 1,200-mile jump into the Marianas to recapture Guam and seize the Japanese stronghold of Saipan, which is only 1,500 miles from the southern tip of Japan itself. Determined to prevent this attack from succeeding in their own front yard, the Japanese sent hundreds of planes against the U.S. task force in one of the greatest air battles of the war.

"A GREAT VICTORY": Radio Tokyo babbled that "the Japanese Navy in the near future will win a great victory." The Japs' reasoning was that U.S. Naval forces, pegged down like a tent around the invaders of Saipan, would be running short of fuel, ammunition, bombs and planes and ripe for attack. The Japanese plan was to launch their aircraft from Jap carriers at maximum range, and loose bombs and torpedoes against the presumably exhausted U.S. force. Then the planes were to land on Guam and Rota, refuel and get home to their mother ships, lying well off to the west. JULY 3

But U.S. Intelligence was working, too: submarines and scout planes had kept Admirals Raymond Spruance and Marc Mitscher well informed. For days they had known that a sizable enemy force was milling around, 500 to 800 miles west of Saipan. On Sunday, June 18, five or six carriers in this force sent off virtually all their planes to the great attack. Others, from land bases, joined them. Spruance knew exactly what to do.

In full morning light the Jap planes arrived off the southern Marianas. They had flown so far that they were almost out of gas when they began to attack. Mitscher sent squadron after squadron of dive bombers to pock the runways and smash the gasoline stores of Guam and Rota, to deny the enemy planes a place to roost.

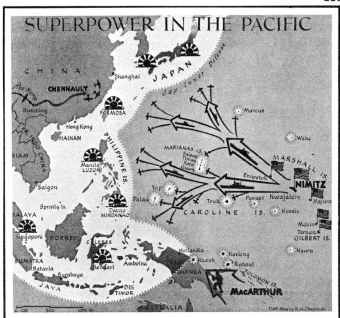

SUPERPOWER IN THE PACIFIC

This map, from the April 24 TIME, *shows the disposition of U.S. forces in the Pacific. Naval units commanded by Admiral Chester Nimitz have moved steadily toward Japan by way of Kwajalein (captured February 6) and Eniwetok (February 20), are sending carrier aircraft on strikes against the Japanese strongholds of Truk, Saipan, Guam and Palau. Saipan would fall on July 9, the Palaus on October 13. Troops under General Douglas MacArthur's command have already invaded the Solomon Islands and are fighting in New Guinea. On the mainland of Asia, the U.S. 14th Air Force under General Claire Chennault is providing air support to Chinese armies.*

Then, as the Jap planes drew near, Hellcat fighters swarmed up from U.S. carriers and took them on. Vapor trails strung across hundreds of miles of sky. Battleships, cruisers and destroyers appeared to be wreathed in fire as they turned the most powerful ack-ack defense in the world upon the few planes which got through the fighters' gauntlet. A quarter of the horizon was polka-dotted with black smoke puffs. The first attack was beaten off on the fringe of the fleet.

An hour later, more enemy bombers broke through. In those furious few hours, 369 Jap aircraft fell to the Hellcats—the war's biggest bag for a single day. Eighteen were knocked down by flak; 15 more were destroyed on the ground.

The last U.S. planes were not taken aboard the carriers until after dark. Then Spruance turned much of his force west, steamed under forced draft all night and much of the day. He was trying to close the range and engage the enemy fleet, now stripped of its air cover.

The westering sun was full in the eyes of lookouts aboard U.S. ships before scout planes gave a fix on the Jap force. It had four or more second-string battleships, at least six assorted carriers, the appropriate screen of cruisers and destroyers and a badly misplaced train of tankers. Hundreds of Helldivers, Avengers and Hellcats swarmed off U.S. carriers' decks. There were only two hours of daylight remaining. This, like the Jap attack, was to be a strike at maximum range. But better planning, better aircraft and better men made it a victory. For agonized hours the waiting fleet steamed, and listened for word from their aircraft. Long after dark, an American voice broke the radio silence: "Two carriers smoking." That was all. More hours passed. Then the planes came thundering back.

Task Force 58 was blacked out. As the first returning plane was spotted, the fleet below sprouted lights: red at the mastheads of battleships, cruisers and destroyers; faint glows on the runways of the carrier decks. A searchlight beam thrust its beaconing finger up into the sky to guide homing planes.

Admiral Marc Mitscher. His dive bombers deny the enemy a place to roost.

Admiral "Bull" Halsey makes a characteristic decision: attack. Page 116.

All of them were desperately low on gas. Some ran dry as they waited their turn to land; their pilots set them down on the Philippine Sea. Pilots and crewmen clambered out aboard rafts, blinked flashlights at rescuing destroyers. There were some bad landings and planes were wrecked on the packed decks; many pilots chose the wrong carriers. But from 95 planes lost to enemy action and "extreme range," all but 22 pilots and 27 crewmen were saved.

In the middle of the night, weary flyers slumped in ready-room armchairs, told Intelligence officers what they had hit:

One *Hayataka*-class carrier sunk; two tankers sunk; a destroyer sunk; another *Hayataka*-class carrier "severely damaged and left burning furiously"; a *Zuikaku*-class carrier hit by three 1,000-lb. bombs; a light *Zuiho*-class carrier hit by two aerial torpedoes; another light carrier perforated by seven 500 pounders; a *Kongo*-class battleship, three cruisers, two destroyers and three tankers damaged. [This battle, which resulted in 16 Japanese ships sunk or seriously damaged, was later known in Navy circles as the "Marianas Turkey Shoot."]

JULY 17 **TO THE VICTOR THE BASES:** Three and a half weeks after landing on Saipan, Marine and Army troops finished the U.S. conquest of the island. Thus ended the bloodiest battle of the Pacific-island offensive; thus was won an air base within 1,500 miles of Tokyo (easy range for B-29 Superfortresses). Best of all, it was a base which could readily be supplied by sea, unlike those in China to which every drop of gasoline, every ounce of explosive, must be flown in.

If U.S. forces had paid dearly for the $14^{1}/_{2}$-mile-long, 75-square-mile island, its futile defense had cost the Japs infinitely more: 8,914 enemy dead were buried in the first three weeks; hundreds more were entombed in caves sealed by dynamite or bulldozers; 1,500 more were killed in a final, banzai-yelling counterattack two nights before the end.

JULY 24 **ADMIRALS' WEEK:**

¶ On Saipan, Vice Admiral Chuichi Nagumo made his honorable exit. Onetime hero of the Empire, Nagumo commanded the carriers in the Pearl Harbor attack, lived to see his fame dimmed when he lost four of five carriers in the Battle of

Midway. After Saipan fell, U.S. soldiers found his corpse. He had, quite obviously, committed hara-kiri.

¶ Nagumo's subordinate on Saipan, Rear Admiral Yano, went out the same way when the last charge was beaten off. Less successful was elderly Lieut. General Yoshiji Saito. He started to make the charge, faltered, tried to take his own life, failed. His adjutant finished him off.

RETURN OF THE FLAG: A radioman at Pearl Harbor adjusted AUG. 7 his earphones, tapped out "Go ahead." The first message came in: "This news is from Radio Guam. Nothing heard from you since 1941. Greetings." Thus last week the liberated area of Guam signalized its return to U.S. possession.

THE NATURE OF THE ENEMY: To the Marines on Saipan, the suicide of Japanese soldiers in the last days of the battle for the island was an old story. But there were 20,000 civilians on the island, too, and many of them elected to die for the Emperor, or perhaps to escape a conqueror represented by Jap propaganda as hideously brutal. In this dispatch, TIME Correspondent Robert Sherrod describes the gruesome deeds, incomprehensible to the occidental mind, which followed the U.S. victory:

"I crossed the airfield and got to the edge of a sheer, 200-ft. cliff where nine marines from a burial detail were working with ropes to pick up the bodies of two of our men, killed the previous day. I asked one of them about the stories I had heard about Jap suicides.

"'You wouldn't believe it unless you saw it,' he said. 'Yesterday and the day before there were hundreds of Jap civilians—men, women and children—up here on this cliff. In the most routine way, they would jump off the cliff, or climb down and wade into the sea. I saw a father throw his three children off, and then jump down himself. Those coral pockets down there under the cliff are full of Jap suicides.'

"He paused and pointed. 'Look,' he said, 'there's one getting ready to drown himself now.' Down below, a young Japanese, no more than 15, paced back & forth across the rocks. He swung his arms, as if getting ready to dive; then he sat down at the edge and let the water play over his feet. Finally he eased himself slowly into the water.

" 'There he goes,' the marine shouted.

"A strong wave had washed up to the shore, and the boy floated out with it. At first, he lay on the water, face down, without moving. Then, apparently, a last, desperate instinct to live gripped him and he flailed his arms, thrashing the foam. It was too late. Just as suddenly, it was all over: the air-filled seat of his knee-length trousers bobbed on the water for ten minutes. Then he disappeared.

"I turned to go. 'This is nothing,' the marine said. 'Half a mile down, on the west side, you can see hundreds of them.' "

AUG. 21 **THE NOOSE TIGHTENS:** For the Japs there was no longer protection from U.S. air power in distance. They got the final proof last week when B-29 Superfortresses made the first incendiary raid on Japan. Target: Nagasaki.

Flames spread like wildfire through the city's flimsy wood and paper buildings while demolition bombs thumped down among seaport, naval-station and manufacturing installations. The B-29 crews took pains to make it a precision job. The big craft were over the city for an hour and a half. Bombermen reported antiaircraft fire and fighter opposition "weak to moderate."

SEPT. 11 **PERISCOPE RESCUE:** A U.S. submarine prowled around a Jap-held island. From the bridge her commander watched Navy planes raiding enemy installations ashore. One of the planes was hit by flak. A parachute bloomed, and the pilot, Ensign Donald Brandt of Cincinnati, flumped into the water two miles offshore.

When the sub moved in for a rescue, Jap shore batteries opened up on it. Shells landed so close that the skipper was forced to submerge. Then & there, he invented a brand-new rescue technique.

With only the top of his periscope above water, the skipper eased his craft close to the airman. Twice Brandt paddled away, thinking it was a Jap sub. Said the Skipper: "The Jap shelling finally got so bad he was willing to catch anything that came his way."

When finally Brandt got hold, the sub slowly moved out of range. It took an hour to do it without drowning the man in tow. As it was, Brandt's head was under water a good half of the time. Then the submarine surfaced at last and took him aboard. Airman Brandt was grateful but "a little beat up."

WHAT IT'S LIKE: Like millions of other kids fighting the war, OCT. 2 Seaman Jack Cooper had his next leave mapped out. He was going back to Elkhart, Ind., marry his girl Helen (he called her "Big Eyes"), put away some home-cooked meals. Like tens of thousands of others, Cooper never made it. Radioman on a Navy torpedo plane, he was shot down in the Pacific by the Japs, drifted for weeks alone on a rubber raft. More than a month later a Navy vessel found the frail craft with Cooper's body and on paper leaves in his wallet a record of what a kid thinks about as he dies slowly and painfully. Wrote Cooper after three weeks adrift:

"July 6 - Mom: Wings are in sewing kit, am entitled to all stars and more. Be sure to check ins. etc. 10,000 ins. Roses to remind me of Helen. I've always loved her. Love kisses same for you mom, dad and all.

"July 8 - Weak. Can't catch fish . . . no rain . . . love big eyes.

"July 10 - Rain last nite very weak land close somewhere.

"July 12 - Little cloudy no planes no land headed north P.M. Jap saw me . . . strafed, hit me, in both legs . . . bandaged them . . . drifting E.

"July 12 - Very weak from loss of blood . . . land in sight . . . no food since the 4th . . . 6 ounces of water left. . . .

"July 14 - Caught one small fish last PM . . . very slight breeze SE. If this is my last day tell my big eyes to be happy with someone else. I'm back to salt water . . . God bless you all.

"Surprise July 15 tell Helen I found God be happy love. No rain for 2 weeks . . . to Helen I loved her until the end— Jack. I love mom dad and all wish I eat some of her cooking."

Cooper missed rescue by four days.

PAUSE FOR ESTIMATES: Both the U.S. and Japan took stock OCT. 9 of the war in the Orient.

Facing certain defeat, the Japs could only take steps to ward off the final assault as long as possible. The U.S., confident of ultimate victory, saw its progress seriously retarded by defeats in China. Everywhere, the key question was asked: how long will it take to defeat Japan after V-E day? After picking the best brains in the State, War & Navy Departments, the OWI came up with an answer: "One and a half to two years is considered an absolute minimum." [Victory over Japan came in August 1945, some three months after victory in Europe.]

OCT. 16 **TOUGHEST YET:** After nearly four weeks the Japs still held out on Peleliu's Bloody Nose Ridge, and in a small pocket on nearby Angaur Island. A picture of the task on the U.S.'s newest and hardest-won Pacific island came last week from TIME Correspondent Robert Martin: "Peleliu is a horrible place. The heat is stifling and rain falls intermittently—the muggy rain that brings no relief, only greater misery. The coral rocks soak up heat during the day and it is only slightly cooler at night. Marines are in the finest possible physical condition, but they wilted on Peleliu. By the fourth day there were as many casualties from heat prostration as from wounds.

"The mountainside caves which the Japs defended so doggedly were the incarnate evil of this war. They were built at staggered levels so that it was almost impossible to reach one without being fired at from another. These American kids are incredible. They went in despite their losses, fully conscious

In thick island mud and driving rain, U.S. troops fire a howitzer at Japanese positions. Says a correspondent: "These kids are incredible."

of the horror ahead of them, suffering unspeakably from continuous, 24-hour-a-day fighting. But it was even more than they could take.

"Peleliu is incomparably worse than Guam in its bloodiness, terror, climate and the incomprehensible tenacity of the Japs. For sheer brutality and fatigue, I think it surpasses anything yet seen in the Pacific."

PROMISE FULFILLED: In the captain's cabin of the 77-ft. PT- OCT. 30 boat he lay on the tiny bunk, beaten, burning with defeat. Corregidor was doomed and with it the Philippines, but one leading actor in the most poignant tragedy in U.S. military history would be missing when the curtain fell. Douglas MacArthur, Field Marshal of the Philippine Army, four-star General in the U.S. Army, had left the stage. It was the order of his Commander in Chief.

The General was seasick; his wife chafed his hands to help the circulation. They could travel only by night; by day Jap aircraft ruled the skies and they had to skulk in coves. At last the PT put in at Mindanao; a battered Flying Fortress took the MacArthurs on to Australia.

That was in mid-March 1942. The MacArthur who flew into Australia then was the picture of what had happened to the U.S. in the Pacific. He was rumpled and untidy and probably for the first time in his life he looked his age. He was 62.

But he was not really beaten. In Adelaide he made the promise that the U.S., bewildered and shaken by the Japs' victorious campaign, heard with renewed hope. "I came through—and I shall return."

Last week, on the flag bridge of the 10,000-ton, 614-ft. light cruiser *Nashville,* stood a proud, erect figure in freshly pressed khaki. Douglas MacArthur had come back to the Philippines, as he had promised.

He had slept well, eaten a hearty breakfast. Now with his corncob pipe he pointed over the glassy, green waters of Leyte (rhymes with 8-A) Gulf, where rode the greatest fleet ever assembled in the Southwest Pacific. Around him were hundreds of transports. On the horizon loomed the majestic battleships of Admiral William F. Halsey's Third Fleet—some of them ghosts from the graveyard of Pearl Harbor. Beyond the horizon steamed the greatest concentration of water-borne air power in war's history—Vice Admiral Mitscher's fast carrier task groups.

There was not a Japanese surface craft in sight. Only one enemy plane ventured out to attack. It dropped one bomb harmlessly into the sea.

Five hours after the first wave of Army infantrymen dashed across the shell-pocked beaches, General MacArthur and his party filed down a ladder from the *Nashville*'s deck into a landing barge. MacArthur sat upright in the stern of the barge. When it grounded in shoal water, he walked down the ramp and waded ashore. He was wet to the midriff, but the sun glinted on the golden "scrambled eggs" on his cap as he faced a microphone. To Filipinos his first words were the fulfillment of a promise. Said Douglas MacArthur: "People of the Philippines, I have returned. By the grace of Almighty God, our forces stand again on Philippine soil. . . . Rally to me. . . . Let every arm be steeled. The guidance of Divine God points the way. Follow in His name to the Holy Grail of righteous victory."

To his Chief of Staff, Lieut. General Richard K. Sutherland, MacArthur said the same thing in homelier language: "Believe it or not, we're here."

NOV. 6 **VICTORY AT SEA:** All summer long the Japanese naval high command had planned for the next inevitable meeting with the U.S. Fleet. The blow must be struck when the U.S. amphibious forces entered the last island defense line, Japan-Ryukyus-Formosa-Philippines. The Japs devised an ingenious plan involving three separate task forces converging from different directions. Last week they snapped the plan into execution, after the Americans' surprise landing on Leyte.

Result: a disastrous defeat from which the Empire's once proud navy would never recover. When the battle ended:

¶ Twenty-four Jap warships were on bottom: two battleships, four carriers, nine cruisers, three flotilla leaders and six destroyers. Possibly sunk were a battleship, five cruisers and seven destroyers.

¶ Damaged when they left the Philippine Sea were six battleships, five cruisers and ten destroyers.

¶ Of 60 warships sent into action, only two escaped without hurt; the 34 that limped home, broken and smoking, would clog their repair yards for months while U.S. planes hammered at them to put them out of business for keeps.

Two or three days before the battle, U.S. submarines in the South China Sea surfaced in darkness and radioed what they had seen: major Jap fleet units advancing northeast from Singapore.

Admiral Halsey disposed his Third Fleet. Long-range scouts from Mitscher's carriers spotted the Japs' central and southern forces, ploughing through the Sibuyan and Sulu Seas. Mitscher sent off powerful forces of Hellcats, Avengers and Helldivers against both Jap fleets. The complicated battle thundered on.

That same afternoon, a land-based search plane spotted the Japs' northernmost force. By then the Japanese plan of encirclement was completely revealed, and "Bull" Halsey had a hard decision to make. His characteristic decision was: attack. He and Mitscher charged north through the night at high speed with most of the fast carrier groups and fast battleships.

The Japs' southernmost fleet reached the scene of battle first. The first-quarter moon had set early, and the morning darkness was deep in Surigao Strait. At the southern end, squadrons of PT boats lay in ambush. As the battleships *Huso* and *Yamasiro* entered the narrows with their screen of smaller vessels, the PT's attacked. The tiny, bucking craft scored some hits, lost several of their number.

Still the Japs came on. Now it was the U.S. destroyers' turn. At 3:30 a.m. they attacked with torpedoes. Then hulking Rear Admiral Jesse Barrett Oldendorf put into effect his policy of "never give a sucker an even break." If the Japs were suckers enough to try to drive through the Strait, he meant to let them come. They came, into the twelve-mile-wide pass between Hingatungan and well-named Desolation Point.

It was Oldendorf's moment. His ships laid down a semi-circular wall of fire. Laying it down were five battlewagons salvaged from the wreckage of Pearl Harbor: the *California, Tennessee, Pennsylvania, West Virginia,* and *Maryland.*

The Japs slowed from 20 knots to twelve. They hesitated as their leading ships caught fire; then they turned and ran. MacArthur proclaimed that every ship was sunk; Nimitz hedged, saying all units were "sunk or decisively defeated."

NOV. 13 **LEY de POLLO:** Tiring of C and K rations, a private first class on Guam bagged a brace of chickens, was on his way to the mess when he was intercepted by the chaplain.

"Where did you get those chickens?" asked the chaplain.

"Shot 'em, sir."

That was a slip. The chaplain was mentally thumbing the rule books as he repeated, dubiously, "Shot them, eh?" The private first class quickly amended:

"Yes, sir, shot 'em in self-defense."

CLOSE, BUT NO CIGAR: General Douglas MacArthur prefers to watch, not duck, when enemy planes attack. It was so at Corregidor; it was so last week at Leyte. A .50-caliber bullet from a Jap strafing plane pierced the wall of his command post building, passed within a foot of his head.

Said MacArthur, eying the bullet hole: "Well, not yet."

NOV. 20 **"YES OR NO":** The Battle of Leyte Island went into its fourth week, and it was less than ever the pushover it had seemed at first. By the week's end the Japanese had more troops on Leyte than they had when MacArthur's men landed on Oct. 20. Douglas MacArthur said last week that his troops had wiped out the original 35,000 defenders. But the Japs by steady reinforcement had replaced them, then had landed 10,000 more.

The arrival of a new Japanese commander in the Philippines was the surest indication of the islands' importance in the plans of Tokyo's High Command. General Tomoyuki Yamashita's arrival in Manila was announced with a flurry by Tokyo Radio. Fat-faced, Nazi-loving Yamashita, brutal, able conqueror of Malaya and Singapore, Bataan and Corregidor, was quoted as saying: "The only words I spoke to the British commander during the negotiations for the surrender of Singapore were: 'All I want to hear from you is yes or no.' I expect to put the same question to MacArthur."

RESCUE AT WOTJE: Nine months after the U.S. power drive in the Central Pacific left them to "wither on the vine," Japanese garrisons on four atolls in the Marshall Islands still held out last week. Almost daily they were pounded by aircraft, often they were bombarded by surface ships.

Helpless, suffering with the enemy, were hundreds of Micronesian natives against whom the U.S. had no grudge. So U.S. warships recently steamed at night into Wotje lagoon, defying thousands of hate-filled Japs. Native guides who had escaped and promoted the rescue attempt were sent ashore to wake the sleeping villagers. Soon a weird flotilla of outrigger canoes was paddled to the warships. More than 700 natives were taken aboard, with their poultry and pigs. The Japs were left on the vine.

Battle of Asia

The U.S. was engaged in two major efforts on the mainland of Asia: 1) to combine with the British in a campaign to recapture Burma, which had been lost to the Japanese in 1942; and 2) to assist the Chinese in their battle against the Japanese by establishing supply routes and deploying an air force from bases in India and southern China. This was the famed U.S. 14th Air Force commanded by General Claire Chennault.

STILWELL: Ever since the Japs ran him out of Burma nearly MARCH 20 two years ago Lieut. General Joseph W. Stilwell has been on the hunt for enough troops and supplies to fight his way back. News from Burma last week indicated that "Vinegar Joe" was making at least a small start in the land of names that sound like unpronounceable grunts.

To his divisions of Chinese, General Stilwell had finally managed to add at least part of a division of U.S. jungle-trained infantry under Brigadier General Frank Merrill. Purpose of Uncle Joe Stilwell's latest drive is to march across northern Burma over some of the world's cruelest, most miasmic terrain, clearing Japs from the path of the new Ledo Road which hopefully will connect with the old Burma Road. Thus eventually a route to China may be opened to supplement supply by airplanes flying the "hump."

To the list of World War II specialists in close combat— Edson's and Carlson's Marine Raiders, British Brigadier Orde Charles Wingate's Raiders, Mountbatten's Commandos, U.S.

Generals Joseph Stilwell and Frank Merrill. In the jungles of Burma they fight for places that sound like unpronounceable grunts.

Army Rangers—another has been added. It is Merrill's Marauders, first U.S. foot soldiers to fight on the continent of Asia. Merrill's troops arrived in India in October as volunteers, soon got used to the Burma jungle. From Ledo last month they began their 100-mile circling march to the rear of Japanese concentrations, averaging 20 miles a day down crude trails. To avoid ambush, intelligence and reconnaissance squads always patrolled the trails ahead of and behind their columns. Last week they were repaid for all their discomforts, all their meticulous training: the stunned Japs were completely surprised to find U.S. troops throwing a road block across their only supply line in the Hukawng Valley.

MARCH 27 **COCHRAN AND COOGAN:** In the tortuous mountains and jungles of Burma last week Southeast Asia Commander Admiral Lord Louis Mountbatten made his boldest move since arriving in the Far East five months ago. Near the key Japanese base of Myitkyina he sent U.S.-manned gliders and troop transports, filled with British Indian troops, to land back of enemy lines. It was the first Allied airborne operation of the Asiatic war.

The operation was commanded by Colonel Philip G. Cochran of Erie, Pa., who won five medals as a fighter pilot in North Africa, even wider acclaim as the model for "Flip

Colonel Philip Cochran is both a car-
toon character and a real hero.

General Wingate of the Raiders fol-
lowed Yoga, spoke Arabic, won battles.

Corkin," Cartoonist Milton Caniff's hero of *Terry and the Pirates.* First glider pilot to land was a handsome Flight Officer, one-time child movie star Jackie ("The Kid") Coogan, first husband of blond Pin-Up Girl Betty Grable.

EXIT WINGATE: One evening Major General Wingate, in command of British troops operating behind the Japanese lines in Burma, had to make a rush visit to his air commando force. A terrific tropical storm was raging at his base airstrip, but he climbed into a Mitchell B-25 and took off. He did not arrive at his destination. APRIL 10

That night a transport plane noted a fire high in the mountains. Next morning General Wingate's air officer, Colonel Philip Cochran, U.S.A.A.F., sent out search planes which spotted burned-out wreckage on the mountainside. Last week ground searchers reached the spot and reported that all the occupants of the plane, including Orde Charles Wingate, one of the military geniuses of World War II, were dead.

Thus perished Wingate of the bushy beard, originator, trainer, brains and spark plug of the Burma Raiders. Wingate was one of those talented originals that some alchemy of British culture occasionally produces. Like Lawrence of Arabia (a distant cousin), Wingate was an eccentric and an artist in unorthodox military operations.

He ate raw onions between meals, frequently carried an alarm clock dangling from his hand in place of a watch, scrubbed his hide regularly with a stiff tooth brush. He followed Yoga, was a physical fitness fanatic, refused to smoke but enjoyed good food and wine. He read widely—from Plato to comic strips—and remembered everything. He knew the Army manuals and the lives of all the great generals by heart. He spoke fluent Arabic and Hebrew. He loved to bait brass hats.

Wingate built his force, a motley crowd of intellectuals and cutthroats, partly from tenderfoot Tommies, partly from native troops. He whipped them into a lean, knife-happy fighting force that last year slipped deep into Japanese lines, cut railroads, blew bridges, slipped out again two and a half months later.

Wingate's axioms: shake a civilized white man out of the narrow trough in which he lives and he can beat the Japanese in jungles. Human beings can store up energy as a camel stores up water. Trained men can keep going for weeks with little food and drink.

MAY 1 **NIGHT LANDING:** War Department files finally opened up. Washington told how U.S. Colonel Philip Cochran landed "up to a division" of Wingate's Raiders deep behind Japanese lines in Burma, in one of the great Allied airborne assaults of the war. That weird first night, 27 big C-47 transports hauled their double tows of gliders up to a rough, gullied clearing in the jungle. The glider pilots cut loose, hoped for the best as they headed down for the clearing.

Said Cochran's second in command, U.S. Colonel John R. Alison: "We were in complete darkness because we didn't dare turn on any lights. Gliders were landing at all angles. Men were running all over the field shouting instructions. Often those trying to help wounded men off the field would have to duck out of the path of a landing glider."

Fiction Writer James Warner Bellah, now an infantry lieutenant colonel, made the flight, told how 50 men sweated to haul glider wrecks from the landing path.

"Screams tear the night and the wrecker crew claws into the wreckage with bare hands to get at the injured. A British surgeon is already inside doing something under a flashlight, something quite frightful with his *kukris* (Gurkha sword) after his morphine has stilled the screaming. And there is a quiet North Country voice in there. 'Don't move me—this is where I hit—and this is where I die.' And somebody's damned good sergeant goes out on the tide."

That night 500 men were taken in, 30 killed, 33 injured. Of 54 gliders dispatched, 37 arrived, eight landed safely elsewhere, nine among the enemy. Six nights later transport planes had shuttled into newly built airfields thousands of men, more than 500,000 lb. of stores, 1,183 mules, 175 ponies.

PICK'S PIKE: Allied troops in north Burma and southeast JULY 17 China were only 26 miles apart across the savage mountains. They fought toward each other in wild, monsoon-sodden terrain. But even if they succeeded in joining, it would be only a token. The real consideration in this remote, Godforsaken battleground is a road.

When the road is done, it will link the Calcutta railhead of Ledo in India with China. Only then will Lieut. General Joseph W. Stilwell and his Chinese allies coming from Yunnan have made their objective. The road will also complete a backbreaking, distasteful job for dambuilder Brigadier General Lewis A. Pick—now a highway builder and the boss of Pick's Pike.

Straight-backed, six-footer Pick once said: "I can keep up with Stilwell as fast as he can drive the Japs out of this area." He did. With 9,000 American engineer troops, a regiment of Chinese engineers and 10,000 native laborers, he had completed 167 miles of road and six airfields. Last week he was working on the next 77-mile stretch to Mogaung, through rain that averaged an inch a day, had already washed out some of the 700 bridges on the twisting road.

Actually, the Ledo road was as much a drainage as a road-building problem. Drainage was Pick's specialty. His heart was still in the Missouri River Basin of the U.S., where he had been onetime Division Engineer. From this job came "Pick's Plan," a series of dams and reservoirs to tame the Missouri.

"I like to control water," Pick ruefully told an interviewer in Burma. "Here, on this road, water tries to control me."

While the Americans and Chinese under General Stilwell were driving across Burma, the Japanese moved south through China dealing out stunning defeats to Chiang Kai-shek's armies. When it became clear that a series of U.S. air bases set up in South China would soon be overrun, General Chennault began making plans to pull out.

SEPT. 25 **THE TASTE OF DEFEAT:** TIME Correspondent Theodore H. White described the debacle in which the Japanese drove Claire Chennault's air force from its principal advance base in South China:

"We and the Chinese had been fighting south of Hengyang for a fortnight when the big break came. The weather had been cloudy all the way up the valley; never could we pour in all the air support in our power till the day we said goodbye to Kweilin. Then the sun shone clear and unchallenged and then it was too late.

"The Japanese were there in force and they were mobile, ahorse, afoot and truck-fed. They could marshal superiority in numbers at any point they chose. They had a fifth column of diabolical proportions. Behind the elbow of every soldier stood the fear of a traitor; the fifth column was among the refugee flood on southbound trains, collecting information, firing buildings, shooting at sight.

"We had hoped to hold the Japs in Hwangshaho Pass, 90 miles from Kweilin. But four days ago, the line gave. Kweilin, with its airfields, had to be evacuated—destroyed, abandoned, leaving the Japanese only its ruins, and it had to be done in 36 hours.

"At dawn, a B-25 and the last transport would take off, carrying Brigadier General Clinton ("Casey") Vincent and his tactical staff including Col. David Lee ("Tex") Hill. On the ground then would remain only the last demolition men to blow the last field, the last building; and Major George Hightower to make sure no strays were left behind at the last minute. Midmorning of the last day brought in Generals Stilwell and Chennault to confer with local U.S. officers and the Chinese commander. Stilwell okayed the final decision—blow it and get out.

"From the east came a glow of red silhouetting the fantas-

tic Walt Disney shapes of the Kwangsi mountains—our sub-
sidiary airfields were already burning. There came the rolling
rumble over the hills as the bombs let go in distant runways.
At our own field alone we had 550 buildings to blow. Our in-
vestment at this field came to $70,000,000 U.S.

"Our shacks and barracks were all tucked away into the
clefts and flanks of the improbable hills. In each, demolition
crews had set up a barrel of gasoline. A sergeant stood at the
doorway with a carbine; someone else fixed his flashlight on
the gasoline drum in the dark and the carbine fired—once,
twice, three times. Gasoline trickled from the holed drums
and its fumes filled the rooms. Then the sergeant would fire
again, and the fumes would catch with a shooshing, explosive
flash.

"In some of the shacks there was ammunition—rifle and
pistol clips careless men had left behind. These popped everywhere. In one shack a store of tracer bullets went up in the
air, casting white, blue and red arching pencils like Roman
candles over all the hills.

"It was almost dawn when we came to blow the fighter strip.
Demolition bombs hammered the air all about us with their
concussion. I found Casey and Tex together, as I had always
known them, packing in their room. There were six bottles of
whiskey left and we took them along. Casey stuffed a useless
pillow into his baggage. 'My wife gave me that,' he said. 'I'll
be damned if I leave it for the Japs.'"

VICTORY DEFERRED: Last week the Japanese did not drive OCT. 2
directly into Kweilin; they circled it to the south. But this
made little difference; they were already in sight of their objective: driving the Fourteenth U.S. Air Force out of southeast China.

While the situation in the field was worsened, so has the
morale of China's Army. This year's Japanese campaigns have
been a series of defeats for the Chinese because:

¶ The underfed troops had to live off the peasantry and often
were so rapacious that they alienated their own people.

¶ The morale of officers deteriorated equally. They often
padded their ration rolls with fictitious names, sold the extra
supplies for living expenses.

¶ As a result there have been cases this year of Chinese troops disarmed by their own people; other cases when officers took the few trucks that the Chinese Army had and used them to save their household goods (four high officers were shot for this after the fall of Changsha).

One element of hope in the situation is that its gravity is forcing the Chinese to pull themselves together. A few weeks ago Chiang Kai-shek began to take steps to reform the draft machinery. One of his ablest generals, Chen Cheng, is pushing a reorganization of the Army.

But the next big step to redress the debacle in south China will probably have to wait for the fall of Germany. With the diversion of material no longer needed for Europe, the volume of war supplies for Asia will grow more rapidly.

NOV. 6 **THE GENERAL GOES HOME:** To leathery, hard-bitten General Joseph W. Stilwell went the final practical proof of what the textbooks had told him 40 years before at West Point: there is more to war than just fighting. Last week "Uncle Joe," hero of Burma and the U.S.'s No. 1 soldier in China, was summarily relieved and ordered home.

The White House announcement, published only three months after Stilwell had been made the Army's sixth four-star general, was a crisp, close-mouthed paragraph. It gave no explanation of General Stilwell's unceremonious removal from his glamorous list of jobs as 1) Chief of Staff to General-issimo Chiang Kai-shek; 2) Deputy to Admiral Lord Louis Mountbatten, Commander in Chief of Allied Forces, Southeast Asia; 3) U.S. Commander of the China-Burma-India theater.

But informed newsmen could and did speculate, and on one point they were agreed: somehow Soldier Stilwell had been caught in the swirling crosscurrents of global politics and washed off his feet.

As a soldier, General Stilwell had reached a hero's height since the grim spring of 1942 when he retreated through Burma and marched over the mountains into India with his famous summary of an inglorious campaign: "We got a hell of a beating." Since then he had trained a new army, fought back across north Burma through the monsoon, had all but finished the opening of a new supply road to China across jungles and mountains. Army men, who knew about Chinese-speaking Joe Stilwell's blunt forthrightness, reflected that his job called for the diplomacy of a super-Eisenhower.

In September of this year, when China's military situation was at its grimmest in five years, Stilwell came back to Chungking to see his chief, the Generalissimo. With him came another American soldier. Suave, worldly Major General Patrick Hurley, emissary of the White House in high diplomatic affairs, settled down in Chungking to confer with the Generalissimo and work out a new solution for the Asia Command.

In the middle of this delicate diplomatic situation, something unexpected happened. Something like an ultimatum was delivered to the Generalissimo, insisting that he give Stilwell full command of the Chinese armies. Whatever may have been its justification, it was a proposition that no self-respecting head of a state, at war more than seven years, could accept. The sequel was inevitable. Stilwell and Chiang must part.

MILESTONES

DEATH REVEALED: The New Deal, 10, after long illness; of malnutrition and desuetude. Child of the 1932 election campaign, the New Deal had four healthy years, began to suffer from spots before the eyes in 1937, and never recovered from the shock of war. Last week its father, Franklin Roosevelt, pronounced it dead.

DIVORCED: By Doris Duke Cromwell, 30, "richest girl in the world": James Henry Roberts ("Jimmy") Cromwell, 47, ex-Minister to Canada; after eight years of marriage, her first, his second.

BORN: To Frank Sinatra, 26, Swoonster, and Nancy Sinatra, 24: a first son, their second child, Francis Wayne; in Jersey City.

DIED: Piet Mondrian (Pieter Cornelis Mondriaan), 71, Holland-born dean of rectilinear abstract painters; in Manhattan. The gentle, jazz-and-orange-loving hermit, heavily influenced by Pablo Picasso, always said that regular curves made him nervous; deplored the necessary circularity of records and oranges.

MISCELLANY

APÉRITIF: In Detroit, Fred Maechtle decided to end it all, turned on the gas, waited patiently for several hours, finally got hungry, lit a match to find some food, blew up the house, escaped with burns.

CORNUCOPIA: In Yakima, Wash., Messrs. Lemon and Cherry arranged to sell the Plum Apartments on West Chestnut Street to an apple grower from Cherry Hill.

THE OLD WORLD: In Stockholm, Swedish youths were introduced to jitterbugging by a group of interned U.S. aviators. Said a spectator: "I assume they get married afterwards."

FOREIGN NEWS

France

In the period between the German occupation of France in 1940 and the Allied invasion in 1944, the Allies dealt with a French Committee of National Liberation, which had its headquarters in Algiers. For a time the committee was presided over jointly by General Charles de Gaulle and General Henri Honoré Giraud, a hero of World War I who had strong U.S. support and initially served as French High Commissioner in Algiers. But General de Gaulle was bitterly opposed to General Giraud and, as the latter's influence began to wane, de Gaulle became the dominant figure and the Allies were obliged, somewhat reluctantly, to deal with him alone.

JAN. 10 **TIME FOR DECISION:** In his tree-shaded villa, overlooking Algiers bay, General Charles de Gaulle served port and caviar to handshaking representatives of eleven nations which, in some form or other, have recognized the French Committee of National Liberation. By next January, the men of Algiers hoped, a reception could be held in liberated Paris.

Behind the Algiers Committee lay some seven months of painful, slow accomplishment; ahead, its hardest task. What the Committee wanted now, on the eve of invasion, was full recognition as the provisional government of France.

London and Washington seemed to have three choices: 1) recognition of the Algiers government now or soon after France is invaded; 2) support in one way or another of Vichy's Marshal Henri Pétain; or 3) an attempt to postpone the whole issue, deal with France during the invasion interim as a military area. The overwhelming testimony of Frenchmen, in France and out, was that either alternative to recognition of the Algiers Committee would lead to bloody disaster: Frenchmen slaying Frenchmen, bitter hatred between Frenchmen and their "liberators."

ADIEU, GIRAUD: In his marble Algiers mansion General APRIL 24
Henri Giraud, Allied protégé, waited vainly for Allied help.
He had not "accepted" General Charles de Gaulle's decree
removing him as Commander in Chief. Now word came that
the Gaullist Government had retired him, at full pay, to the
"reserve command list." Old Soldier Giraud saw that the
fight was lost. To his troops he bade a dignified farewell:
"Men pass, but France is eternal."

Never had Charles de Gaulle ridden so high. His government had liquidated the most vexing symbol of Allied intervention in French affairs. It was accepted by the Allied High
Command as the authority for the France that would be liberated. From London came word that General Dwight Eisenhower had invited General de Gaulle to talk over problems
of civil administration.

"DEAR RUSSIA": In Tunis, General de Gaulle pointedly MAY 15
reminded the U.S. and Britain that France has another
friend. Said he: "Toward the west the French want to be a
center of direct and practical cooperation while they want to
be permanent allies in relation to the east—that is to say first
in relation to dear and powerful Russia." De Gaulle's loving
phrase in French: *". . . la chère et puissante Russie."*

THE SYMBOL: Last week the French Committee of National MAY 29
Liberation and the 100 earnest, arguing men who make up
its Consultative Assembly formally declared themselves the
Provisional Government of the French Republic. That made
the slope-shouldered, big-boned man with the pursed mouth
and the melancholy eyes the Provisional Premier-President
of what he calls the Fourth Republic. The Committee became a Cabinet, the Assembly a sort of Chamber of Deputies.
The symbolic power of Gaullism had triumphed over the
doubts and fears of the U.S., of Britain, of a vocal minority of
Frenchmen. One simple fact about De Gaulle is that De Gaulle
the man does not amount to a great deal—now. The De Gaulle
who counts is De Gaulle the symbol—the half-seen, half-
known figure who to millions of Frenchmen personifies the
French will to survive, to kill Germans, to lay Germany forever low, to restore France to greatness.

Charles André Joseph Marie de Gaulle, 6 ft. 4 in. tall and

53 years old, is very French indeed. The De Gaulles were petty aristocracy, provincial squires, not well off. Papa taught philosophy. For hulking Charles, the family determined on St. Cyr, the West Point of France. Charles entered low, graduated high—in 1911. As an honor student, he had the privilege of choosing his regiment. He chose the 33rd Infantry, commanded by a Major Pétain.

De Gaulle had to nurse his dreams. He inveighed against the doctrines of static defense (the Maginot Line). He urged an elite, mechanized, relatively small army of attack. Almost nobody listened except the Germans, who applied his teachings in the development of the streamlined *Wehrmacht.* Just before the Germans fell upon France, he wrote one last memorandum, warning of the danger in trusting to the forests in lieu of proper defenses. Nobody paid attention. Frustrated, agonizingly sure that *he* might have saved France, Charles de Gaulle went into battle. Five weeks later, Paris had fallen.

Then in a dismal old Loire château, the Ministers and the generals assembled to deliberate the fate of France. Premier Reynaud presided, flanked by Generals Pétain and Weygand. The rest gathered around the long table, with young General de Gaulle, Reynaud's Undersecretary of War, inconspicuously seated near the lower end. They had a distinguished visitor, Winston Churchill.

Coldly General Weygand analyzed the situation. Hopeless, he said; nothing to do but give up. Churchill had no answer; Dunkirk had robbed him of everything except the will to fight. It had robbed Pétain of everything. He decided to surrender.

As the meeting broke up and the bowed men filed out, some of them in tears, De Gaulle sidled up to Churchill and begged for a word. Resistance could go on, he said; France was battered but not beaten. Would Churchill stand behind him if he tried to bind the falling parts together, arrest the toboggan of doom? Churchill knew almost nothing of this stiff, self-conscious giant. Gloomily he gestured his agreement. A British destroyer took De Gaulle to England.

On June 18, 1940, De Gaulle's words bombarded France from a BBC studio: "France has lost a battle. But France has not lost the war." The Fighting French movement was born that day.

A stubborn man with a single, overriding idea set out with nothing but his voice and Churchill's backing to prove that France was still a power. Once when Churchill pressed hard for some adjustment which struck De Gaulle as a backward step, he drew himself to his full, unshapely height: "Mr. Prime Minister, now that at last you have Joan of Arc on your side, you are still determined to burn her." As time went on, Churchill's patience with his solemn, intransigent protégé wore thinner and thinner.

A year ago the headstrong headman of Fighting France forced his way into grubby, squalling Algiers, administratively a part of metropolitan France. Reluctantly, General Eisenhower had granted him permission to take a hand in the snarled affairs of the floundering, Vichy-tainted regime of luckless Admiral Darlan and, after Darlan's assassination [December 1942], of befuddled General Giraud.

SNUBBED AGAIN: On the Sunday before D-day, General JUNE 19 Charles de Gaulle flew to England from North Africa. The touchy French leader could hardly fail to be touched by the reception committee which met him: Prime Minister Winston Churchill, Foreign Secretary Anthony Eden, Lieut. General "Beedle" Smith (busy chief of staff for busy General Dwight Eisenhower), other British and U.S. bigwigs.

On the rail trip from the airport to London, cigars and cigarets were lighted, conversation flowed smoothly. General Smith told General de Gaulle that the invasion of France had been set for that night but that a brief delay was necessary. Meanwhile, would General de Gaulle read the text of General Eisenhower's proposed D-day address to France, and suggest whatever changes he thought advisable?

All Sunday night in London the French leader worked on the script, altering words here & there, inserting statements. On Monday he called at General Eisenhower's headquarters with a practically new draft. There he was flatly told that changes were impossible: recordings had been made, leaflets printed. The important thing for General de Gaulle to do now, he was told, was to draft a speech of his own to follow General Eisenhower's.

The long-frustrated, oft-snubbed French leader blew up, exclaimed: "I cannot follow Eisenhower!" Then he turned on his polished heel and strode off. Behind him he left turmoil. The U.S. generals wanted to be tough. The British statesmen wanted to be tender; they asked that they be allowed to handle the situation.

They had to work fast; obviously the French must hear from De Gaulle on D-day. Winston Churchill's Cabinet thrashed the problem all afternoon & evening. At midnight word went to Algiers' Ambassador Pierre Viénot that General de Gaulle must speak over the radio, or Prime Minister Churchill would have to speak on the situation before Parliament. Diplomat Viénot hurried to his chief's apartment. There he found Charles de Gaulle energetically pushing a pen at his desk. "You must speak!" the Ambassador cried impetuously. "Who said I was not going to speak?" retorted the General. "I am in the middle of writing it now."

Thus the first crisis passed.

The next worry concerned the contents of Charles de Gaulle's speech. Americans and Britons desperately wanted to see it before it was broadcast, but, remembering the General's temper, they did not dare make the request. With his speech known only to himself, General de Gaulle hurried to the BBC studio to make a recording. The manuscript was written in almost illegible longhand, with sentences running up & down the margins, words hidden under inkspots, holes torn in the paper by a scratchy pen. But the recording was made.

On D-day, Charles de Gaulle spoke to his countrymen, in his own manner and long after General Eisenhower had spoken. Nothing that he said displeased the Allied command outright; nothing that he said waived one iota of his Government's claim to exclusive sovereignty in France.

JUNE 26 **THE RETURN:** Across the choppy Channel plowed the French destroyer *Combattante,* with the Tricolor whipping smartly from her taffrail. From the bridge General Charles de Gaulle looked toward the shore of invaded Normandy. For him this was a solemn hour. He was coming back to *la patrie.*

A U.S.-made duck carried Charles de Gaulle from ship to beach. A British-driven jeep bore him inland. In Bayeux, first French town liberated by Anglo-American arms, loudspeakers blared the news of the General's coming. Hurriedly shops closed, Tricolors were unfurled. The people went into the

General de Gaulle, a towering figure, is mobbed by Frenchmen in Normandy. Six hours later, he leaves behind a new government.

streets. At last the General appeared, his tall figure towering above everyone, his face taut and set. The bishop and the sub-prefect greeted him. The townsfolk trailed him to the park. There, bareheaded under a Tricolor mounted with the Gaullist Cross of Lorraine, flanked by the Union Jack and the Stars & Stripes, Charles de Gaulle said: "We will fight by the side of our Allies. Our victory will be a victory of a free people." Then he sang *La Marseillaise* with his countrymen.

Then, after six hours in the homeland, Charles de Gaulle went back to Britain. He left behind, in one corner of France, a new Government.

PARIS IS FREE!: The news that made the whole free world SEPT. 4 catch its breath last week was the news that Paris was free. It was one of the great days of all time. For Paris is the city of all free mankind, and its liberation last week was one of the great events of all time.

This event was reported by the first U.S. newsman to enter Paris, TIME's Chief War Correspondent Charles Christian Wertenbaker: "I have seen the faces of young people in love and the faces of old people at peace with their God. I have never seen in any face such joy as radiated from the faces of the people of Paris this morning. Your correspondent drove into Paris with eyes that would not stay dry, and we were no more ashamed of it than were the people who wept as they embraced us.

"We had spent the night at General Leclerc's command post, six miles from Paris on the Orléans-Paris road. Here the last German resistance outside Paris was being slowly reduced, while inside the city the Germans and the F.F.I. fought a bitter battle that had already lasted six days. Late in the afternoon a French cub plane flew in 50 yards above the Cathedral of Notre Dame, on the Ile de la Cité where the F.F.I. had its headquarters, and dropped a message which said simply: 'Tomorrow we come.'

"At 6 o'clock in the morning General Leclerc's tanks began to move. We maneuvered our Jeep just behind the General's armored car and drove fast toward the Porte d'Orléans. The people, who up to now had made small groups beside the road, suddenly became a dense crowd packed from the buildings to the middle of the street, where they separated to make a narrow line for the General's car to pass through. No longer did they simply throw flowers and kisses. They uttered a great mass cry of delight that swelled and died down and swelled to a greater height. They cried: *'Vive De Gaulle!'* and *'Vive Leclerc!'* But one word repeated over and over rose above all the other words. It was: *'Merci! Merci! Merci!'*

"Close to the golden dome of the Invalides we stopped. There was fighting in the streets ahead. A tank stopped before a house and for ten minutes pumped bullets into it. We left the Jeep and walked down the Boulevard des Invalides to the corner of the Rue de Grenelle. To the left, in the Ecole Militaire, there were a few German snipers. Down toward the Quai d'Orsay many Germans were giving battle.

"The streets were full of people—Resistance groups armed with any old rifles, white-clad doctors and nurses carrying stretchers, and citizens old and young who, in spite of the danger, could not stay at home on this day.

"De Gaulle is at the War Ministry, still nursing a sore throat. German prisoners are paraded through the streets, frightened but mostly well treated. Snipers are still shooting. The Chamber of Deputies on the Quai d'Orsay is still burning. But Paris is not badly damaged. When the last German is killed or captured, Paris will still be Europe's most beautiful city and Paris will again be French."

DE GAULLE'S DAY: At 18 minutes past 3 on the afternoon of Saturday, August 26, General de Gaulle bent his tall, awkward body below the Arc de Triomphe and laid on the Tomb of the Unknown Soldier two bunches of flame-colored gladioli. The flame at the tomb still burned.

As the General turned to start his march down the Champs Elysées, the person closest to him was a Negro in a dirty white shirt, his arm in a sling made of a dirty towel. He was one of the bravest fighters in Paris' week-long battle for liberation, and there was something significant in the nearness of this symbol of a new, militant, common man's France. And behind them marched the most bizarre parade that ever trod this historic avenue.

There were cars of every kind but new ones, piled high with people. They waved flags and handkerchiefs, saluted, made the V sign. One girl sat on the hood of an old car, her arm aloft, her eyes burning with joy and pride. A captain sat on a tank, his hand held stiffly at attention, tears streaming down his face. Perhaps not since Bastille Day had the people of France celebrated such a victory.

In front of the Hôtel de Ville the shooting started. Dozens of cars and Jeeps jamming the square were suddenly slowed by a narrow street. A machine gun let go from the top story of a high building across from the Hôtel de Ville. Then other machine guns and rifles fired from above. Everything stopped. People dived under cars, trucks, jeeps, while every man who had a gun or a pistol—and hundreds had—started firing. The thousands of pedestrians in the square stampeded, scattered, fell flat, piled three or four deep in places. The shooting spread. Soon there was shooting all over Paris.

It was plainly pre-arranged by the Vichy fifth columnists who, unlike the German soldiers, could not give themselves up. As the first shots rang out at Notre Dame, Generals Leclerc and Koenig tried to hustle De Gaulle through the door. De Gaulle shook off their hands and never faltered. While the battle began outside he walked slowly down the aisle. Before he had gone many paces a machine pistol fired down from above. At least two more joined in, and from below the F.F.I. and police fired back.

While the firing continued De Gaulle continued his slow

walk up the aisle toward Cardinal Suhard and Monsignor Beaussart, who never faltered either. A *Te Deum* was playing from the organ where the machine pistolers were hidden.

The ceremony was brief. De Gaulle walked back down the aisle as slowly and as calmly as he had gone up it. Thus ended his first great public appearance in Paris. If there had been any doubt about his acceptance by the French people, this hour finished it.

SEPT. 11   **AT CHARTRES:** In the middle of the courtyard was a growing pile of grey and blondined hair. At the Chartres police station patriots were shaving the heads of women collaborationists. There were old ones who had operated black markets. There were young, blowsy ones who had sold themselves to the Germans. The women, their shaved heads bowed, were lined up against a wall.

Every once in a while the crowd would boo as more women, with expressionless faces, were hustled in to be shaved.

Said a girl from the Resistance: "It is cruel and unnecessary. They are soldiers' women, and tomorrow they will be sleeping with the Americans. What difference does it make? I have worked for liberation. Three times I have been questioned by the Gestapo. And I do not demand such a thing as this."

Frenchwomen sit with shaved heads. The trimming was done as punishment for collaborating with the Nazis during the occupation.

A murmur went through the crowd. The Tricolor was going up on the tower of the cathedral. Beside it waved the Stars & Stripes. Spontaneously the crowd began to sing the *Marseillaise*. The shaved women raised their heads and sang with the rest.

SCARS: Ugly scars left on the body of Paris by Nazi terror came to light last week:

¶ In the Ivry suburb, nameless graves held the remains of an estimated 75,000 persons shot during the occupation.

¶ In the Sûreté Generale on the Rue des Saussaies, Gestapomen had tortured prisoners with near-freezing baths, electric currents, beatings. Scratched on the walls of cells: "Long live eternal France! . . . Never confess! . . . My God, I have confidence in Thee!"

¶ At the Air Ministry's rifle range on the Boulevard Victor, the Germans had built an asbestos shed in which they threw flames at prisoners, or burned them alive with scorching air. The asbestos walls bore the imprints of the palms of men, women and children who had tried to escape.

¶ In the old Jewish quarter around the Rue Ste.-Croix de la Bretonnerie, the Germans had set up a ghetto. Only 10,000 of 100,000 Jews who used to live there still remained. They straggled out last week to meet American visitors. Broken by hunger, torture, humiliation, they were Paris' most sadly joyous beings.

TALLY HO!: Last week all France went hunting—and the quarry was man. The patriots were having their long-looked-for day. In city streets and country woods, Frenchmen and their wives and children tracked down the Germans and collaborationists like animals. Sometimes the quarry was dispatched out of hand. More often, by an instinct for justice and law that was stronger than vengeance or terror, the quarry was jailed.

In Annecy, on a rifle range where the Germans had killed many a Maquis, an F.F.I. firing squad snuffed out 24 *SS* and Gestapomen.

Rumor said that the Gaullists had 700,000 names on their blacklist. Subprefect Edgar Pisani of the Paris Special Police promised a fair trial for every accused person. He said: "We

SEPT. 18

want to be deliberate and methodical. Some inevitably will get away but we are bound to catch up with the great majority sooner or later."

OCT. 16 **A SLINKY, BACKLESS "LIBERTY":** Although the Germans had not yet been driven out of France, an old Parisian institution (and big Parisian business) returned. Liberation fashions were barely a month old, the season of style shows was on.

The spectators were almost as arresting as the mannequins. One *Parisienne* wore black lace bobby socks with matching lace earrings. Past a dead elevator (no electricity) they clattered up four flights of blue carpeted stairs, sat down and glorified the gilt chairs in the long showroom. A sprinkling of WACs, a handful of beadyeyed U.S. officers lined the wall. Appraising eyes watched pretty, pert mannequins strut, simper, pirouette.

New fashions appear in Paris soon after the Germans leave, under the old familiar names: Molyneux, Lanvin, Schiaparelli, Lelong.

All last week famous couturiers displayed their 1944 creations. Most of the familiar names were back: Molyneux, Lanvin, Schiaparelli, Lelong. The trend was pronounced: skirts full and short, waists small, shoulders wide, sleeves mutton-legged. Designers used material lavishly, too lavishly for U.S. and British women limited by regulations and rationing.

The old Parisian skill was evident. Lelong put jeeps on charm bracelets. Agile, aging (70) Madame Jeanne Lanvin showed a slinky, black, backless, low-front evening dress called "Liberty." She also offered a simple frock of palest pink named "Free France."

Sales were disappointing. Prices were high. Dresses ranged from $200 to $900, coats from $500 to $1,000. Moaned one famous couturier: "What shall I do with all this nonsense going on? All my best customers are in concentration camps, because of course they were working for Vichy."

RAISED TO THE FOURTH POWER: The Big Three became a NOV. 20 Big Four last week, and France became one of Europe's four ruling powers. Simultaneously, Washington, London and Moscow announced that France had been added to the European Advisory Commission (the U.S., Britain, Russia) established a year ago to consider "the treatment to be accorded Germany." Said the Big Three: "Conscious of the part France will inevitably play in maintaining the future peace of Europe, the Provisional Government of the French Republic is invited to full membership."

ON TO MOSCOW: Armed with a bronze plaque for the City of DEC. 11 Stalingrad, General Charles de Gaulle climbed into his transport plane and zoomed off on the first leg of a trip to Moscow.

Switching later to a train, he arrived in a blinding snowstorm. At the flag-decked Kursk Station, a Red Army Guard of Honor stood at attention. A Red Army band played *La Marseillaise* and the Soviet Hymn. Down 100 yards of red carpet marched People's Commissar for Foreign Affairs Viacheslav Molotov and a reception committee of fur-coated, fur-hatted, felt-booted Russian and Allied dignitaries.

For five minutes De Gaulle kept them waiting. Then, muffled in a fur-lined khaki greatcoat and red cap, he detrained, saluted, shook hands with beaming Commissar Molotov. While Soviet newsphotographers cranked their cameras, General de Gaulle spoke into a microphone: "On behalf of the people of France, I pay homage to the gallant people of the Soviet Union." Then, his long nose and ears blue with cold, he sped to the Foreign Office's guest house. A few hours later he disappeared into the Kremlin.

HOME TO PARIS: Two planes, bound on fateful missions, went opposite ways in Europe's troubled air last week. One plane was carrying General Charles de Gaulle toward Moscow. The other carried his most formidable rival, Maurice Thorez, Secretary of the French Communist Party, from exile in Moscow to Paris. Three weeks ago De Gaulle had cleared the way by pardoning Thorez for military desertion.

DEC. 18 **TIRED BUT HAPPY:** From Moscow's Kursk Station General Charles de Gaulle chugged off for home, one day last week, in a swirling Russian snowstorm. He was sleepy but happy, for in his pocket was a treaty of alliance and mutual assistance between Russia and France. It pledged the signatories to cooperate in the war against Germany "until complete victory," provided for joint safeguarding of Europe from new aggressions after the war.

As he ended his 16-day visit General de Gaulle said: "I am sure the days we have spent here will leave their mark on the history of this war and I believe, too, they will leave their mark on the peace for the good of all men. Long live Soviet Russia!" Shaking hands with Foreign Commissar Molotov, he added: "Thank you for everything."

Well might he say so. The Russian alliance had bettered his bargaining position in international politics, had enormously strengthened his position at home. For France's powerful Communist Party, if it does not actively support De Gaulle, will be bound not to make trouble for him so long as his Government is an ally of Russia.

DEC. 25 **THE FIRST CLASS:** The little girl hurried along a road in Alsace. The first snow lay over the wheat stubble. She was Paulette. Or was she Paulette? Under the Germans she had always been called Paula. She was eleven years old. But she could remember far back—almost five years. She was not quite sure that she could remember when the French soldiers went away. She was not quite sure that she could remember when the German soldiers came. But she could remember something. That something was fear.

Now the Germans had gone again and there was no fear—except that Paulette was terribly afraid of being late. For this morning the new French class began at the Town Hall, with a new teacher. When the Germans were there, everybody had to speak German. French was *verboten*. Now everybody must speak French. It was funny.

The school bell rang. The little girls bustled onto their narrow benches. Sister Elizabeth called the roll. Instead of *"Hier!"*, the little girls answered *"Ici!"*, and giggled at the unfamiliar sound. Then Sister Elizabeth spoke in French, translating phrase by phrase into the Alsatian German dialect: "This is our first class in a long time. There is much to do. All that is needed is a very good will."

The little girls repeated after the teacher: "Do not answer *Ja,* say *Oui, ma soeur. . . . Voici la table . . . Voilà le mur. Voici le crucifix.* This is the table. That is the wall. Here is the crucifix. . . ."

Sister Elizabeth asked Maria Pia and Bernadette to open the windows. From the distant Rhine rolled the thunder of guns. Suddenly, much more loudly, came the roar of planes. Eyes widened in panic, voices shrilled: *"Flugzeuge! Flugzeuge!"* (Airplanes! Airplanes!). The little girls had remembered fear.

Said Sister Elizabeth: "Close the windows and sit down. We will repeat, *Voici la table, Voilà le mur, Voici le crucifix.* —This is the table. That is the wall. Here is the crucifix."

International

THE ISSUE: The sensational news from Europe's battlefronts SEPT. 11 last week threatened to overshadow the emergence of a sensational development in Europe's political set-up:

¶ The only effective government of Poland, Lublin's National Committee of Liberation, was preponderantly Communist.

¶ The Marshal of the Yugoslav Army was a Communist.

¶ For the first time in history, Communists held cabinet posts in the governments of France, Italy, Rumania, Greece. They might soon hold similar posts in the governments of Bulgaria, Czechoslovakia, Finland, eastern Germany.

MOMENTOUS MEETING: One of the most momentous politi- OCT. 23 cal meetings in history was taking place in Moscow last week. It was a meeting not only of two of the world's great men—Prime Minister Winston Churchill and Marshal Joseph Stalin, but a meeting of heads of two of the world's great empires. They were meeting on the eve of victory. Each had successfully steered his country through the most perilous military crisis in its history. Now they faced the almost equally perilous crisis of peace. Both men and both their nations passionately wanted and desperately needed peace. On the political decisions they made, on their attitude to one another, the world's peace hinged for perhaps a generation.

The beginnings were auspicious. The official good-will reception of the visiting Britons by the Russians was staged for all the world to see. And seldom, if ever, had anything like it been seen in Moscow.

Up to the British Embassy dashed the U.S.-made car with bulletproof windows that the Soviet Government had placed at Winston Churchill's disposal. Other U.S.-made limousines brought 38 other guests. They were bound for a four-hour, 14-course lunch with Stalin. Stalin wore his simplest Marshal's uniform—no decorations. Churchill wore his uniform as honorary colonel of a Sussex regiment—four banks of decorations.

The guests were no sooner seated than Russian Foreign Commissar Molotov proposed a toast: "To the health of Churchill, whom we are so glad to welcome here."

Churchill responded: "To Stalin. Very glad to be here again."

Churchill toasted again: "It is a sign of a great man and a great nation to be able to be magnanimous and generous. Marshal Stalin has been most generous in the compliments he has paid the Allies."

Stalin broke in: "That was not just a compliment—it was the truth."

Churchill went on: "Thank you. But we want you to know that all the world realizes it was the Red Army that clawed the guts out of the filthy Nazi war machine. To the Red Army."

During the strawberry parfait and champagne Stalin rose again and toasted: "To those who worked for the peace of the world at Dumbarton Oaks. But the Allies must be prepared for peace."

There was one uninvited presence at the feast, but nobody toasted him. He was Adolf Hitler, who had done what centuries of British and Russians had failed to do—bring Britain and Russia together.

WORKMEN & SOLDIERS: Down to Moscow's rain-swept OCT. 30 airport dashed the great-great-great-great-great-great-great-grandson of the Duke of Marlborough—Winston Churchill. With him dashed the cobbler's son from Tiflis. Never before had Joseph Stalin made such a good-will gesture to any visiting foreign statesman. Stalin was all smiles. He had been ever since his talks with Churchill began in the Kremlin ten days ago.

Much of what they accomplished would not be revealed until later. For the present, the achievements were set forth in an official communiqué in which words were strictly rationed.

If words when used by statesmen mean anything, the communiqué meant:

1) The Polish problem was nearer solution, but not yet solved.

2) Britain had practically relinquished its political interests in Yugoslavia.

WINTER OF DECISION: It looked as if liberated Europe had NOV. 27 been liberated chiefly for hunger and disorder. From Greece to Holland there was social and political crisis. Western Europe's economic structure, looted by the Nazis, shattered by bombing, gutted by the resistance and war, had all but collapsed. Most factories lacked raw materials. Few railroads were running. Food was scarce. Liberated Europe foresaw a winter of hunger.

This was the economic crisis. It inflamed the social and political crisis. As a result of the Nazi occupation, traditional government, law, justice and political parties had broken down or were discredited. As a result of the resistance, Europe's people were armed. Almost everywhere the Communist parties fought to keep them armed. Almost everywhere insistence on disarming them caused Government crises.

Scarcely anywhere did Britain and the U.S. offer a political leadership intelligent or tough enough to counteract the Communists or sufficient economic aid to quiet the unrest.

To most Europeans democracy, U.S. style, was a new experience. Many, perhaps most of them emerging from fascist domination, had been eager for it. But because its deeds were falling far short of their hopes, they were in a mood to judge it harshly. Unless the U.S. and Britain acted quickly to retrieve the ground they had lost, they might win the war but lose Europe. For Europe, and for the world, this was a winter of decision.

DEC. 11 **FIVE CRISES:** Europe's economic and political crisis was reflected in the crises of five cabinets—those of Greece, Italy, Belgium, Rumania and the Polish Government in Exile. But the focus was on Greece. Greece was dangerously near, if not already in, civil war.

In Italy Premier Ivanoe Bonomi was still trying to find somebody to join his Cabinet. Communists, Socialists and Actionists had tried to form a cabinet around Count Carlo Sforza. But British Ambassador Sir Noel Charles blocked the move. Britain, he said, did not consider Sforza a reliable man. Few political parties wanted to share the onus of governing Italy under Allied control during an economic crisis. All were waiting for the north to be liberated. And meanwhile recurrent street fighting between monarchists and republicans—a new thing in Rome—was a grave portent.

In Rumania, Radio Bucharest flashed another message: "Premier Constantin Sanatescu and his entire Cabinet have resigned." No details were given.

In Belgium, following a fortnight of riots in Brussels, the Chamber of Deputies met behind a wall of British tanks and bayonets, voted, 116 to 12, to retain Premier Hubert Pierlot. The Communists continued to shout: "The Pierlot Cabinet is condemned by the mass of people." Through the newly opened port of Antwerp, people expected Allied food.

In London the Polish Cabinet crisis simmered. Premier Tomasz Arcizewski was trying to hold together a Cabinet of anti-Russian Socialists, democrats and laborites.

Europe's crises were threshed out in Britain's House of Commons. To a perturbed and sometimes heckling House, Foreign Secretary Eden explained that Britain's policy in liberated Europe has a threefold purpose: 1) to achieve victory; 2) to keep order behind the lines of the Allied armies; 3) to provide fair and untrammeled elections of governments and parliaments.

"In trying to pursue this policy in a state of confusion and tension, we are not dominated by a desire to set up a government of the right in this place, or of the left in that. We're trying to give the countries concerned the best chance they could have in expressing their own will. Their young people have known little else than working against the law. It is bound to take a little time for them to adapt themselves to new conditions."

Great Britain

MAN OF ENGLAND: In astonishing numbers, the American MARCH 6 soldiers flooding into England go to gawk through the iron fence at Buckingham Palace in the hope of seeing the King. Says a cockney, also gawking: "He's a decent bloke, you know. Works hard. I wouldn't have his job." Says G.I. Joe: "Yeah, not much chance for promotion."

Four years and six months have passed since King George VI told his people: "We are at war. We can only do the right as we see the right."

Britain and her Empire, her people and her King have changed. The looming question for Britons and their king is no longer whether they can avert disaster, but how they will fare in victory—and with whom they are going to share it.

One of the Britons girded for the climactic year of Europe's war, and for the peace, is King George VI. His highest duty is to be one of Britain's 46,000,000. In a fashion which no other people can wholly understand, and which no Briton needs to understand, he *is* Britain, or he is nothing.

In the trembling years of 1940 and 1941, King George spent nearly a third of his time among his people. He joined the Navy on its prowls around Britain. He even had his own personal bomb. After his office on the north side of the Palace had been blitzed, he moved across the hall. There, at work one day, another bomb spattered the room with broken glass, plaster and dirt. The King, like all his subjects, was proud of his bomb, bored his friends telling about it. Never in British history has a monarch seen and talked to so many of his subjects or so fully shared their life.

Throughout the war, George VI's daily routine has been rigorous, unsensational, inelegant. Like every other Briton who can manage it, he has his cup of morning tea, a black Indian blend, in bed at about 8 o'clock. By 9:30 he has bathed, dressed, breakfasted and glanced at the morning papers. When he is in London he then meets one of his two secretaries in his office. The secretary is loaded with papers. Among them are the latest secret dispatches from the Admiralty, War Office and Air Ministry.

From 11 a.m. to 1 p.m., he sees people. In a typical week he saw five admirals, two air marshals, two British generals and two American (Eisenhower and Spaatz).

Prime Minister Winston Churchill used to see the King one morning each week. Their sessions grew so long they were absorbing each other's entire half-day. Now Churchill lunches with the King one day a week, usually Thursday. Over grilled sole, or cold roast beef, washed down with whiskey and soda, the Prime Minister talks about the war, or the latest gossip of Downing Street.

After dinner, the King may play a few phonograph records from an enormous collection of jazz recordings he owns. He doesn't go for classical music.

The war has given him a new and tempered toughness, a new confidence, an easier manner. As Duke of York he was shy, hesitant in public, agonized by his stuttering. Now he walks with dignity. He is still only 5 ft. 8 in. tall and slightly built. But he seems a bigger man.

APRIL 17   **APRIL LAUGHTER:** This joke was going around in jampacked pre-invasion Britain:

A British soldier and a U.S. soldier were standing in Piccadilly Circus when a dilapidated car drove up. Said the Yank: "What a wreck! Do you know what we would do if a car like that drove up in Times Square?"

"Well," mused the Briton, "if you treated it as you treat everything else over here you'd either drink it or kiss it."

MAY 15   **THE CAVENDISHES & THE KENNEDYS:** William John Robert Cavendish, 26 years old, Marquess of Hartington and a Captain in the Coldstream Guards, proposed to marry an American, a Boston girl named Kathleen Kennedy. The Marquess had been mentioned as a suitable suitor for the hand of Princess Elizabeth. Kathleen's father was Joseph P. Kennedy, wealthy, Irish, and no admirer of the British. He had been a popular U.S. Ambassador to the Court of St. James's, who had later thrown away his popularity and then some by voicing dim views of Britain's chances in the war. What was more, the Kennedys were good Catholics; the Cavendishes have been strenuously Protestant since the 16th Century.

The Marquess' parents, the Duke and Duchess of Devonshire, and his grandmothers, the Dowager Duchess of Devonshire and the Marchioness of Salisbury, not to speak of the Kennedys, might have seen it coming. Kathleen had been going with the Marquess since 1938, when Ambassador Joe brought her to London. Paddling about London on a bicycle and working at an American Red Cross Club in Knightsbridge since last summer, Kathleen continued to see the Marquess.

But the actual prospect of marriage hit the Cavendishes hard. One of England's oldest and loftiest family trees swayed perceptibly.

The Cavendish family first appeared in 1366, when Sir John, the lord of Cavendish Overhall, acquired a seat on the King's Bench. In 1530 Sir William placed a firm foundation under the family fortunes while serving as a commissioner for Henry VIII. Bluff King Hal had yet to put away Catholic Catherine of Aragon, but was already breaking up the church monasteries and preparing to establish the Protestant Church of England. A share of the extensive Catholic lands fell to Sir William Cavendish.

At the beginning of World War II the family owned some 180,000 acres, and ranked well up among the "twelve families that own England." The Cavendish motto: *Cavendo Tutus,* Secure by Caution.

If Ambassador Joe had a motto, it might well be *Operando Tutus,* Secure by Operating. Joseph Patrick Kennedy's father came over from Ireland, became the mellow-voiced boss of Ward 2 in East Boston. Joe was a newsboy, candy butcher, bus operator, Harvard graduate ('12), bank president, shipbuilder, film magnate and a Wall Street operator. Then he

The Marquess of Hartington marries Kathleen Kennedy of Boston—mingling nationalities, religions, mottoes. Her brother Joe stands behind them.

became first chairman of the Securities & Exchange Commission under Franklin Roosevelt, and last peacetime Ambassador to the Court of St. James's. At the time of prohibition repeal, Joe secured the U.S. distribution of Haig & Haig, King William IV, other famed brands. The venture was successful.

Ever since the business with the monasteries, the Cavendishes have been unswervingly Protestant. In recent years they have been known as positively anti-Catholic. Before the Catholic Church will issue a dispensation permitting marriage with a non-Catholic, there must be agreement that all offspring will be brought up in the Church. Lord Hartington declined to marry in the Church, or to agree that future Cavendishes would be Catholic. Kathleen decided to marry anyway. The Duke, the Duchess, the Dowager Duchess and the Marchioness capitulated.

Last week the Marquess of Hartington repaired to the Chelsea Registry Office. Fifteen minutes later Kathleen Kennedy arrived in delphinium pink suede crepe, a short mink jacket and a little hat of pink & blue ostrich feathers. Lieut. Joseph Kennedy Jr., U.S.N.R., came to give his sister away. Seven minutes later, in the bare, plain registry room, livened only by carnations on the table, Kathleen became the Marchioness of Hartington. [Brother Joseph, a pilot, died on a bombing mission three months after the wedding. The Marquess died in battle four months after the wedding. Kathleen lost her life in an airplane crash in 1948.]

"EACH MAN TO 'IS POST": The heart and mind of Britain JUNE 19
may have been across the laden English Channel last week, but Britons did not show it. On D-day plus one, the Regent's Park Zoo decided to build a new elephant house, put the parrots on its upper floor, move the insect collection to the second floor of the new antelope house.

Charlie Evans, Cockney dustman, plugged steadily at his job of collecting garbage in Chelsea. He worried a bit about his son Charles, his son-in-law George, both in the Royal Navy, both probably somewhere in the Channel. But what got him proper hot was a report that Prime Minister Winston Churchill wanted to go to France with the troops. Said Evans: "'E knows 'e mustn't go out of the country. 'E's Minister of Defense, and if they tried something 'ere where would we be without 'im? In times like these it's each man to 'is own post." [Churchill visited the Normandy Beachhead that week just the same.]

On June 13 the first V-1s, small pilotless German aircraft delivering large bombs and launched from sites in France and Belgium, began dropping on London, causing enormous damage. In seven weeks the "buzz-bombs" killed 4,785 people, seriously injured 14,000, damaged 800,000 homes, of which 17,000 were demolished.

DAMNABLE THING: From the start London knew the robot JULY 17
bomb for what it was—a new weapon of terrible power. It was a weapon which struck again & again & again, 18 hours at a stretch. Even its sound-effects were potent: a throaty roar, then a sudden silence when the jet motor stopped and the bomb dived; then the blast. It kept thousands of Londoners in deep shelters. It drove other thousands to the country. It kept thousands, at work above ground, in a state of sustained apprehension which the Great Blitz never matched. As inaccurate as it was impersonal, it was a weapon precisely

designed for sprawling London, precisely calculated to raise havoc with civilian life.

Last week the world was told what London was putting up with. Winston Churchill partially cracked the censorship, told all that security allowed.

From what he told, Britons got an eerie glimpse of an invisible war—enemy technicians racing to perfect their new destroyer, Allied technicians piecing together jigsaws of information and racing to contrive counter measures.

The Allies also had dropped 50,000 tons of bombs on laboratories in Germany, on the launching ramps in France. But the Germans surmounted this drenching attack by devising easily moved, easily hidden ramps.

The robot's power to disrupt was greater than its power to kill. Said Churchill: "Everyone must go about his business and when the long day is done seek the safest shelter he can find."

On London streets dignified Britons forgot their dignity. Sir Kenneth Clark, director of the National Gallery, was standing in a bus queue when he heard the roar, felt the silence. Unashamedly he ran, threw himself in a doorway. The queue was wiped out.

In pubs and cafés, chatter stilled while diners and drinkers ducked under tables. The Government opened eight new

A victim is removed from the rubble after a buzz-bomb attack on London: a throaty roar, a sudden silence, then the blast.

shelters, 100 feet underground. Special trains evacuated 15,000 children a day.

On Sunday morning, June 18, the Rev. Dr. Leslie Owen was conducting a service for officers of the famed Brigade of Guards when a robot roared overhead, silence fell, and the bomb burst through the roof. Outside, 86 Guards standing at attention did not flinch. They were unhurt. But many were killed in the chapel.

General Dwight D. Eisenhower called the robot "a damnable thing," added: "From the German's point of view, the flying bomb gives him a cheap air force." Not since the blitz had Londoners hated the Germans so intensely. [On September 8, the V-1 was joined by the V-2, a more devastating weapon. A true rocket, the V-2 was a revolutionary invention. Designed by German engineer Wernher von Braun, it was the ancestor of all rockets—military and space—developed since by both Russia and the U.S. After the war Von Braun came to the U.S. and played a leading part in U.S. rocket development.]

ONE-THIRD OF A PETTICOAT: Clothes-rationed British wom- AUG. 28 en last week remembered a sad song of coupons that amused them earlier in the war:

> *If you spent them all at once*
> *You could be looking dandy,*
> *But by November or December*
> *You would look like Gandhi.*

Britain's women are not yet down to dhotis. But the British Board of Trade found that in one year the average woman now buys: one dress, two pairs of gloves, four ounces of knitting wool, two yards of material, one pair of knickers (underdrawers), no vests (undershirts), one-fifth of a nightdress, one-fourth of a suit, one-third of a petticoat.

LIGHT: This week hundreds of thousands of London children SEPT. 18 will see a wonder they have never seen before (or cannot remember seeing)—a lighted city. This week the lights will go on again in London. They will not all go on, yet—but the five years (1,843 nights) of total blackout will be over.

SEPT. 25 **BLITZ SCORE:** About a quarter of London will have to be rebuilt after the war. Bombs (Blitz I) and robombs (Blitz II) have left few streets in the world's largest city without ruins or cratered lots, few buildings undamaged. Last week Reconstruction Minister Lord Woolton totted up the damage.

Blitz I killed 42,000 Britons, injured 50,000, destroyed 84,000 homes, damaged 1,500,000. Blitz II killed 10,000, injured 28,000, destroyed 23,000 homes, damaged 1,104,000.

Most Londoners preferred bombs to robombs. At its peak the robomb blitz destroyed or damaged 17,000 houses a day, a destruction rate never equaled in the much longer bomb blitz.

A million Londoners are homeless, hundreds of thousands are living in "acute discomfort." Lack of labor, materials, time have made it impossible to rebuild wrecked houses. This winter at least 10,000 Nissen-type Army huts will dot the London landscape as emergency shelters. But they will shelter only a fraction of the homeless.

At week's end robombs again began falling on London. Londoners, who had cautiously raised their blackout curtains for the first time in five years, promptly lowered them again. On dimout night the city continued to look like the inside of an inkwell. As long as the bombs kept coming, London would go back to being sensibly dark.

OCT. 16 **CAUSE & EFFECT:** London's *Time and Tide* reported a delayed buzz-bomb story. In London a robomb hit a house in which an old man was taking a bath. Nothing was left but debris, so there did not seem to be much use searching for the body. But rescue squads dug in, presently dug out the old man, dazed but otherwise unhurt, and still sitting in the bathtub. Said he: "I don't know how it happened. I just pulled out the plug and the house blew up."

DEC. 25 **THE OUTLINE OF CHURCHILL:** Splenetic Herbert George (*Outline of History*) Wells is a historian whose interest in the remote past is based on his interest in the immediate present. He also brandishes words like a Martian. From the sickbed where he has lain for months, the 78-year-old socialist last week sent London's pinko *Tribune* a sizzling, unsolicited philippic entitled *Churchill Must Go.*

Cried Wells: "Winston Churchill, the present would-be British Führer, is a person with a range of ideas limited to the adventure and opportunities of British political life. The country meant to fight and he delighted in fighting. For want of a better, he became the symbol of our national will for conflict, a role he has now outlived.

"The British Prime Minister's mind is now plainly in a phase of extreme reaction. His ideology, picked up in the garrison life of India, on the reefs of South Africa, the maternal home, and the conversation of wealthy, conservative households, is a pitiful jumble of nonsense. He has served his purpose and it is high time he retired upon his laurels before we forget the debt we owe him.

"We want him to go—now—before he discredits us further, for his own sake as well as ours. The matter is urgent. If we do not end Winston, Winston will end us." [The British electorate turned Churchill out of office in July 1945 and swept the Labor Government of Clement Attlee into power.]

"BOB HOPES": Londoners had a new name for the German rocket bombs: "Bob Hopes." The name was a contraction of "Bob down, and hope for the best."

Germany

"IT MIGHT BE HIS LAST": Berlin posters cried birthday greetings to the Führer: "Our walls may crumble but our hearts stay firm." Tiredly Propaganda Minister Joseph Goebbels eulogized: "Even the greatest of leaders of history will be faced with occasional setbacks." Discreetly the radio did not play the refrain, *Today Germany, tomorrow the world!*; instead it broadcast a Handel concerto, Beethoven's *Eroica*. On his 55th birthday Adolf Hitler spoke not a word. Cried the BBC: "Yes, flags out on Hitler's birthday. Flags out—at half-staff! It might be his last." [It was not. Hitler and his longtime mistress, Eva Braun, committed suicide in his Berlin bunker on April 30, 1945, ten days after his 56th birthday.]

MAY 29 **HUNGER:** Inside Germany, home-front morale sprang little fissures. Basic trouble: a food shortage. In Berlin a 27-year-old woman was beheaded for snatching another woman's purse. Execution for such trivial offenses was decreed to help stop the flow of stolen ration cards into the hands of speculators.

JUNE 5 **FOR WORLD WAR III:** In a blue-bound, looseleaf "Memo for Company Instruction," the German High Command announced that every German family must average four children. Reason: "Every stout boy born in 1943 can become a brave soldier in 1963."

THEY WHO CANNOT LAUGH: German nerves tautened:
¶ The High Command ordered the word "catastrophe" eliminated from all military reports and "the vocabulary in general."
¶ The authorities sought ways to cheer the dour people. Amid Berlin's debris 72 movie theaters kept open; they held high priority in air-raid repair. A flower show in the capital featured half a million tulips. The radio urged: "The human body and mind need the stimulating reactions of the laughing muscles. He who cannot laugh lives in vain."

JULY 31 **CRACK OF DOOM:** Bomb-weary Berliners sat down to another dreary dinner. From radio loudspeakers came pleasant music, scheduled to be followed by a useful lecture on the extermination of rats. The lecture never came. Instead a tense voice clipped in: "Today an attempt was made on the life of the Führer with explosives."

Around the world as in Berlin the tense voice sounded like the crack of doom. The one question that flashed through every mind was: is this the end, the crackup? Had the long-awaited struggle between Hitler and his generals begun?

The voice went on: "The Führer suffered no injuries except light burns and bruises. He resumed work and, as scheduled, received the Duce." Wounded with Hitler were twelve of his military advisers, some of them seriously. That was all.

For hours the fate of Hitler and of Germany, which was in some degree the fate of every man, woman & child in the world, was shrouded behind an invisible, hermetic barrier. Seven hours later Hitler himself spoke on the air. He said: "German men and women: I address you for two reasons: first, so that you shall hear my voice and know that I am unhurt and well and, second, so that you shall hear the details of a crime that has no equal in German history.

"An extremely small clique of ambitious, unscrupulous and at the same time foolish, criminally stupid officers hatched a plot to remove me and the staff of the German High Command. The bomb that was placed by Colonel Graf von Stauffenberg exploded two meters (about two yards) away from me on my right side. It wounded very seriously a number of my dear collaborators. One of them has died.

"At an hour in which the German Army is waging a very hard struggle there has appeared in Germany a very small group, that believed that it could thrust a dagger into our back. It is a very small clique of criminal elements, which will now be exterminated quite mercilessly."

¶ Among those executed immediately were bomb-tossing Colonel Graf Claus von Stauffenberg, member of Hitler's own personal staff; Colonel General Ludwig Beck, onetime Chief of Staff, who fought Hitler's intuition in 1938, had since been in retirement.

Meanwhile people in the outer world peered at the blood-and-iron orgy and wondered. What they felt about the misfired assassination was neatly and stoutly said by Prime Minister Winston Churchill: "They missed the old bastard— (British newspapers had him say "bounder") but there's time yet." [According to Gestapo records, 7,000 Germans were arrested as a result of the attempt on Hitler's life. An estimated 5,000 were executed—including, according to some reports, more than 50 officers of the German General Staff.]

TENTATIVE V: As the first U.S. armor rumbled into the first SEPT. 25 German town, Roetgen, Germans froze and stared. Then a German made a tentative V-sign. A woman started to cry. Finally a *Hausfrau* approached with an offering—a skirtful of green apples. Against orders, the G.I.s passed out chocolate.

It was like that in half a dozen little forest towns along the border, as fear gave way to sullenness and sullenness to little offers of assistance. But in Wallendorf, frenzied civilian snipers picked off the first patrols, shot down rescuing medical corpsmen. Wallendorf was burned to the ground.

OCT. 23 **DEATH ON THE DOWNGRADE:** Trim, broad-faced Erwin Eugen Rommel rose with Hitler from the street brawls of pre-Nazi Germany. No *junker* but a schoolteacher's son, he became the ranting Führer's bodyguard, military adviser and top-drawer hooligan. When Hitler rang up the curtain on World War II, Erwin Rommel was a colonel, commanded an *SS* division that fought in Poland.

Hitler, who sometimes knew a good soldier when he saw one, gave Rommel a free hand with the *"Plan Sud"*— Rommel's scheme for securing an African-Middle Eastern German empire. On the Baltic shores Rommel simulated desert conditions, trained the *Afrika Korps* with super-heated barracks and artificial sandstorms. By March 1941 he went to Libya, to pull the faltering Italians out of defeat.

Arrogant, autocratic but a resourceful, daring tactician, he restored the art of bluff and ambush to modern big-scale war. He tied up much of Britain's military strength for nearly two years and at his peak he stood at El Alamein, 65 miles from Alexandria. Then Rommel and his *Afrika Korps* began the downhill trail. He was soundly defeated at El Alamein by an abler general—Sir Bernard L. Montgomery—and by a superiority of power. Even so, his 1,500-mile retreat across North Africa was masterly. Had his career ended then, he might have been one of military history's heroes.

The Germans were still convinced he was a topnotcher. At 52, Germany's youngest field marshal, he took command of an army group in France. In Normandy, Rommel and the German Army were swamped. By July 17 it was clear that Rommel was again a defeated commander. That day, as Rommel sped down a French road in his staff car, an Allied fighter pilot dipped down for a burst. The car smashed up, Rommel was wounded. This week Berlin announced that he was dead. [What Berlin did not announce was that Rommel had swallowed poison on orders from Hitler for his part in the July bomb plot to kill the Führer.]

THOUGHT FOR THE SEASON: For Christmas, Propaganda DEC. 25 Minister Joseph Goebbels excogitated a thought in keeping with the season: every good German's idea of peace, he wrote, is a world in which "the Olympic games provide the only conflict."

Argentina

FORCED BREAK: A small crowd gathered in the rain last week FEB. 7 in front of Buenos Aires *Casa Rosada* (Pink House), heard President Pedro Pablo Ramírez announce that Argentina had broken diplomatic relations with Germany and Japan. The last and most reluctant nation of Latin America had put a tentative foot in the United Nations camp.

SOBERED PERÓN: Last week, as usual, U.S. policy in Latin APRIL 24 America was up against an obstacle: Argentina, which refused to be a Good Neighbor. Foremost, though not the loudest leader of this recalcitrance was Colonel Juan Domingo Perón, at present serving slightly behind the scenes as Acting Minister of War.

Colonel Perón, now tall, handsome and 48, was brought up on his father's ranch in bleak southern Argentina. His boyhood was like that of a healthy, western Yankee. He played and fought with the local boys, rode wild horses, hunted wild turkeys. He entered the Army's Military Academy, became a sub-lieutenant at 18, a full lieutenant at 20.

A fine athlete, he distinguished himself in boxing, fencing and track. A good scholar, he wrote books on military affairs (one of which praised Germany). Always in his mind and on his lips was the conviction that the Army was the purest, finest, most *Argentine* thing in Argentina. While in charge of troops in Mendoza in 1941, he started a "crusade for spiritual renovation"—which worked out as a scheme to staff the Argentine Government with idealistic, hard-working and deeply nationalistic young Army officers.

Few Argentine officers answered this description. But the idea spread, quickly crystallized into the GOU, an amorphous organization of officers below the rank of general. The letters mean *Grupo de Oficiales Unidos* (Group of United Officers), later idealized into *Gobierno, Orden, Unidad* (Government, Order, Unity). When the military revolution of June 4, 1943 knocked unpopular President Ramón Castillo out of power, the GOU took charge. It has since split up into factions. But Colonel Perón's influence with some of these groups is still the basis of his power.

U.S. correspondents find nothing wrong with Perón personally. He is well-mannered, well-dressed without being particularly stiff or foppish. He can tell a good joke, enjoy a joke at his own expense. A widower, he has a pretty, 17-year-old daughter, María Inez. He likes to cook, to fish, to hunt, and to be with a charming movie star named Eva Duarte.

Colonel Perón denounces Communism and admires German military efficiency. But Colonel Perón does not practice European Fascism. Nazi money, Nazi influence operate in Argentina. But Perón is a home-grown Argentine authoritarian, not a Nazi stooge. Perhaps he would like to be a real dictator; at present he is merely a brainy man who generally outmaneuvers the other militarists, mostly numbskulls. [In 1946, with the help of movie actress Eva, whom he had married, Perón became dictator of Argentina.]

Canada

JAN. 10 **FORM CHART:** At the start of her fifth year of war, Canada added up some figures, made form chart on the Dominion's performance:

¶ Of 725,000 Canadian men & women now in uniform, all but 70,000 are volunteers. The 70,000 draftees are liable for service on the North American continent only. Of the total 37,800 are women.

¶ The Dominion has now become fourth largest producer of munitions among the United Nations. Seventy per cent of her manufacturing plant now working on war orders has produced $6,500,000,000 worth of material.

FEB. 7 **THE OLD ARMY GAME:** To soldiers applying for overseas service, military authorities in Toronto last week handed a

form reading: "This application will be made out in tripli-
cate on forms F M B 2783, which is obsolete, and therefore
the first 16 questions will be answered on substitute form
F M B 813, copies of which are not available at present."

VICTORY FOR PAPA: When his five daughters were born in MARCH 27
1934 he ran dazedly away to hide, crying: "A man like me
should be kept in jail." As any father would, he made a scene
when control of his new daughters was taken from his hands,
given to a Government-appointed board of guardians. It was
another affront to his paternal dignity when the girls were
kept in aseptic isolation in a fancy hospital-home of their
own. For almost ten years Oliva Dionne had nursed a wounded pride. Last week he won a great victory.

In Ontario's Legislature, Attorney General Leslie Black-
well introduced a bill, which will make Papa Dionne sole
guardian of his wealthy ($50,000 a year income, plus a six-
figure reserve), renowned Quintuplets. Ontario courts hence-
forth will supervise only their business contracts. Otherwise,
from July 1 on, Oliva Dionne will have full authority over
all his children.

In an $80,000 stucco-and-stone mansion, built with Quint
profits near Callender, he will live with the healthy, chubby,
stolid Quints, Mama Elzire, the less famed Dionnes—Ernest
(19), Rose (17), Thérèse (15), Daniel (13), Pauline (11),
Oliva Jr. (8), Victor (5).

Oliva Dionne has changed in the past decade. Before Marie
Reine Alma, Emilie Marie Jeanne, Cécile Marie Emilda, An-
nette Lilianne Marie and Yvonne Edouilda Marie were born,
ten years ago next May 28, he was a shy, thin, weather-
beaten, unlettered farmer grubbing a living for his brood
from 200 unproductive acres near Callander, Ont. He still
farms the same soil (hay, oats, cattle), but only in a super-
visory way. He wears neat business suits, looks more urban
than rustic. He is assertive now, aware of his responsibilities,
no longer thrown off balance by publicity and whoop-
de-do.

When Quint Guardian J. A. Valin, a judge who is now 86,
recently resigned, the Province re-examined the guardianship
setup. Its decision: unnecessary "intervention should not
persist." A contributory factor: public opinion has turned

more & more toward Oliva Dionne ever since the late Dr. Allan Roy Dafoe, also a Quint guardian and the physician who had delivered them, was photographed in 1939 in New York City wearing a pink mortarboard and a sign reading: "Doctor of Litters."

JULY 17 **FATAL FASHION:** The Royal Canadian Navy solemnly passed a word of warning to bearded sailors and sailors who had thought of growing beards. The Navy's Newfoundland Command, concluding a post-mortem on the sinking of the frigate *Valleyfield,* found that a man overboard can be fatally choked by a heavy beard full of oil and salt water.

OCT. 16 **HIGH-GRADING:** An Ontario mining-commission report last week revealed a staggering yearly theft, highlighted a persistent racket that has become almost a tradition. Said the commission: a million dollars worth of gold is stolen every year from Ontario's mines by high-graders.

High-graders are miners who sneak rich bits of ore out of mines in their hair, ears, mouths, between their toes, between slices of bread in their dinner pails, or who raid staked claims which are not yet producing. They peddle their loot to "receivers" who melt the stolen ore into "buttons" worth $4,000 to $5,000 each. Then "carriers" tote the buttons, usually hidden in multiple-pocket corsets, into the U.S. Most of the gold reaches New York City, where refiners pay $30 an ounce for it, sell it in turn to the U.S. Treasury.

Almost all producing mines require miners to strip as they leave their jobs, undergo inspections. In some cases, suspicious-looking miners are X-rayed. Nevertheless gold still disappears.

NOV. 13 **NO COMPULSION:** A crisis in the Canadian Government has been simmering for weeks. Last week it boiled over. Out as Defense Minister went bulky, ruddy James Layton Ralston.

The cause of the crisis was the question of Canadian Army reinforcements. Evidence had been piling up that reinforcements for Canada's overseas army were inadequate. To assay these reports, Defense Minister Ralston had toured the battlefronts. Now, at a series of secret, full-dress Cabinet meetings in Ottawa, he demanded a change in government policy.

He insisted that the Dominion's 70,000-odd "Zombies" (soldiers drafted for home-defense service only) should be sent overseas.

Prime Minister William Lyon Mackenzie King and a majority of the Cabinet listened for ten days, remained unconvinced. They felt sure that if they decided to change policy now, they would be opening the door to serious internal ruptures, perhaps even to bloody riots such as occurred in conscription-hating Quebec during World War I. But Mr. Ralston was adamant. At last Mr. King accepted Ralston's resignation, which had been in his hands, undated, for two years.

To the vacant post the Prime Minister appointed popular General Andrew George Latta McNaughton, who less than a year ago was relieved as commander of Canadian Army troops overseas by Minister Ralston himself.

Even the Winnipeg *Free Press,* friendly to the King administration, was sharp in its rebuke: "The departure of one Minister of Defense and the appointment of another does not add one man to our striking force. The problem today is exactly what it was yesterday."

CHAOTIC COMPROMISE: The jampacked public galleries were DEC. 4 sober and attentive. On the floor, Prime Minister William Lyon Mackenzie King and his new Defense Minister, General Andrew G. L. McNaughton, faced a tense House of Commons, summoned to hear the facts about the Army's reinforcements crisis. The Prime Minister picked up a piece of paper. Loudly and clearly, head bobbing, he read an order-in-council. The Government had decided to compel home-defense draftees ("zombies") to serve overseas.

Parliament and the country were stunned: Mr. King had suddenly abandoned his lifelong opposition to conscription. Only one day before, the Prime Minister himself had reiterated: "I do not believe that conscription is necessary." Terrific public pressure had forced him to change his mind.

The greatest pressure of all came from rank-&-file members of Mr. King's own Liberal Party. In caucus, they told the Prime Minister that the people were outraged. The voters were asking: Does Quebec rule Canada?

Reluctantly, Prime Minister King gave in. He told the

House that 16,000 of the Dominion's 60,000-odd zombies would be compelled to go overseas in the next few months. But they would go only to Europe (not to the Pacific war). And only "to the extent necessary." Great Compromiser King had compromised again.

DEC. 18 **WHAT WIVES SHOULD KNOW:** For the 23,000 wives whom Canadian soldiers have married in Britain, the Canadian Government this week published a 40-page pamphlet telling the girls what to expect in their husbands' country. *Welcome to War Brides* contains everything from geography lessons to shopping hints, and a glossary explaining, for example, that in Canada a joint is a roast, a spanner is a wrench, and corn is wheat.

Typical advice:

¶ "Canadians are very democratic and take a dim view of people who try to impress them."

¶ "You will be asked hundreds of times how you like Canada. If you can make your answer an enthusiastic 'I love it!' you will make friends right and left."

¶ "If you should unwittingly convey the impression that you regard Canada as in any way a dependency of Britain, you are likely to find that many people will temper their welcome with coolness."

China

In 1944, the seventh year of her war against Japanese aggression, China faced not only a determined enemy but immense internal problems. The Communists controlled a large area in the north and were exerting increasing political pressure on Generalissimo Chiang Kai-shek's Nationalist government. What remained of Free China was so riddled with inflation and graft that Chiang was forced to divert much of his attention from military matters to economic and political problems.

AUG. 28 **POWDER KEG:** Last week the long-smoldering quarrel between Kuomintang and Communist Governments blew up in a shower of sparks. From the Secretary of the Chinese Communist Party Chou En-lai came an ugly cry: "There is danger of civil war."

After five years of armed truce, blockade and counterblockade, the Kuomintang and Communist Governments last May began haggling over unity terms. Chungking offered to recognize the Communists as a legal party but demanded that they acknowledge Kuomintang suzerainty. Yenan (Communist capital) countered with sweeping proposals for national economic and political reform.

Negotiations continue, but, said a Chungking spokesman: "It is like a Hottentot talking to an Eskimo."

BEYOND CHINA'S SORROW: Communist China now claims 80,000,000 people and 1,000,000 square miles of territory. For five years it has been a land of mystery to the outside world. Last May Chungking lifted its blockade, let foreign correspondents enter the Communist Border Region. Only last week did reports from Yenan, the Communist capital, tell what life is now like there.

The Border Region, a wilderness cut into wild shapes by streams, broken by valleys and woodland, is generally fertile, but there is little rainfall. The Communists are slowly changing the face of this churlish land. Where the soil is cultivable, they have planted crops. Villages have plenty of pigs and chickens. The typical village home is an arched cave, whitewashed and faced with wood.

Yenan, the capital (pop. 25,000), is a city of caves cut in tiers in the slopes. One of its cave hospitals has eight stories. Its university (enrollment: 2,000) is a labyrinth of classrooms and dormitories. Everywhere on stone walls and cliffsides appears the four-syllable slogan coined by the government's able chief, Mao Tze-tung: "Move your own hands!" Meaning: "He who does not work shall not eat."

In parts of the Border Region, the old landlord-tenant system is preserved with modifications. Rent and interest have been cut. Landlords may not evict tenants. Tenants must pay their rent on time except in cases of crop failure when both sides share the loss. Why doesn't the Communist government get rid of the landlords and divide the land? The Communists say: In wartime, civil peace is necessary; otherwise whole

Communist boss Mao Tse-tung: "He who does not work shall not eat."

Chiang Kai-shek. He smashes every tea cup on the floor. Page 164.

classes will be pushed into the enemy camp. The first goal now is the defeat of Japan. Next, China's feudalism must be uprooted.

DEC. 18 **TIRED NATION:** China was deadly tired. Since 1911 she had been going through a convulsive social revolution. Since 1937, almost singlehanded, she had been holding off the Japanese invaders from without. At the same time she had held off the Communists from within.

Generalissimo Chiang Kai-shek himself had fought the Communists, had fought the Japanese. When it was no longer possible to hold against the Japanese, he had organized the retreat. In Chungking he had organized the resistance. By an act of inflexible will, the Generalissimo had held together China's battered, wasting strength. He knew there were abuses—there are always abuses. But reforms must wait until the more urgent purpose was achieved—victory which will make reforms inevitable. But victory had always been predicated upon real help from the Allies.

Last month it became clear to tired Chiang Kai-shek that reforms could not wait for victory—that Allied help, until then too little, would be too late, that China, as usual, must rely upon China. Somehow China and Chiang found the strength. Chiang gave his armies a new, energetic Minister of

War—young able General Chen Cheng. Just as important, Chiang had reorganized his civil administration. To China's No. 2 job, Acting President of the Executive Yuan, he appointed China's ablest administrator, his brother-in-law, Foreign Minister Tse-veng ("T. V.") Soong.

In 1940 T. V. had flown to Washington to negotiate an urgently needed loan. He talked with Franklin Roosevelt, played poker with the RFC's Jesse Jones, the Treasury's Henry Morgenthau. He had come with a business proposition: For $100,000,000 worth of supplies China would continue to pin down 1,125,000 Japanese troops. By saving China from collapse, the U.S. could buy time to prepare for war with Japan. T. V. drove his bargain. Pearl Harbor proved his point.

A fortnight later the Generalissimo cabled his appointment as Foreign Minister. T. V. became a peripatetic global emissary shuttling between Chungking, Washington, London, Quebec, New Delhi. He signed the Declaration of the United Nations. But, like all China, he soon found that the priorities of Allied global strategy made Allied aid to China a dribble.

Last October T. V. went home. Over a Chungking tea table, frustrated Chiang Kai-shek upbraided his brother-in-law for the meager trickle of foreign aid. Hot words passed between them. According to one story, the Generalissimo ended the angry conversation by smashing every teacup on the floor.

For a year T. V. lay low. But many an old China hand knew that T. V. would come back in China's next crisis. In effect, T. V. last week was China's Premier. The road to victory was still up the sharp sides of mountains. But with T. V. at work again, there was a new faith that China would one day get over the hump.

Czechoslovakia

German troops had marched into Czechoslovakia in the spring of 1939 and Adolf Hitler had issued a decree declaring that the country ceased to exist. The Czechs lived under a harsh German rule until 1944 when the Soviet army moved in to drive the Germans out.

MARCH 27 **THE ART OF SURVIVAL:** Five years, to the week, after German boots had hit the cobblestones of Prague, and the solar plexus of the world, the Czechoslovak Government ordered its people to join, in "an army uprising," the approaching "Army of Liberation."

The call came from London. The "Army of Liberation" was coming from Soviet Russia. There was not too much reason to expect that the call can be heeded by nine million Czechoslovaks who, in chains and humiliation, are forced to produce huge quantities of weapons for their German masters. But to survive is an obsession with Czechs; it is also their greatest talent.

The man who administers Czechoslovak foreign policy may set a powerful precedent for the liberation of Europe. Foreign Minister and No. 2 man of the first Government in Exile preparing to go home is Jan Masaryk. In his person, career and present predicaments the whole Continent might recognize itself.

Masaryk tries hard to live down his name. He is a chip off a colossal old block: Professor Thomas Garrigue Masaryk, his father, was not just the creator of Czechoslovakia but a sage of world stature. Burdened by a father who belonged to history, young Jan preferred to clown his way out of such embarrassment. He is as handy with unprintable stories as the Great Old Man was with the terms of Aristotle.

Today, "young" Jan Masaryk is 57 and the most popular diplomat in London. Full of bounce and zest and a bravura that was once described as "something out of the pages of Dumas," the tall (6 ft. 2 in.) extrovert has a selling power that could make Eskimos buy iceboxes.

Last December, in New York, Jan Masaryk said: "We intend to live our own life in our own way and we know that Russia will respect our way of living." And added: "Russia is fighting with us to destroy once for all time the German *Drang nach Osten* and we know that without Russia in Europe there is no stopping it."

As motto of the Republic he created, Jan's father selected two humbly confident words: *"Pravda vitezi"* (Truth prevails"). One truth is: the Czechs are a liberty-loving European people. Another truth is: the Czechs are prepared to conform with any power that assures their national security. Another and most immediate truth is: to this day, the only power current to reach Central Europe with respectable voltage comes from Russia.

Whatever truth prevails, the Czechs are above all resolved to survive. Asked what his postwar program was, shrewd, sensible Jan Masaryk gave students of the craft the most pointed diplomatic statement of modern times: "I want to go home." [After the war Jan Masaryk served as Czech Foreign Minister until 1948 when he died under mysterious circumstances. His body was found outside the window of the Foreign Office and there were rumors that he had been thrown to his death by the country's new Russian masters.]

Greece

"OUR DEAD DEMAND IT.": To Cairo by plane from London APRIL 24 hurried King George of the Hellenes to steady the rocking boat of the Greek Government in Exile. Promptly he promised a government "composed largely of Greeks who have lived in their country under enemy occupation." Promptly he persuaded liberal Sophocles Venizelos to take the premiership.

Popular Premier Venizelos knew what most Greeks in the Middle East urgently wanted: a broadened government capable of administering liberated Greece until elections could be held.

At week's end occupied Greece sent her first envoy to the new exile government: George Papandreou, 56-year-old leader of the Social Democratic Party. Bitterly, passionately, the refugee spoke of Greek suffering under the Nazi heel, urged national unity: "From their graves our dead demand it."

RETURN TO REASON?: A tall, stoop-shouldered man with a MAY 8 mighty tongue and a little mustache took office in Cairo last week as the third Greek Premier within a fortnight.

George Papandreou (rhymes with hey you) had left occupied Athens less than a month ago. Premier Sophocles Venizelos had turned out to be a stopgap, and he stepped down the minute he caught sight of the dynamic newcomer. Unable to form a cabinet right away, energetic Mr. Papandreou ruled alone. He uttered such firm, authoritative commands that Cairo Greeks first blinked, then cheered. Said the man from Greece: "Our watchword shall be one nation, one government, one army. I have no doubt at all that after the ignominy of recent weeks there will now be a general return to reason."

DEC. 18 **CIVIL WAR:** For Greece, Britain, Europe, it was a week of tragedy, a week of decision.

The hills of Athens echoed and reechoed to the boom of bombs. Against a sullen sky loomed the Parthenon, monument to the ruin of Europe's most serene civilization. Across it flashed the shadows of strafing Spitfires. On the sides of the Acropolis and in the streets of Athens, where British soldiers and Greek Leftists stalked each other with Tommy guns, were the ruins of the hopes born of liberation. Splashes of Greek and British blood slowly clotted on the pavements. Athens, where the word democracy first achieved political meaning, was a battleground for two forces, each claiming to defend democracy.

An armed showdown had come between the Communist-cored EAM and its fighting wing ELAS on the one side, and the coalition Government of Socialist Premier George Papandreou with the backing of the British occupation forces, on the other. Ever since the police fired on a forbidden EAM demonstration, called to protest the surrender of its arms, open warfare had raged in the ancient capital.

Because the battle lines were everywhere all Athens was a no man's land in which few unarmed civilians dared to venture. Martial law and the general strike ordered by EAM paralyzed all public services. Shops closed, trams stopped, streets emptied. Conditions at Athens' Hospital of the Evangelist had been bad enough before the fighting began. Now so many civilians had been wounded that patients lay on mattresses on the floor. After the first mass funeral, nobody found time for more burials. Since several cemeteries were being used as guerrilla strong points, naked corpses were piled up in mortuaries like cordwood.

The struggle went on all week. British troops and the British-trained Mountain Brigade methodically cleaned up street after street only to have ELAS riflemen, clad in civilian clothes, infiltrate behind them.

At week's end the British-held area was still only an island in a hostile sea.

SECOND WEEK: In Greece the civil war raged on. For the sec- DEC. 25
ond successive week men fought and died in the streets of Athens. The outcome was inconclusive—ELAS had not enough arms, the British not enough troops to win the city.

At night Athens was awesome. The darkness which engulfed the city was periodically pierced by flares parachuted by the R.A.F. to reveal ELAS troop movements. The floating flares also revealed the Parthenon in a new, glowing beauty. The Acropolis was again a fortress. Under cover of night British paratroopers descended on the historic eminence, found it unoccupied. All round them was ELAS-land, but the skytroopers were confident they could hold the precipitous heights against any assault. The only troops which had ever taken the Acropolis by storm were the Persians (in 480 B.C.).

Italy

Benito Mussolini, who had ruled Italy as Premier since 1922, resigned in July 1943 soon after Allied forces invaded Sicily. Mussolini was succeeded by Marshal Badoglio, a venerable hero of World War I, and the new Italian government dissolved the Fascist party, surrendered to the Allies and declared war on Germany. Allied troops invaded Italy itself in September 1943, but Nazi troops under Field Marshal Albert Kesselring put up a stiff resistance. As the year began, two-thirds of the country, including Rome, was still in German hands.

GENTLEMEN OF VERONA: While *Fascismo* still paid divi- JAN. 17
dends, Count Galeazzo Ciano supped as well as any. Wedded to Mussolini's daughter, the waspish, predatory Edda, and openly called the heir apparent, he swooped through his

duties as Foreign Minister with minimum effort and maximum profit.

Ciano was no fool. He saw the writing on the wall well ahead of the other stalwarts of the Fascist hierarchy, began making quiet plans to save himself. Mussolini took over the portfolio of Foreign Affairs, made his son-in-law Ambassador to the Vatican. But he let Ciano save face with a seat on the Fascist Grand Council, and it was there that Ciano pulled down his house of cards about his ears: when the Council voted to oust Mussolini last July, Count Galeazzo's vote went against his father-in-law.

This week in Verona, capital of the Nazi manipulated Fascist "Republic," Ciano was condemned to death by a puppet court, shot next day.

APRIL 3 **DYSPEPTIC DUCE:** Benito Mussolini's eye had lost its glitter. Eight months had leafed away since his fall from power in Rome. In his Nazi-guarded villa on the shores of North Italy's Lago di Garda, he donned his grey general's uniform, began the day's mock routine of a mock Duce.

No windy halls were here, no balconies for strutting. Laurel and cypress shut in the rococo house; stained glass windows kept its rooms in decadent twilight. Benito Mussolini shuffled to his desk, shuffled through a morning's paper work. His three physicians—two Italians, one German—had warned him sternly: a dyspeptic Duce could not live like a lion.

There was lunch with his wife, Donna Rachele, Son Vittorio, Son Bruno's widow and daughter. Then an hour of chess and strolling through the grounds, not too far from the Nazi Elite Guard or the air-raid shelter hewn from solid rock.

At 3 o'clock began the day's main chore: conference of state, sessions of the Fascist Republican cabinet. Of the old gang, Benito Mussolini had few left. Most influential of his fellow puppets: tall, peasant-tough Marshal Rodolfo Graziani, chief organizer of the Fascist Republican Army which helps the *Wehrmacht* curb restive northern Italy.

By 8 o'clock the Duce's stomach ulcers could stand no more. The household gathered for supper. Afterward, the man who once said, "I shall make my life a masterpiece," browsed in a book, chatted quietly. Punctually at 10, he shuffled to bed.

Count Ciano is shot for voting against his father-in-law, Mussolini. Page 169. *Lieut. Colonel Charles Poletti sells everyday democracy to the Italians.*

PRACTICING DEMOCRAT: On a moonlit street in the heel of MAY 1 Italy a British soldier uttered a cry of pain, fell with a stab wound in his back. Angry Tommies beat through the dark village, could not find the assailant. This vignette of violence had a moral: it happened in a town where a Fascist still held office. Here, as in most of the liberated land, things were not going well.

But there was hope. In particular, an Italian-American from New York had brought to bear a great deal of political savvy, a great ability to personify democracy to Italians who had never seen it in action. This paragon is Lieut. Colonel Charles Poletti, onetime Lieutenant Governor of New York, now Regional Commissioner for Naples, Salerno, Benevento and Avellino.

Colonel Poletti took hold last February. He began by renovating his four-story, red-painted, Renaissance *prefettura* near the Naples waterfront. He had bomb debris cleaned up, plumbing repaired, elbow grease applied to slick up the place. Explained one of his subordinates: "You can't sell democracy in an outhouse."

Then Lieut. Colonel Poletti began selling democracy to Italians. He saw all callers. In wrinkled uniform, slouched behind a huge desk, he listened to complaints, cracked jokes, gave out facts, usually ended interviews with a pep talk reminding Italians of their responsibilities and opportunities. Visitors were flattered by hearing their own language, by the deft touch.

It did not take long for Lieut. Colonel Poletti to put war-shocked Naples on the way toward recovery. Now the city gets regular street washings. Over the radio the Regional Commissioner appeals to Italian patriotism to help stamp out black markets. He has granted labor unions collective bargaining, encouraged a manufacturers' association. In the suburbs, too, he has restored democratic forms of government, helped industrialists, workers and peasants get representation on local councils, prodded the average Italian into talking over public problems in public meetings.

JUNE 19 **"PURE OF FASCISM":** Last week, to the Grand Hotel in liberated Rome came the leaders of the Socialists, Christian Democrats, Social Democrats, Communists, Liberals and the Action Party. In the South these men had effected a coalition. Now they were to meet the chieftains who had worked underground in Rome.

Arrangements made in southern Italy were bound to change when the tougher, industrial, politically sophisticated North got its first voice in free Italy's affairs. But no one outside of Italy had expected so abrupt a change, so soon after the North met the South.

Out went Marshal Pietro Badoglio, the old royalist who had held on through thick & thin until he reached Rome. In as Premier, Minister of War and Minister of Interior went white-haired Ivanoe Bonomi. His Cabinet, carefully balanced between North & South, included representatives of all six parties, four leaders of the Roman underground. Said Bonomi of his Cabinet: "No one, absolutely no one, with any Fascist connnections at all is in it; only men pure of Fascism."

JULY 17 **TUSCAN MASSACRE:** As the Germans were preparing to retreat from the little Italian town of Civitella, Italian Partisans shot three of them. That evening, a German commandant issued an ultimatum: Civitella would be burned to the ground by seven next morning, unless the villagers surrendered the culprits. No informer appeared.

At seven next morning, a German tank, mounting a flame-thrower, rumbled slowly through the village street. As it passed each house, its fire-spitting nozzle licked a blast of flame through the open window. The sleeping mothers and children were burned to death where they lay; the houses went up in flames. Then the tank turned and blocked one end of the street.

At the open end of the street German soldiers appeared. They rounded up the men, about 150 of them, herded them to the public square. There German machine guns were waiting. The machine guns chattered.

One old man, two women, a few Partisans who had watched helplessly from a distance made their way to Eighth Army headquarters near by, reported what they had seen. Little Civitella, nine miles off the main highway, has never been described by that careful German traveler, Karl Baedeker. But Italians will remember it.

DEFLATION: In Rome an astonished *carabiniere* officer AUG. 14 blinked, gasped. Never had he seen so many pregnant *romanas* trudging back from visits to the countryside. He remembered Mussolini and his medals for motherhood. But Il Duce was gone. Could it be that his works were marching on? The suspicious *carabiniere* decided to investigate, uncovered a widespread fraud. In fitted containers under their clothes the "pregnant" women were delivering olive oil to Rome's black market. A few days of prenatal checkups yielded ten tons of oil.

Japan

NEW SAMURAI: To the honored ranks of the warrior classes JAN. 3 last week were admitted the little people of Japan, the ragged and hungry factory workers. It was an admission that this was total war, and all Japan was told that *Bushido* [code of the Samurai] was not an exclusive spiritual cloak for those who fight it; it was also for those who produce. Said Tokyo radio: "Step by step and moment by moment the enemy is approaching our mainland. To support the spirit and follow the souls of the 4,500 men on Tarawa and Makin who preferred death to dishonor is the best way to fight. The 100 million people of Japan must arouse themselves and must follow the glory of the 4,500 heroes."

In the appeals made to the workers three points could be discerned: 1) Japan fears collapse of her supply lines to the conquered territories; 2) Japan hopes for a compromise peace; 3) Japan has abandoned the offensive, is now desperately waging a defensive war.

JAN. 17 **NEWS FROM NIPPON:** Japanese postal and press censorship ranks with the world's tightest; outsiders usually hear only what Nippon wants them to hear. But to the U.S. last week, through secret channels, came a rare, uncensored letter from Japan:

"The economic situation is as you possibly imagine—corruption in every department of life, the black market has become a national institution. Tokyo has become a city of troglodytes: holes everywhere. The hospitals are full of broken limbs, as during the nights zealous patriots dig holes into which other zealous patriots fall at dawn. It is excellent firstaid practice but bandages are scarce (doctors have the right to own five).

"The local population is getting per month: one slice of meat; one cake of soap and a little oil; a minute quantity of fish and one egg. Only children have the right to milk."

JULY 31 **THE SHADOW BEFORE:** A political earthquake shook Japan's war structure. When the heavings subsided, Tokyo had a new, two-faced Cabinet, geared to continue fighting the war vigorously—or sue for a negotiated peace.

General Hideki Tojo bowed before the Emperor, confessed his many failures. As Premier, holding most of the strategic Cabinet posts, he had bet on the wrong team in Europe, had led his country into war. As War Minister and lately Chief of the Army Staff, he had lost Saipan, was still bogged down in China. As Munitions Minister, he had failed to achieve sufficient war production at home. Tojo resigned with his whole Cabinet.

Into his shoes, but as Premier only, stepped another two-fisted Army man, General Kuniaki Koiso, 64.

Poland

UNDER THE JACKBOOTS: Out of the wild marshes and the APRIL 17
dark forests strode soldiers of Poland's Underground Army.
They bore aloft their country's red-&-white flag, marched
into the Russian lines, presented "declarations of collabora-
tion" to Red Army commanders: "We meet the forces of the
Soviet Union on Polish soil as our co-belligerents in the fight
against our common enemy, Germany. We bring to your
knowledge that there is in existence in these territories an
administration secretly organized by the Polish State."

Thus in London last week, the Polish Government in Exile
described the first meetings of Polish and Russian forces.
They were meetings fraught with uncertainty: can the Polish
underground and the Red Army cooperate on soil whose own-
ership is bitterly disputed by their respective Governments?

Poland's underground fighters have been toughened and
tempered by four bloody, silent years of warfare with the
Nazis. Poles are proud that the Nazis have never found a
Polish Quisling. A few small-fry Poles have collaborated; the
nation's true leaders have preferred torture and death.

Poles call their secret state the legitimate heir of Poland's
prewar Government. The *émigré* Cabinet is the secret state's
head until elections can be held. The hidden state within
Poland runs an administrative system, army, political forum,
courts, press, radio and even schools under the Gestapo's
jackboots.

Underground couriers shuttle fantastically from Poland to
Britain across the face of the shackled Continent. Inbound,
they drop by parachute into Poland's night from Allied planes.
A secret radio network has operatives who carry transmitters
in handbags, dodge from hideout to hideout. Underground
courts pass judgment on ultrabrutal Gestapomen. Special
squads carry out the sentences. Several months ago death was
decreed for Gestapoman Franz Buerckl, Governor of Warsaw's Pawiak Prison. One day, as Buerckl walked the streets
with wife and child, a Polish fiddler whipped a tommy gun
from his violin case, shot Buerckl down.

Opposed to the *émigré* Government in London is Poland's young Partisan underground, led by Polish Communists. Just how the two undergrounds will react to each other

and to the Russian occupation remains to be seen. But the Polish people have not forgotten an old tradition of resistance to foreign masters; their undergrounds have kept a stubborn nation alive for the day of reckoning.

AUG. 7 **MISSION TO MOSCOW:** Rugged Stanislaw Mikolajczyk, Premier of the Polish Government in London, hurried to No. 10 Downing Street. Winston Churchill had urgent news for him; Joseph Stalin, who did not recognize the London Polish Government and had just recognized the Polish Committee of National Liberation, had agreed to see Mikolajczyk.

With the tense haste of a man who knew it was now or never, Stanislaw Mikolajczyk summoned his Cabinet. The hard facts of power politics stared them in the face. Their own survival and the inner peace of Poland lay in Russia's hands. Neither Britain nor the U.S. was likely to risk good relations with Russia for a forlorn Polish cause. Before them lay a message from the Polish underground: "We who are fighting the Germans must work with the Russians."

SEPT. 4 **FIVE YEARS OF WAR:** "We lack food and medical supplies. Warsaw is lying in ruins. The Germans are murdering the wounded in the hospitals. They are driving women and children before their tanks as screens. Our sons are dying. Hear us Holy Father, Vicar of Christ."

This despairing cry of a nation in agony, slicing through the international joy over the liberation of Paris, was radioed last week to Pope Pius XII in the name of the women of Warsaw.

In Paris the U.S. and French forces had arrived in the nick of time to save the patriots. In Warsaw, no rescue had come to the underground forces, which for a month had stood off the German Army. R.A.F. flyers in Italy had made the 1,750-mile round trip to drop supplies and a few weapons. So far the Russians, some ten miles away, had dropped nothing.

DEC. 25 **"GRIM, BARE BONES":** Prime Minister Winston Churchill had a Christmas present for the Poles—partition. To a House of Commons still seething with the Greek crisis, he announced that with Britain's consent, Russia would extend her western frontier.

Churchill was grim as he exhumed the "grim, bare bones" of the Polish question. He reported: "It was with great pleasure that I heard from Marshal Stalin at Tehran that he, too, was resolved upon the creation and maintenance of a strong, integral, independent Poland as one of the leading powers in Europe. I am convinced that that represents the settled policy of the Soviet Union."

The U.S. was shocked. It should not have been. Power politics still dominated Europe, and the past masters of power politics were the masters of the Kremlin. Ever since Winston Churchill's last visit to Russia there had been little doubt that, for a free hand in the Mediterranean, he had been forced to grant Russia a free hand in Poland and the upper Balkans. Poland was the sacrifice.

Rumania

When King Carol of Rumania went into exile in 1940 for the second time (he had abdicated once before, in 1925), the throne went once more to his son, Mihai, who was then 18. But most of the real authority was in the hands of General Ion Antonescu, who appointed himself marshal and Conducator (leader) of Rumania and ruled the country as a dictator. Antonescu turned Rumania into a German satellite, and Rumanian oil from the fields at Ploesti helped fuel the Nazi war machine.

PASSAGE TO PEACE: Terror swept the Bessarabian plains, JAN. 17 driving the peasant folk and bourgeoisie like leaves in a rising storm. The Red Army was less than 70 miles away and advancing westward from the Kiev bulge. Behind the crumbling German front, Rumania trembled.

FLIP-FLOP: Rumania flip-flopped last week out of the war on SEPT. 4 the German side into the war on the Allied side.

The Red Army's mighty shove shook the royal palace, jolted young King Mihai into the realization that it was time to do something. Young Mihai reached first for his Tommy gun, then for a microphone.

To Rumanians he broadcast: "Rumania has accepted an armistice offered by the Soviet Union, Great Britain and the United States. From this moment all hostilities and other activities against the Soviet armies as well as the state of war with Great Britain and the United States cease."

Promptly Moscow warned the new Government: "The help of the Rumanian Army to the Red Army in the liquidation of German troops is the only means of speedily concluding an armistice between Rumania and the Allies."

Promptly the new Rumanian Government declared war on Germany. The Berlin radio snarled: "Perfidy." The *Wehrmacht* angrily attacked Bucharest; at week's end, said Nazi sources, the capital was ringed and cut off from the rest of the country.

SEPT. 18 **KING'S COUP:** To the A.P.'s Joseph Morton, King Mihai last week told the story of his dramatic palace coup which flip-flopped Rumania from the Axis to the Allied camp.

Seven times since early 1942 the young King and his young aides had planned to overthrow old hatchet-faced Marshal Ion Antonescu, the Nazi-loving dictator. Seven times they had to call off the plot.

On Aug. 23, Mihai sent for Antonescu. The dictator, following his practice of keeping the King waiting, arrived an hour late. He left his bullet-proof automobile, with glass an inch thick, a gift from Hitler, in the courtyard. Several other automobiles loaded with armed bodyguards parked behind it.

The King waited in his palace study. Beside him was his aide-de-camp, now Premier, General Constantin Sanatescu. In an adjoining room sat his Marshal of the Court, Baron Ion Mocsonyi-Styrcea, his good friend, now Foreign Minister, Grigore Niculescu-Buzesti, and his secretary Mirce Ionnitiu. In a third room, an officer and three members of the King's Palace Guard waited his signal.

When Antonescu came in, he and the King shook hands. Then—

Mihai: I have a wire from the front and the situation looks disastrous. What are you going to do about it? Are you or are you not going through with the armistice?

Antonescu: I am going through with it but there are some conditions to be met. I want a guaranty from the Allies that they will land in Rumania and guarantee it for us against the Russians.

Mihai: That is so absurd it is not worth discussing. How do you expect the Allies to guarantee us against their own Allies?

Antonescu: I will not move. If necessary I will retire to Transylvania and fight there.

Mihai: You will have to make an armistice or resign. This time you have gone too far.

Styrcea and Ionnitiu, both excellent shots, took pistols from their pockets and stepped in at the main doorway. Then—

Mihai: I am very sorry, but I have explained the situation to you and you must make a choice.

Antonescu: I will not resign and will not leave this country in the hands of people that I am not sure about.

The King reached with his foot for a pushbutton hidden under the carpet to summon the soldiers. Before he could reach it, however, they tramped in. The soldiers silently forced Antonescu up the stairs to a small fireproof vault that his father King Carol had built to safeguard his stamp collection. There they locked him in.

Antonescu's bodyguards were invited to come inside for coffee. As they lifted their cups, servants slipped the pistols from their holsters, took them prisoner. That night Mihai proclaimed Rumania's surrender to the Allies and the overthrow of Antonescu. [After the war, General Antonescu was convicted of war crimes, and in 1946, when King Mihai rejected his appeal for clemency, the former dictator was executed.]

FEAR IN RUMANIA: Before the Russians entered Bucharest, OCT. 23 the people were plain scared. The Red Army entered the city and quietly passed through, leaving small contingents behind.

But more Russians came, Russians who had been fighting Germans and Rumanians from Bessarabia to Stalingrad and back again. They came to a country rich in everything they had done without for more than three years. They came with only the barest minimum of supplies. They started requisitioning. Some started looting. Some got drunk and started taking women. For a while the Red Army went on something like a spree.

Their officers needed cars. With little or no ceremony they took them where they found them—sometimes right off the street. They needed quarters, and requisitioned them. And the Russian soldiers found an easy way to get watches: they walked up to somebody on the street, asked the time, looked at the watch and, if they liked it, took it.

Russia

JAN. 31 **THE SLEEPER:** When founding father Vladimir Ilyich Ulyanov (N. Lenin) died 20 years ago last week, Russia's foremost biochemists, and anatomists were ordered to preserve the frail little man's mortal remains for posterity. A black and red marble pyramid was erected on Moscow's Red Square. Inside the embalmed body was laid out in a quiet vault where the people could file silently by. War closed the tomb's door, but last week Moscow scientists made their annual report: "Excellent color in the skin, firmness and elasticity of connective tissues, flexibility of the joints and elasticity of the muscles, along with excellent preservation of the features of the face. It looks like Lenin sleeping." [A similar technique was used later to preserve the body of Stalin, which was displayed next to Lenin's until 1961 after Stalin was denounced by Khrushchev and his remains were removed from the tomb.]

FEB. 7 **TRIP TO KATYN:** Ten miles out of Smolensk, at a place called Goat Hill, overlooking the Dnieper, a light snow was falling on the slender leaning birches, the bare oaks, the tall evergreens and the huge mounds of frozen sand with the black boots sticking out. A party of visitors that included ten foreign correspondents and Kathleen Harriman, 25-year-old daughter of U.S. Ambassador W. Averell Harriman, stumbled over the rough ground, past pits the size of tennis courts, to where Dr. Victor Prozorovsky, senior medical expert of the Atrocities Commission, stood on a freshly turned heap of red sand. He was directing Red Army men as they hacked out frozen, mildewed Polish corpses, arranged them on wooden stretchers for autopsies.

The correspondents and Kathy Harriman saw thousands

of corpses; the authorities said that Katyn Forest contained some 12,000. Then the party went into one of four large grey-green army tents. It was warmer inside and the stench was overpowering. Dr. Prozorovsky ripped open a corpse numbered 808, sliced chunks from the brain like cold meat, knifed through the chest and pulled out an atrophied organ. "Heart," he said, holding it out to Kathy. Then he slit a leg muscle. "Look how well preserved the meat is," he said. Each skull revealed a small hole at the back, generally another through the forehead, showing that the Poles had been butchered by pistol, fired from behind. Eleven doctors were averaging 160 post-mortems daily.

The correspondents were told that medical evidence indicated that the bodies had been in the ground about two years; the Germans have claimed that the Russians killed these Polish prisoners of war in March 1940. The Russians say that the Germans found the Poles still locked in camps when they reached Smolensk in July 1941, slaughtered them all by the end of September. They say that German Construction Battalion #537, housed in a large *Dacha* half a mile away, carried out the executions.

Tall, blue-eyed, full-lipped Anna Alexeyeva told of having worked for the Germans in that *Dacha*. Trucks filled with Polish prisoners, she said, had rumbled by the *Dacha* in August and September 1941. Afterwards, from Katyn Forest, would come the regular sound of firing, "as if one were pounding with a hammer." Then the men would come in with blood on their tunics and get drunk.

In the afternoon the party went to the Smolensk Soviet Building to watch the Atrocities Commission in session. They heard the Commission conclude that: 1) the Germans had killed the Poles in August and September 1941; 2) later the Germans, knowing that they would have to leave, sought to cover up evidence of the crime by opening the graves, removing dated documents.

When the correspondents were permitted to put questions, one asked why, if the slaughter had been in August or September, many of the corpses wore fur-lined coats. The Russians said that fall nights were cold in Smolensk and the prisoners probably had no other outer garments. Russian censorship permitted the correspondents to cable this searching question and its none too convincing reply. [The question of the massacre was brought up at the Nuremberg war crimes trials after the war, but the Soviet representatives at the trials had nothing more to say about it. In 1952, a special committee of the U.S. House of Representatives conducted its own investigation of the massacre and concluded that the Russians had committed it "not later than the spring of 1940."]

JULY 17 **RHAPSODY IN RED:** The Soviet Government last week tightened up its already tightened divorce laws, otherwise encouraged the production of more babies, and sent the Moscow press into rhapsodies on the bourgeois subject of motherhood.

Cooed *Isvestia*: "In human speech, there is nothing more pure and exalted, nothing more tender and holy, than the word 'mother.'" Declared the Communist Party's *Pravda:* "Motherhood is the inexhaustible source of human rapture." *Pravda* then quoted the late Maxim Gorky:

"Without sunshine there are no flowers. Without love, there is no happiness. Without woman, there is no love. Without the mother, there is neither poet nor hero."

OCT. 9 **"GET THEE BEHIND ME, SATAN!":** The Soviet Government has been very reluctant to let its citizens travel outside Russia. But last week, with Red armies overrunning Rumania, Bulgaria and entering Hungary, more Russians than ever before were face to face with the blandishments of the other world.

In *Pravda* and *Red Fleet,* famed Soviet Author Leonid Sobolev tackled the *Get thee behind me, Satan* problem with humor. He warned Red Army men who had seldom seen luxury goods in Russian shop windows, that "a lot of outward tinsel will dazzle your eyes." He warned them "not to believe in the deceitful phantoms of a false civilization." Some of Sobolev's "deceitful phantoms": sleek automobiles, bright advertisements, well-to-do homes with shutters mysteriously drawn to hide "cheap luxuries," fat businessmen with gold watch chains.

Other foreign perils were short, knee-length skirts, stockingless legs, and "wonderful shoes with the full bare heels showing." Said one of Sobolev's characters, a Red Army man, drawing on his experience: "Probably not enough material to finish the shoes."

Spain

PICTURE STORY: An allied observer visited the State Depart- JULY 31
ment, graphically illustrated current political trends in Spain
with a story about pictures. The pictures were on General
Francisco Franco's handsome desk.

A year ago, when the observer visited Franco, there were
three of them—a large, autographed photograph of Pope
Pius XII, flanked by large, autographed photographs of Hitler and Mussolini. When he called again eight months later
the pictures were still there.

But when he went to see Franco less than a month ago, two
of Franco's heroes had disappeared. Gone were Hitler and
Mussolini. Only the Holy Father remained on Franco's table.

Sudan

CEILING ON WIVES: Bearded, greying Sir Sayed Abdel Rah- JULY 24
man el Mahdi Pasha grieved to see his subjects forego the joys
of marriage because the price of wives had soared. The most
diligent young Sudanese could not hope to save the $400 a
buxom maiden's parents asked; $100 brides were never of
much account.

Rich, benevolent Sir Sayed had a reputation as an apostle
of Allah to maintain. Although his fighting father had killed
General "Chinese" Gordon, King George V had forgiven
and knighted the son. Now Sir Sayed determined to break the
market, enable his followers to obey the Prophet's injunction:
marry and beget sons.

In the spacious, broiling, tented square behind his rambling
mansion at Omdurman, on the upper reaches of the Nile,
sharp-eyed parents, bright-eyed youths and soft-eyed maidens
gathered last week for bargain day. From tent to tent the
bridegrooms raced, making their selections. The price was a
flat $8 per wife, rich or poor, pretty or plain, young or not,
with Sir Sayed footing the difference. Then Sir Sayed, tall in
his flowing black *galabia,* appeared upon his pillared porch
to intone the Koran's marriage service. Upwards of 300 cou-
ples took the vows at Omdurman and blessed his name.

Turkey

Though it had signed a treaty with France and Great Britain in 1939 pledging to aid them in the event of war, Turkey remained neutral throughout most of World War II, convinced that Germany would win. The Turks finally declared war on Germany in February 1945—three months before the war's end in Europe.

FEB. 21 **TOO SOON:** In Ankara last week the Turkish General Staff suspended talks with a British military mission after a month of palaver. Premier Saracoglu immediately called in foreign correspondents and gave them a 50-minute exposition of Turkey's present position.

The effect of his talk: Turkey is still sympathetic to the Allied cause but is not yet ready to fight for it. The Turks seem to feel that jumping into the war now is like jumping into an uncharted river.

AUG. 14 **NAZIS PACK UP:** In Ankara, Turkey's diplomatic break with Germany closed one of the country's biggest businesses—the $1,000,000-a-month Nazi Near East espionage system.

At Izmir, departing German diplomats burned so many papers that they set fire to the consulate. As the Germans had locked themselves in for privacy, the firemen found themselves locked out.

The Turks arranged for five trains to carry out the departing Germans. At the end of three days they had only enough applicants to fill one sleeping car. The rest of the *Herrenvolk* preferred Turkish internment to the discomforts of home. When German Ambassador Franz von Papen went home, his servants immediately started looking for jobs.

And in Istanbul an old friend of the Nazis was missing. Thomas Ludwig (or Lewine), Gestapo agent and "honorary Aryan," had a trap door in front of his desk which, in his heyday, he used to snap open by means of a concealed button. Said he:

"In this work one must be prepared to spirit away undesirable elements without a trace." Last week Ludwig himself had vanished without a trace.

Yugoslavia

The Germans had overrun Yugoslavia in 1941, but they had not conquered it. The 17-year-old king, Peter, fled to London; groups of guerrillas fled to the hills and organized a resistance that tied down entire divisions of German troops. One resistance hero was General Draja Mihailovich, whose rightist group known as the Chetniks (from a Serbian word meaning "company") was supported by the British and bore the brunt of the early fighting. But by 1944 another leader was attracting greater attention—Marshal Josip Broz, a Communist better known by his underground name of "Tito." He led a group of some 100,000 Partisans, many of them women.

INCIDENT ON GREEN MOUNTAIN: When the war began, Olga JAN. 3 Dedier was a dark-haired girl with a medical degree and a passion for skiing. She worked in Belgrade's anti-Fascist youth movement, often made flapjacks for her journalist husband Vladimir, who learned to like them in America. In the war's first year she bore a daughter, Militsa.

In a hospital bed in Cairo last week Lieut. Colonel Vladimir Dedier of the Partisans gave some old friends among the correspondents later news of his wife. Major Olga Dedier of the Medical Corps had been hit in the left shoulder by a bomb fragment during an engagement on Bosnia's Green Mountain last June. Marshal Tito was wounded that day, too, and the Germans almost surrounded and annihilated four of his best divisions. Vladimir saw Olga fall and ran to pull her into a ditch, out of reach of the *Stukas.*

There were no other doctors and no medicaments. For nine days, while the Partisans slipped out of the trap, Olga staggered after them. Vladimir brought her berries to eat and occasionally raw horse meat. On the tenth day her ragged arm was amputated. When one of the few remaining shots of heart stimulant was brought to her, Dr. Olga said: "Save it for those who will live." Then she said: "Tell our little daughter she has something to learn from her mother."

Next day she died and Vladimir dug her a shallow grave with a pocketknife. Her service revolver he took as souvenir. Militsa is now a ward of Marshal Tito. [Vladimir Dedier later broke with his hero, Marshal Tito, and in 1955, after bitterly criticizing the Yugoslav government, he was expelled from the Communist party. He was not imprisoned, however, and became an author and a professor of history.]

JAN. 31 **HELP FOR TITO:** Marshal Tito's Yugoslav Partisans checked several German offensives and, at some points, again went over to the offensive. Last week they recaptured Jajce, Tito's capital in Western Bosnia.

The guerrillas have few trucks and armored cars, have to make up the lack with bravery and footwork. In the ice and cold of the Balkan winter they need, first of all, good shoes. That is why, near Lipovac in Western Bosnia, shoeless Partisans attacked a column of 400 lorries transporting German reinforcements, hit them fast and hard, then withdrew to the snowy mountains. Hundreds of Partisans at last had shoes, taken from Hitler's hated soldiers.

JULY 17 **FOR UNITY:** Yugoslavia's bright-eyed, bustling Premier Ivan Subasich at last put together a new Cabinet. It was a notable achievement—Yugoslavia's nearest approach yet to a national Government, a sharp defeat for General Draja Mihailovich and his intra-nationalist Serbs, a solid victory for Communist Marshal Tito and his Partisans.

Dr. Subasich had traveled 9,000 miles: from the U.S. to Britain to Yugoslavia and back to Britain. He had bridged the chasm between young King Peter and Marshal Tito. He had found a way to reconcile British and Russian interest. He came up with a Cabinet of veteran, moderate politicians representing Yugoslavia's Croat and Slovene groups and those Serbs who had fallen in with Tito.

Marshal Tito had played an astute hand in his parley with Premier Subasich last month on the Dalmatian island of Vis. The Partisan leader did not insist on Communist representation in the Government. No lover of the monarchy, he agreed to serve under Peter for the duration; after the war a national plebiscite would decide the King's future. In return, Marshal Tito won the support of Yugoslavia's Government.

OCT. 9 **AREA OF DECISION:** Russia's Red Army lunged last week across the Danube into Yugoslavia. British forces landed on the coasts of Albania, on the islands of Dalmatia, inched into Greece. From two sides of the Balkan *massif,* Europe's two greatest powers were approaching a junction in the Balkans. Waiting at this mountainous meeting place of empires was a man who had newly risen into political history after a cryptic lifetime in the political underground: Yugoslavia's Marshal Josip Broz Tito.

He had begun as plain Josip Broz. He had scarcely begun to learn his father's blacksmith trade when the shot which killed the Austrian Archduke Franz Ferdinand at Sarajevo, shot young Josip Broz into the Austrian Army. Then Josip Broz was captured by the Russians—or deserted to them. It was 1915. He was 19. The Russians packed him off to Siberia, where he joined the Red Army and fought through the hard, bitter years of Russia's civil wars.

Just a decade after he marched away from the smithy, Josip Broz returned to Croatia, but not to blacksmithing. His job was to organize a metal-trades union. As a Croat, a Communist and a trade-union organizer, Josip Broz soon found himself in jail. He stayed there five years. He was tortured. But to Communists, jail is a commonplace, torture an annealing experience. What busy Comrade Broz was doing between his release from jail circa 1930 and his sudden emergence in Yugoslavia in 1941 is mostly his secret.

Tito emerged from underground obscurity for a brief moment during Spain's Civil War when he was among a handpicked group of Communists behind Franco's lines. He was next heard of in France, working in the section of the underground whose function was to dispatch men from all over Europe and the U.S. to fight in Spain. He did not reappear again until the Nazis overran Yugoslavia.

For a long period Tito was unknown to the outside world. Then in 1943 British Brigadier Fitzroy Hew Royle Maclean, who had lived with the Partisans as head of an Allied military mission, put down what he had observed about Tito in a report that landed on the desk of Prime Minister Winston Churchill. That report, and Britain's need for any fighting ally, convinced Downing Street that its warm smile for King Peter's exiled Government, and its cold shoulder toward Tito, would have to be reversed.

Churchill acted. A shake-up occurred in the Yugoslav

Government in Exile. This year the blacksmith's boy of Klan-
jec became Marshal and Provisional President of Yugoslavia.

DEC. 4 **NEW POWER:** A plan for the formation of a new Balkan state
—federated Yugoslavia—was announced officially from Moscow last week. A new chapter in Balkan and European history
had begun.

Scarcely a month had passed since the Red Army entered
Belgrade. Sappers had removed 4,158 mines, 7,270 unexplod-
ed bombs, 76,298 live German shells, most of the hidden German soldiers. Partisan boys drilled in streets over which
stretched banners emblazoned with new Yugoslavia's red star,
Russia's hammer & sickle. Big pictures of Russia's Stalin,
Yugoslavia's Tito stared side by side from every shop window.

At the gate of the Royal Palace, fierce, shabby Partisans
mounted guard. But the palace was an empty symbol, young
King Peter, exiled in London, might never live there again.
Boys & girls of the Serbian Anti-Fascist Youth Congress
chanted: "We don't want Peter, we want Tito."

For three weeks the Partisan National Liberation Committee had been busy creating, on paper, the new Yugoslavia.
Twice Tito had flown to Moscow, conferred with Stalin and
the People's Commissar for Foreign Affairs, Viacheslav M.
Molotov. Last week a plan for the reorganization of Yugoslavia was evolved and British-supported Dr. Subasich took
it, not to London for the approval of Prime Minister
Winston Churchill, but to Moscow for Stalin's O.K. After
three days of Kremlin conferences, Stalin approved. Said the
official Soviet communiqué: "The Soviet Government wel-
comes Marshal Tito's and Prime Minister Subasich's efforts
to unite all truly democratic national forces and to create a
democratic, federative Yugoslavia."

PEOPLE

"Names make news." In 1944 the following names made the following news:

BETTY GRABLE was the year's biggest box-office draw, exhibitors reported to *Motion Picture Herald*. She was the first female winner since SHIRLEY TEMPLE (1935-38). Second biggest: BOB HOPE. Still among the top ten: Air Force Captain CLARK GABLE.

DWIGHT DAVID EISENHOWER wrote to an old friend of his 82-year-old mother in Abilene: "Next time you call on my Mother, tell her I am well and miss her all the time. I only wish that planes flew fast enough that I could spend one day with her and be back here the following day for work. I would go A.W.O.L. that long!"

FRANK ("The Voice") SINATRA, patent-leather-lunged idol, opened a three-week engagement at Manhattan's mammoth Paramount Theater, got the usual screaming reception from 30,000 bow-tied, bobby-soxed fans, who caused such a commotion that the Police Department responded with 421 policemen, 20 policewomen, 20 patrol cars, two trucks.

ORVILLE WRIGHT flew the giant new 57-passenger Lockheed Constellation at Dayton's Wright Field. The 72-year-old aeronaut was up for almost an hour, piloted the great plane for five minutes. His comment: "Wonderful!"

FRED ASTAIRE, having danced his way through a six-week U.S.O. tour of the European theater, arrived in Manhattan, reported that when doughboys asked, "How does it feel to hold RITA HAYWORTH (or GINGER ROGERS) in your arms?", he invariably replied: "Fine—they're swell dancers." Groaned the doughboys: "Aw, that's not what we meant."

MAJOR JAMES STEWART, tall, gangling cinemactor, received the Distinguished Flying Cross—for his leadership in a raid on aircraft factories, at Brunswick (20 U.S. planes lost). As an Eighth Air Force squadron commander, he was the pilot-leader of 20-odd B-24s on eleven missions over Germany.

HUMPHREY BOGART, Hollywood's No. 1 he-man (*To Have and Have Not, Casablanca*), announced that he had separated from his wife, ex-Cinemactress Mayo Methot. Bogart, who nicknamed his wife (also his yacht) "Sluggy" and bragged about their many private and public fights in six years of marriage (on their fifth anniversary, he gave Sluggy a rolling pin), kept mum about the reasons. Hollywood newshawks pointed out that Methot was for Dewey, Bogart for Roosevelt.

WILHELMINA, Queen of the Netherlands, escaped unhurt, lost two bodyguards, in a direct bomb hit on the house in which she was staying near London.

LIEUT. JOHN F. KENNEDY, second son of the ex-Ambassador to Britain, was given the Navy and Marine Corps Medal for "extreme heroic conduct" in rescuing two sailors when a Jap destroyer sliced his PT boat in two.

W. C. FIELDS, great, greying, polyp-nosed comedian, whose propensity for strong spirits is famed, lay abed in Los Angeles' Queen of Angels Hospital, his nose in a sling, roundly denying reports that he had fallen flat on his face. Fields: "I never reach my face when I fall flat because I can't get past my nose. I was leaning too heavy on a cane getting into bed. The cane slipped and I fell. It hurts quite a bit, y'know, and I have to resort to medicinal mixtures."

LIEUT. COLONEL HENRY CABOT LODGE JR., 42, who resigned his Senate seat last February to do some real fighting overseas, captured a four-man Nazi patrol singlehanded. The grandson of famed post-War I Isolationist Senator Henry Cabot Lodge let his Jeep driver tell the tale: "Colonel Lodge had spotted the Germans a long way off. When we got close to them, Colonel Lodge pulled out a pistol, leaped out of the Jeep, and the prisoners threw their hands in the air."

SPORT

CRAPS MANUAL: Don't cheat yourself at craps—use the cor- MARCH 6
rect odds. This is the advice of John Scarne, professional magician and gambling authority for *Yank* magazine, who worked out the mathematics of the armed forces' No. 1 sport. By last week he had sent copies of the odds (printed on cards small enough to paste into helmets) to more than 2,000,000 servicemen. Scarne's table:

Against Passing
6 to 5 (30¢ to 25¢) against 6 or 8
3 to 2 (15¢ to 10¢) against 5 or 9
2 to 1 (10¢ to 5¢) against 4 or 10
8 to 1 (40¢ to 5¢) against double 2 or 5
10 to 1 (50¢ to 5¢) against double 3 or 4

On the Come-Out (First Roll)
35 to 1 ($1.75 to 5¢) against double numbers
17 to 1 (85¢ to 5¢) against 11
11 to 1 (55¢ to 5¢) against 4 or 10
8 to 1 (40¢ to 5¢) against 5 or 9
8 to 1 (40¢ to 5¢) against crap (2, 3, 12)
5 to 1 (25¢ to 5¢) against 7

Scarne figures that craps is an almost perfect gambling game: the shooter has a 49.293% chance of winning. Other Scarne conclusions: 1) soldiers gamble $300 million a month; 2) most of their games are on the level.

CENTAUR: The most famous figure in the most dashing of MAY 1
sports died last week in an airplane—a Mustang fighter he had been flying over Salisbury, England. Most U.S. citizens never saw a game of polo, but people who got no closer to one than the rotogravure sections knew that Tommy Hitchcock played it. For nearly 20 years he was the greatest polo player in the U.S. and probably in the world. He turned a short-passing game into a fast, hard, long-walloping one. He

was a whirlwind at infighting, and probably the most powerful and accurate hitter of all time.

Three years ago 41-year-old Tommy Hitchcock won a commission in the Army Air Forces. "Polo is exciting," he once remarked, "but you can't compare it to flying in wartime. That's the best sport in the world." When he died he was a lieutenant colonel doing tactical research for the Ninth Air Force.

JULY 24 **IT'S A GRAND WEAK GAME:** Baseball's Midsummer Night's Dream—the annual All Star game—was more like a dull nightmare. Not a single home run was scored. The American League team failed to make even a single extra-base hit. When it all finally came to an end in Pittsburgh last week, the Nationals had won by 7-to-1, the most lopsided score in the twelve-year-old series.

But baseball, in the throes of its third wartime year, is doing much better than anyone had thought possible. Talent had never been so weak and unpredictable, but neither had it ever been so evenly distributed. This happy circumstance was no fault of management. To spur their teams into early leads, dugout bosses had grabbed up 4-F's, imported foreigners, recalled rusty old men, hired war workers on their days off, distributed daily doses of vitamins.

One team and one player had especially good sporting value to offer in baseball's Ersatz Epoch. The team: the St. Louis Cardinals, which were $10\frac{1}{2}$ games ahead of the runner-up Pittsburgh Pirates. The player: Mel Ott, the New York Giants' right-fielding manager, scored his 1,741st big league run on June 21, breaking the great Honus Wagner's alltime record, hung up in 1917. Ott also holds National League records in home runs (483), runs batted in (1,749), extra base hits (1,013). At a time when most veterans begin to relax, 35-year-old Ott was last week leading both leagues in home runs for the season (20).

AUG. 14 **McGILLICUDDY'S 50TH:** In spite of the heat (96°) and the transit strike, Philadelphians—29,166 of them—jammed into Shibe Park for a jamboree. The hot time was in honor of one Cornelius McGillicuddy, 81. Connie Mack had finished a half-century of big-league baseball management.

A jazz band let go, Abbott & Costello clowned. Master of Ceremonies Ted Husing stepped to the microphone near home plate to read a telegram from Franklin Delano Roosevelt: "My sincere and best wishes on your Golden Jubilee. May your score card continue to wave from the dugout."

As Connie Mack strode, thin and vigorous, toward home plate, the crowd rose to its feet. His hair was slicked down, he looked almost boyish in his dark brown Sunday suit and sport shoes. Then Connie Mack beckoned from the dugout, one by one, some of the most effulgent guests who ever gathered to do homage to a baseball veteran. They were the members of his personally picked, all-time, all-star team: George Sisler, "the greatest first baseman ever" (now a Brooklyn Dodgers scout); Eddie Collins, second base (Boston Red Sox general manager); Frank ("Home Run") Baker, third base (Maryland farmer); Honus Wagner, shortstop (Pittsburgh Pirates coach); Bill Dickey, catcher (U.S. Navy); Lefty Grove, pitcher (Maryland farmer); Tris Speaker, center field (Cleveland wine distributer); and George Herman ("Babe") Ruth, right field (who lives on annuities in Manhattan). Absent were Lieut. Commander Mickey Cochrane, catcher, who failed to get leave, and Ty Cobb, left field, who wired from his California retirement that he had a bad case of poison ivy.

When Connie Mack's dream team had lined up on either side of him, all dispute over his selections was drowned in one gasping verdict from the crowd: "Whatta ball club!"

EXPLOSION: Lieut. Colonel Earl Blaik is a patient, meticulous man; wartime West Point and its hard-studying, hard-drilling Cadets are right out of a football coach's dream. For six weeks Army Coach Blaik had carefully nursed his blessings, polishing his flashing T attack, proving his line, patiently preparing for a pay-off. Last week, souped-up to their mental and physical peak, the Cadets exploded against Notre Dame. NOV. 20

The Irish, anticipating the worst, had cooked up a complicated 5-3-2-1 defense, with guards in the end positions and tackles in the guard spots; Army found soft spots all along the Notre Dame line, particularly at left tackle. Notre Dame put up a desperate aerial barrage; Army intercepted eight passes (five led to touchdowns). Above all, Army blocked for keeps—on set plays, downfield, everywhere.

Glenn Davis and Felix ("Doc") Blanchard. Their Army team, shooting down an enemy air assault, gives Notre Dame its worst beating ever: 59-0.

A ferocious block by Fullback Felix ("Doc") Blanchard helped Quarterback Doug ("Hard Luck") Kenna sweep right end for the opening touchdown. It was Army's first touchdown against Notre Dame in five years, and it stimulated the killer instinct in the Cadets' cheering section. "Get more . . . get more," they chanted, and the West Pointers poured it on. Halfback Glenn Davis, with All-America stamped all over him, carried the ball eight times for 83 yards, scored three touchdowns. As the avalanche rolled on, the Cadet rooters changed their chant to: "Hit 'em again . . . hit 'em again . . . harder . . . harder." The final score, 59-to-0, was the worst beating Notre Dame ever took. [Both Blanchard and Davis were named to the All-America team in 1944, 1945 and 1946.]

DEC. 4 **THE BOSS:** Everybody knew that Judge Kenesaw Mountain Landis' contract as Baseball Commissioner might not be renewed. He had done much for baseball, earned the deep respect of both players and owners; but he was hardheaded and crusty, had stepped on a lot of toes during his quarter-century of rule. He was also old and sick. Club owners and sportswriters alike speculated about his successor. Then suddenly, a fortnight ago, the Judge took a turn for the worse. A joint committee of the National and American Leagues rushed to Chicago, solemnly recommended him for another seven years in office. It was a kindly gesture. Last week, baseball's 78-year-old czar died of a heart ailment.

Kenesaw Mountain Landis almost always wore a scowl, never pulled a punch. When he became the $42,500-a-year kingpin of organized baseball in 1920, the game reeked of the Black Sox scandal. He promptly decreed that the eight Chicago players involved, although acquitted by a civil court, be barred from the game for life. From that solid beginning, he ruled supreme.

As professional baseball's one-man judge, jury and police force, Judge Landis had the power to cancel a World Series, banish an owner or manager, void any deal at any time. Truculent, profane, razor-sharp, he had only to look down his nose to make everybody hop. Most times they didn't like it, but his kind of tyrannical power was good for the game, and baseballers knew it.

Although few knew it, Judge Landis had his own peculiar sense of humor. One favorite story: he and his wife, Winifred, were getting out of a cab to attend the Chicago opera; observing how slippery the sidewalk was, the Judge called to his wife, "Be careful, dear, or you'll break your goddam neck." But stubbornness was his best-known quality, and it never served him—or baseball—better than it did two years ago. When the service draft hit major-league rosters and some club owners wondered about giving up baseball for the duration, the Judge doggedly insisted that, unless some law prevented putting nine men on the field, the game would go on.

END OF A PERFECT YEAR: The build-up was terrific. Sport DEC. 11 pages groaned with the burden of adjectives striving to describe the forthcoming super-colossus. And when Army and Navy finally did get down to the business of beating each other's brains out, it certainly was a game of games.

Glenn Davis breaking loose, "Doc" Blanchard bulling through (and knocking down, punting, kicking off into the end zone, tackling for keeps, intercepting Navy passes), these were the stars of the year's best backfield. The score—Army 23, Navy 7—fairly measured the edge of the whole Army team. It was West Point's first unbeaten, untied season in 28 years.

THE THEATER

JAN. 17 **"OVER TWENTY-ONE"**—It was a dead cinch that in her maiden stage effort Ruth Gordon the playwright would be kind to Ruth Gordon the actress. It was less a cinch that she would also be kind to the audience. But though *Over Twenty-One* is a collection of comic swatches rather than something cut from whole cloth, it proves a lively evening. Much of *Over Twenty-One* is decidedly *vin Gordonaire,* but it is smoothly decanted.

MARCH 27 **"JACOBOWSKY AND THE COLONEL,"** adapted by S. N. Behrman from a play by Franz Werfel, uses one of the grimmest moments of the war—the fall of France—for half-satiric, half-fantastic comedy. Its comic thesis is that flight from the Nazis makes strange carfellows. A swaggering, snooty Polish colonel and a rueful, humorous, clever Jewish refugee both have to bolt from Paris on the run. The colonel cannot find a car; Jacobowsky finds one but cannot drive. Grandly tossing out Jacobowsky's luggage, the colonel condescends to take the wheel, and off they go—smack toward the Nazis in order to fetch the colonel's pretty mistress. From then on, while the colonel remains majestically helpless, Jacobowsky gets the party out of tight squeezes, ferrets out food, locates gasoline. As the colonel's lady becomes more & more admiring of Jacobowsky, the colonel becomes more & more jealous, issues a challenge, creates an *opéra-bouffe* atmosphere that makes the trip as much a flight from reality as from the Nazis.

THE SIXTEENTH CRITIC: Most non-conformist of Broadway critics is the *World-Telegram*'s wiry Burton Rascoe. He throws vitriol while his colleagues are pouring honey, ecstatically waves his arms while his colleagues are turning down their thumbs.

Featured in last week's *Jacobowsky and the Colonel* was Hollywood's pretty Annabella, wife of Cinemactor Tyrone

Power. The French cinemactress was making her Broadway debut. Critic Rascoe charged from the show to his typewriter, abruptly started off: "An incredibly talentless actress who calls herself Annabella made me so spiritually ill last night that you can stop, right now, if you want to. . . ."

Next day, with knightly gallantry, the Theatre Guild ran an ad in the *World-Telly* headed: "Here's to Annabella from 15 Drama Critics." For her performance, the 15 had showered on her such words as "charm," "sparkle," "warmth," "appealing," "delightful," "fresh as a breeze."

Fresh-as-a-breeze Annabella sent Rascoe a note saying: "Sorry I sickened you," and enclosing a bottle of castor oil.

PUHFICK EXPLANATION: Mae West, asked by a reporter from OCT. 2 *Yank* how she felt about the pasting the critics had given her show, *Catherine Was Great,* gave a forthright reply:

"I never read 'em. I'm a constructive kinda person. Don't believe in readin' destructive kinda trash. The way I figger is those critics came up against a play that was so fine, so sincere, so puhfick they knew there wasn't anything they could write in praise would add to it. So they went off and panned it. See what I mean?"

"BLOOMER GIRL" was a roaring hit before it ever opened. OCT. 16 Even after the superlatives have settled and the hats have dropped from the air, it remains a superior musical.

The plot is pleasantly interrupted by Composer Harold Arlen's music. The yarn is brightly punctuated, too, by Agnes de Mille's varied choreography—a sharp, expressive Civil War ballet, a waltz-drenched first-act finale, and some lively specialities in which *Oklahoma!*-born Joan McCracken is indeed pretty special. To her clean dancing style, she adds pert looks, funny gestures, a comic gift for bellowing a song:

> *T'morra, t'morra,**
> *Livin' for t'morra,*
> *Why is t'morra better than t'day?*
> *T'morra, t'morra,*
> *Lookin' for t'morra,*
> *My aunt became a spinster*
> *That way.*

OCT. 30 **"I REMEMBER MAMA"** is the second smash hit within a year for John van Druten, the author of *The Voice of the Turtle,* and Broadway's pleasantest family album since *Life with Father. Mama* is warm, humorous, sentimental, lightly nostalgic, more than slightly idealized.

NOV. 13 **"HARVEY"** by Mary Coyle Chase is the funniest and most likable fantasy that Broadway has seen in years. Described in one sentence, this yarn about a balmy tosspot who knows an imaginary outsized rabbit named Harvey may suggest all the horrors of relentless whimsy.

Distributed over three acts, Elwood P. Dowd and the hare of the dog that bit him become a delightful adventure in wackiness. Elwood, who on a stage could easily become incredible or dismaying, is played to perfection by veteran Vaudevillian Frank Fay, one of the great vaudevillians and conceivably the greatest master of ceremonies of his day. His manner is almost prim, his delivery slow, his material largely pointless. For one drawled gag like "Had a date with a newspaperwoman the other night—yes, she keeps a stand," there are a dozen droll nothings that are triumphs of timing and intonation.

MILESTONES

DIED: Albert Bacon Fall, 83, arrogant, ice-eyed Secretary of the Interior under President Harding, catalytic agent of the Teapot Dome and Elk Hill scandals (he secretly leased Government oil fields to private oil interests); after a long illness; in El Paso, Tex. First U.S. Cabinet member ever found guilty of a major crime, Fall spent nine months in prison for taking a $100,000 bribe from his friend and onetime associate, Oilmagnate Edward L. Doheny.

BORN: To Gypsy Rose Lee, 29, literate ecdysiast; and Alexander Kirkland, 40, Manhattan actor-producer; their first child, a son; two months after her Reno divorce, one day before his marriage to blond postdebutante Phyllis Adams, 21.

MISCELLANY

SEASCAPE: In Syracuse, N.Y., Rudolph Di Biasio, picked up for being A.W.O.L. by U.S. Navy shore patrolmen, was released after he proved his uniform was the regulation Sea Scout outfit of the Boy Scouts.

MOTHER IMAGE: In Denver, Mrs. Martha Martin got a black eye when a stranger walked up and hit her. Said the stranger apologetically: "I thought you were my mother-in-law."

DRESS DOWN: In Brooklyn, N.Y., Fort Hamilton's WACs received a list of clothing to be laid out on their beds for a rigid inspection, just before the zero hour got the list modified so that they would not be stark naked during the inspection.

$$\boxed{\textbf{MUSIC}}$$

30,00U FLUTISTS: JAN. 3

Flute playing is bad for the morals of the people.—Aristotle.
You ask me what is worse than a flute? Two flutes!
— Luigi Cherubini.

I'll have no flutes in my music.
—James (Schnozzola) Durante.

A living reproach to Aristotle, Cherubini and Schnozzola is the Flute Club of New York which last week held its regular monthly meeting in Manhattan's new City Center of Music and Drama. Some 100 flutists and their friends wandered about the auditorium, filling the air with a high-pitched and rarefied din. Near the door stood one of the club's nonflutist members, one Edwin Rosenblum of Brooklyn, who loathes the flute but cannot resist the morbid spectacle of an army of flutists pilliwinking away at once.

There are some 30,000 professional flutists in the U.S., and nobody knows how many amateurs. From the age of Cleopatra's father, Ptolemy Auletes, down to that of Communist Earl Browder (who used to flute away his time in Leavenworth Prison), many men have been unable to leave the instrument alone. The flute has claimed, among others, Frederick the Great, Henry VIII, George III, George Washington. U.S. Composer Stephen Foster could not play anything else. Charles G. Dawes and George Bernard Shaw are both amateurs.

ROSELAND'S BIRTHDAY: Roseland, on Manhattan's Broad- JAN. 31 way, is the most famous public dance hall in an insatiably dancing nation. Last week it finished celebrating its 25th birthday. Under the electric stars in the ceiling of this huge second-story ballroom, generations of clerks, shopgirls and other widely assorted humans have shuffled and spun to tunes from *Pretty Baby* to *People Will Say We're in Love*.

Roseland's founder, Louis Brecker, has livened up his

soirées with female prize fights, staged an exhibition of yo-yo by the world's champion, held a sneezing contest for hay-fever sufferers. His taste in popular dance music has been catholic and sometimes very discerning. He picked Fletcher Henderson's band, which for years made hot jazz history at Roseland, in 1924 introducing Trumpeter Louis Armstrong to Manhattan. He picked the Wolverines, who introduced Cornetist Bix Beiderbecke.

Today ultra-respectable Roseland keeps only 15 hostesses. They charge 11¢ a dance or $1.50 a half-hour (of which the girls get 7¢ or $1). They are forbidden to leave the ballroom with a patron (although outside dates have led, among other things, to the marriage of Al Jolson and Ruby Keeler). Roseland has 15 well-dressed housemen (ex-wrestlers) who mix with the crowd—often way over 3,000 a day—and stop raucous jitterbugging. The bar serves beer and a sweet, sparkling wine.

FEB. 7 **THAT SONG:**

Mairzy Doats and Dozy Doats and liddle lamzy divey*
A kiddley divey too, wouldn't you?

These iddly-oozy words were spreading fast last week from Tin Pan Alley to any place where a man could go nuts over silly syllables. Most citizens could keep their sanity at least long enough to discover that this apparent double talk was simply nursery talk—it was a paraphrase of an old verse ("Mares eat oats and does eat oats, and little lambs eat ivy. A kid'll eat ivy too, wouldn't you?").

Mairzy Doats was written two years ago by three affable-looking Broadway song writers named Milton Drake, Jerry Livingston and Al Hoffman. Drake got the idea from the infant prattle of his daughter, Niela. Last month Jack Robbins decided to take a chance on it. By last week, with a sale of 350,000 sheet-music copies, it was already the biggest Tin Pan Alley freak hit since *Yes, We Have No Bananas* and *The Music Goes 'Round and Around.*

MARCH 20 **BIG MILDRED:** The popular music field is all a-twitter with canaries—shapely, grinning young women who sing with the dance bands, usually in a somewhat phony Southern accent.

But just about the greatest popular songbird in the U.S. is a shapeless, 190-lb. soprano named Mildred Bailey, who was holding the connoisseurs spellbound when most of her competitors were in bobby socks. Last week big Mildred was still at it. Her massive figure encased in a spangled black gown, she stepped up to the microphone in Manhattan's Café Society Uptown. She looked her audience over with an air of indifference. But when she heaved into such old Bailey favorites as *Rockin' Chair* and *Squeeze Me* something highly authoritative happened.

Mildred Bailey's style, as exemplified in old recordings of such songs as *Downhearted Blues, Thanks for the Memory* and *Bewildered,* has kept record fans combing the secondhand shops for a decade. Grand-daughter of a full-blooded Canadian Coeur d'Alene Indian, Mildred grew up on a farm near Spokane, Wash., went to & from her one-room schoolhouse astride the family plow-horse. At 17 she got her first singing job, at $10 a week, plugging hit tunes at a music store in Seattle.

Because her real name, Mildred Rinker, lent itself too easily to pungent typographical errors ("Blinker, Stinker, etc."), she changed it to Bailey. Her brother Al was then singing with Bing Crosby in one of San Francisco's theaters. Paul Whiteman hired them, and they became the famous Whiteman Rhythm Boys. That was in 1927. Two years later Whiteman signed Mildred.

EXIT CHAMINADE: In Monte Carlo last week death came to MAY 1 the most famous woman composer who ever lived. Frail, white-haired, 86-year-old Cécile Louise Stéphanie Chaminade had been bedridden with a bone disease for more than a decade.

A fluttery little woman fond of long white gowns, Chaminade gave her recitals before banks of potted palms. She claimed that the soul of Beethoven once appeared outside her window in the form of a flame and burned briskly while she played the piano.

Deprived of her royalties by the German occupation (her Jewish publishers in Paris had been liquidated), she died in comparative obscurity. The era that her fragile, saccharine little piano pieces (most famed: *The Scarf Dance*) represented

Niela Bonni Drake. Her infant prattle led to "Mairzy Doats." Page 199.

Cécile Chaminade. Hers was an age of rubber plants and "The Scarf Dance."

had long since closed. Hers had been the age of rubber plants, stereoscopic views and parlor trances over Ethelbert Nevin's *The Rosary.*

MAY 22 BALLET: Troops at camps around Manhattan will shortly have a taste of the ballet. They may very likely enjoy it, for they will see nothing dainty or esthetical in *Fancy Free,* the surprise hit of Manhattan's booming ballet season. It is a lusty piece of knockabout vaudeville, as genuinely native as a buck-&-wing on a xylophone. Three bored sailors tank up and pursue three slick chicks. Some of the action is more like expert pantomine than dancing.

Fancy Free's success has its 25-year-old choreographer in a state of amaze. Sharp-faced pint-sized Jerome Robbins was in & out of little dance groups for six years without getting anywhere. He started plotting *Fancy Free* last June, got the New York Philharmonic's 25-year-old assistant conductor Leonard Bernstein to do the music. Now Hollywood and Broadway will not let Robbins alone. Says he, the son of a corset manufacturer: "Who am I? Just a guy from Weehawken, and all of a sudden—boom!"

SEPT. 25 SHARK SEASON: A clever gang of U.S. racketeers known to Tin Pan Alley as the "song sharks," mulct their victims—

amateur songwriters—for amounts up to $100 apiece. The song shark's most familiar bait is a small ad along these lines: "Send us your poems for expert criticism. You may have a song hit. Upon acceptance, we edit, publish, record your song and bring it to the attention of bands and broadcasting studios."

When the sucker has swallowed the bait by submitting his song, he gets an enthusiastic letter stating that his lyrics are indeed hit material, that with a good tune and publication they can scarcely fail to score. Expenses incidental to publication—tunewriting, arranging, etc.—will, of course, cost a small amount, which must be sent in advance. The sucker sends the money, and is gratified to receive 20 printed copies of his song. He next hears from an apparently different concern (the same shark using a different address), expressing great interest in his published song and suggesting that all it needs is a recording, by an unfamiliar but impressively named orchestra. This can be done for a small fee, and so on.

Several months ago the National Better Business Bureau sent to a large number of suspected sharks the worst sample of lyric writing its staff could concoct:

> *When we said goodbye by the silo*
> *After milking time at time of eve*
> *Sadly you did cry and patted poor fido*
> *As I did march away in khaki sleeve*
> *The cows mewed goodbye, the chores were all done*
> *As I turned and marched away to*
> *Washington, etc. etc.*

By return mail, the sharks beamed encouragement. Comments: "We receive very few lyrics that are as inspired and well-written as yours. It has distinct novelty and originality. It should make a beautiful and appealing song which people would love to sing, whistle and remember ($30 for music and professional copies)."

Song sharks are hard to catch. But they are easy to detect. What gives them away is asking for fees. No legitimate U.S. song publisher ever accepts money for publishing a song.

ARMY & NAVY

JAN. 3   **QUACK HERO:** One Marine hero of the Tarawa battle was Siwash, an artillery battalion's mascot. Siwash is a duck. Landing with his outfit, Siwash spent 36 hours under fire, in the first 15 minutes of his invasion beat the stuffing out of a Jap rooster, attacked and routed a shell-shocked Jap pig. Siwash showed no battle strain at all.

JAN. 10   **NIGHTMARE'S END:** For years the U.S. soldier's grey-green leggings have been a nuisance to him. They are hard to adjust, complicated to lace (especially the left one), have a trick of starting to go adrift at crucial moments. Last week the War Department gave harassed G.I.s better news than a 16-day furlough. The devilish leggings will soon be replaced by leather combat boots ten inches high. The lower part of the boot is laced; the top part, into which the trouser leg tucks, is buckled. Combat soldiers, long envious of the Germans' comfortable, homely field boot, thought it was about time.

A new combat boot replaces leggings that often go adrift.   *Siwash, the Marine mascot. Is it a he or a she? Page 209.*

HOBBY'S ARMY: In England this week, the U.S. Women's Army JAN. 17
Corps had the pleasantly apprehensive experience of being
inspected by the Corps' Commanding Officer. Trim Colonel
Oveta Culp Hobby, head woman of the WACs, found everything in order.

In the clammy English dawn, she saw WACs in maroon
bathrobes (with boy friends' unit insignia sewn on their
sleeves) dashing from tin barracks and scuttling across the
mud—heading for the "ablution hut" to start the day with a
shivery wash-up.

There was not much glamor in it, Hobby's army had found
out. Living quarters were either huts heated by a single stove,
or some drafty English country house. The pay was low. The
hours were long. Discipline was strict. Sometimes there were
bombings. During occasional air raids, some achieved the
WAC ambition: to bolt from barracks, crouch in a slit trench
and duck back to bed at the "all clear" without really
waking up.

Women had turned out to be more awed than men by the
military structure. Colonel Frank U. McCoskrie, who occasionally inspected a line-up, asking questions, once snapped
at a WAC recruit: "Who is the commandant?" Back came
the answer: "Colonel Frank U. McCoskrie." To the next
WAC he said: "What's in that barracks bag?" Gulped the
stiff-legged little private: "Colonel Frank U. McCoskrie."

Essential difference between G.I. Jane and G.I. Joe was
pointed out by a Fort Des Moines recruit who was being
loaded into an already jampacked Army truck. "Hey sergeant," she protested, "have a heart, this bus is full." Said
the tough male sergeant: "Lady, I been getting 18 men into
these trucks and I sure as hell can get 18 WACs in." Wailed
the squeezed WAC: "But men are broad in the shoulders."

HOW TO SURVIVE: The Army Air Forces and the Navy have JAN. 31
both issued books for flyers on how to survive on foot in
jungle, desert, sea and frozen North. Having absorbed 174
pages of advice on getting along in such places as the Solomons and the Arctic, servicemen read hardest an owlish chapter, tagged on to the Navy book, on how to get along in the
U.S. Excerpts:

"In some parts of the U.S. eggs in powdered form are

unobtainable and you will have no choice but to eat directly from the shell."

The Americans "are really a very friendly people. They mean well. Remember their civilization is much younger than that of Europe and Asia. They are just great big overgrown children at heart and should be treated as such."

FEB. 14 **MAN AT WORK:** In Sicily, Messerschmitts circled a nearby hill, but Technical Sergeant Richard Redding, stringing wire atop a telephone pole and a perfect target, worked on. Someone yelled up from below: "What are you doing up that pole?"

"Working," said Redding, too engrossed to glance down.

"How long you been there?"

"About 20 minutes."

"Don't the planes bother you?"

"Hell, no—but you do!"

At the foot of the pole, Lieut. General George S. Patton Jr., who had been doing the yelling, kept his peace.

SWEET VICTORIES: On the operations-tent bulletin board at a U.S. advanced fighter base in Italy good news was pinned up last week: an official commendation by Army Air Forces' Chief "Hap" Arnold. Reason for the commendation: the squadron had shot down eight German aircraft in one day, four in another. Score for three days' missions had totaled twelve kills, two probables, four damaged.

Any outfit would have been proud of the record. These victories stamped the final seal of combat excellence on 99th Fighter Squadron.

Wiry Major George Spencer Roberts, 25-year-old commander of the squadron, pulled at his pipe, told newsmen that so far as he and the boys were concerned, it was just a matter of getting an opportunity and jumping on it.

"We have not turned out to be super-duper pilots—but as good as the U.S. Army turns out," he said. "That's important. Because we had one handicap: people assumed we were not producing because we were Negroes."

FEB. 21 **THE NOSE KNOWS:** Diligently searching its field for war news, *Science Service* emerged last week with a new U.S. secret

New summer uniforms for the women's services: a Palm Beach suit for Marines (left), a khaki tropical outfit for WACs, seersucker for the WAVES and Spars.

weapon in the South Pacific: the human nose. Solemnly the *Service* quoted jungle-veteran Sergeant Delmar Golden:

"You can smell a battalion of Japs a good 500 yards away."

The enemy's special aromatic quality, in the sergeant's opinion, is accounted for by the prominence of fish heads in the Jap soldier's diet.

THERE HE GOES AGAIN: In England, Lieut. General George S. MAY 8 Patton Jr. put both feet in his mouth, where there was obviously room for his cavalry boots as well. In high spirits over his sudden emergence from obscurity and his announced role as commander of a U.S. invasion army, Patton gave a speech of welcome to a mixed U.S. and British audience at the opening of a new club for soldiers.

Said he: "The sooner our soldiers write home and say how lovely the English ladies are, the sooner American dames will get jealous and force the war to a successful conclusion. And then I'll have a chance to go and kill the Japanese."

General Patton went on: "The idea of these clubs could not be better because undoubtedly it is our destiny to rule the world." In Washington, Secretary Stimson quickly and emphatically pointed out that Patton spoke only for himself. In a hailstorm of editorials, the U.S. press asked the General, with varying degrees of asperity, to confine himself to such remarks as "Forward, men" and "Open fire."

MAY 15 **THE NAVY'S LADIES:** The proud U.S. Navy, which used to be exclusively masculine, made a startling boast last week. At its headquarters in Washington, the Navy said, almost half the uniformed personnel are now women. Officers and enlisted personnel of the WAVES have been arriving in blue-clad droves, sometimes at the rate of 1,000 a month, while blue-clad men have been shoving off for sea or overseas duty.

MAY 29 **THE OLD ORDER:** Said a headline on the society page of the New York *Herald Tribune* (with complete correctness but startling effect): "MARINE CORPORAL A BRIDE."

AUG. 14 **"DEAR MOM":** In a recent widely published advertisement appeared this "letter," an advertising copy writer's idea of a G.I.'s dream:

"Dearest Mom: So old Bess has pups again. She had her last litter two years ago—just about this time of year—when everything was so fresh and new. That's what I want to get back to, that world back home where a fellow can give the sort of welcome he ought to give to a litter of setter pups in the spring. Your loving son, Bill."

In Normandy the ad caught the eye of an insulted soldier writer for a service paper called *Le Tomahawk,* who raised a tomahawk and went to work.

"Since the public seems to think that soldiers are simple asses, drooling slush in the face of machine-gun fire," he wrote, "we offer the following copyrighted 'Dear Mom' letters direct from the front:

¶ "Dear Mom: Well, here we are in Normandy. I saw a cute little piggy-wiggy today, Mom, and gracious was he cute. That's what I'm fighting for, Mom—little piggy-wiggies and little ducky-wuckies and little lambie-wambies and, oh, just oodles of young, free things to brighten a brave new world. Your loving son, Joe."

¶ "Dear Mom: We are camped in an orchard Mom, and there are dairy cows grazing in our orchard and the peasants come right out in their wooden shoes and milk them and Mom, one of the cows made fertilizer right where I put down my blankets. Golly, Mom, it sure smelt good and reminded me of you and Dad and old Muley. That's what I'm fighting for, Mom, a world in which there won't be no soldiers putting down their blankets right where old Muley wants to make fertilizer. Your loving son, Junior."

NEW BOSS: To boss its most important new pioneering job in air combat today, the U.S. Army Air Forces last week picked one of its youngest, yeastiest generals. Burly Major General Curtis Emerson LeMay, 37, crack Flying Fortressman, was detached from the European Theater and ordered to China to take command of the A.A.F.'s new B-29s.

Major George Roberts. His fliers easily overcome a handicap. Page 205.

General Curtis LeMay is assigned to China to write the book on B-29s.

Curtis LeMay had seen plenty of combat over Germany, but it was not entirely for bravery that he was picked for the new job. Almost from the day he entered the Air Corps as a flying cadet in 1928, Airman LeMay had been a bug on precise maintenance of military aircraft, had been equally pernickety about how they were flown.

Because the B-29s have a lot of tricks, they also call for a whole set of new tactics. Many an airforceman was ready to bet this week that General LeMay would write that book, too, just as he had developed a dazzling set of new formations for Flying Fortresses. [General LeMay—who was famous for the cigar clenched in his teeth—later commanded the Strategic Air Command and served as Chief of Staff of the U.S. Air Force from 1961 to 1965.]

AUG. 28 **BETTER MOUSETRAPS:** In the Southwest Pacific, U.S. Seabees, who boast that they can repair anything from a watch to a battleship, turned to another activity in their spare time. A Navy officer reported they were making grass skirts and selling them to the natives. Reason for the market: the Seabees' skirt is better than the native product.

OCT. 9 **DUCK OR DRAKE?:** Duck Siwash, the Marine mascot which arrived home last week on leave after starring in beachhead landings at Tarawa, Saipan and Tinian, left the Marianas under a cloud, according to reports reaching the U.S. ahead of him. Reason: "He" had laid an egg.

NOV. 27 **COMPARISON:** Which is the tougher war—in Europe or in the Pacific? To this inevitable argument among veterans, two authorities made curtain-raising contributions.

The New York *Herald Tribune*'s Correspondent Homer Bigart, who covered the Italian campaign, described his reactions last week to fighting in the Philippines.

"I was impressed by the weakness of the Japanese artillery and the failure of the enemy to employ mines with anything like the diabolical thoroughness of Kesselring's army in Italy. Their fire has been woefully ineffective except against an easy, point-blank target. You can drive right up to the front without drawing a storm of artillery or getting blown skyhigh by mines."

But—"the newcomer gets a false sense of security. Hearing none of the usual din of battle, he comes jeeping along, admiring the scenery, when—*ping*—a sniper's bullet shatters his daydreams. Japanese bullets and knee mortars can kill just as surely as von Mackensen's railway guns at Anzio."

Jap fanaticism is also disturbing. Wrote Bigart: "The German rarely tries suicide tactics. When a mission becomes hopeless the German gives up. But the Japanese never does."

From the European theater another two-front observer gave his opinion. Major General J. Lawton ("Joe Lightning") Collins fought in Guadalcanal and New Georgia, now commands the VII Corps on the Western Front. In a recent interview in *Yank*:

"From the purely physical standpoint the Pacific campaigns have been infinitely worse for the private soldier. There he's had to live in the heat and filth of the jungle, worrying about malaria and the fact that a scratch may develop into a tropical ulcer. In the Pacific we're fighting the toughest kind of warfare—amphibious warfare.

"The Jap is a helluva sight tougher. But the Japs are dumb. The Germans are much more skillful tactically . . . much better equipped." [General Collins was U.S. Army Chief of Staff from 1949 to 1953.]

MILESTONES

KILLED IN ACTION: Marine Pfc. Stephen Peter Hopkins, 18, youngest of Assistant President Harry Lloyd Hopkins' three sons; in the Marshall Islands. Stephen, who had preferred active service to Officer Training School, was buried at sea.

DIED: Irvin S. (Shrewsbury) Cobb, 67, famed humorist; Paducah, Kentucky's favorite son; of dropsy, in Manhattan. After his death appeared a long valedictory Cobb had written a few months before. Excerpt:

"When convenience suits, I ask that the plain canister—nothing fancy there, please—containing my ashes shall be taken to Paducah, and that at the proper planting season a hole shall be dug and a dogwood tree planted there and the ashes strewn in the hole to fertilize the tree roots. Should the tree live, that will be monument enough for me."

MISCELLANY

PSHAW: In Texas, a WASP, flying a ferry route, got so hot that she stripped to the waist, hung the garments in the cockpit of her plane, lost them to the wind, radioed Waco for help, was met at the field by a ground crew with averted eyes and a WAC bearing a shirt.

DIRTY WORK: In Manhattan, Charles Wagner, who has been etching clothing on tattooed nudes since the war began (so would-be sailors could pass Navy regulations barring naked figures), was fined $10 for failure to sterilize his equipment.

GROUNDS: In Toronto, absolute judgments were granted in the divorce appeals of Loveless vs. Loveless.

BASIC: In Scenery Hill, Pa., Sandy Bottom, 17, newly enlisted in the U.S. Navy, received the blessing of his father, Rocky.

SOLUTION: In Los Angeles, Alvin Meyers used his last coupons for ten gallons of gas, drove nowhere with it because his four-year-old son filled up the rest of the tank with water and a bottle of vitamin pills.

LOST & FOUND: In Maplewood, N.J., Patrolman Herman Schmidt brawled with three motorists, had his ear bitten off, lost some teeth, his badge and gun. Later in the night police, searching with floodlights, found Schmidt's ear, rushed it to the hospital, where it was sewed back on.

$$\boxed{\text{ART}}$$

JAN. 24   **PETER'S MISS POTTER:** *"Now, my dears," said old Mrs. Rabbit one morning, "you may go into the fields or down the lane, but don't go into Mr. McGregor's garden: your Father had an accident there; he was put in a pie by Mrs. McGregor."*

When Peter Rabbit squeezed under the forbidden gate into Mr. McGregor's garden he also wriggled forever into the lives of millions. Last week news reached the U.S. that Peter Rabbit's creator was dead. The end had come three days before Christmas to 77-year-old Mrs. William Heelis ("Beatrix Potter"), wife of a British solicitor, artist and author of some of the simplest, shortest and fastest moving tales ever written.

The original Peter Rabbit was pulled out of a hat of kindness. In 1893 Beatrix Potter (her maiden name) concocted him in some letters to a sick child. The invalid was enchanted. In 1901 Peter made his book debut accompanied by his brother and sisters Flopsy, Mopsy and Cottontail. Pale, soft, charming—and accurate—watercolors graced the pages of this story. Beatrix Potter had long been an accomplished amateur artist.

FEB. 7   **EXPRESSIONISM'S FATHER:** An historic figure in modern art, little known in the U.S., died last week in Oslo, in his native Norway. Eighty-one-year-old Edvard Munch (pronounced Moohnk) was the founder of the Expressionist school of painting. He was also a legendary eccentric.

Munch was a highly neurotic, misogynous, inward-turning artist who led the revolt of the '90s against the formal, detached, analytical approach of the French Impressionists. Munch and his followers, trying for the highest degree of personal, emotional expression, deliberately set out to step up the passionate style of Vincent van Gogh. Munch's first one-man Berlin exhibition, in 1892, contained 55 screechingly colored, cacophonously designed canvases.

In Norway, when he was still young, Munch fell in love for

the first and last time. In a secluded village where he was painting, he learned that his beloved had shot herself and was dying. Rushing to her, he found the report exaggerated. "Hardly had I entered the room when she sprang out of bed and said: 'You love me, Edvard. I knew you would come.' We quarreled and finally she produced a revolver and threatened to shoot herself. I did not believe her, but of course I had to be chivalrous and put my hand over the revolver. And don't think the bitch failed to press the trigger!" Munch emerged minus part of his left index finger and his desire for marriage. In 1937 Germany banned Munch's paintings.

THE WHITEMARSH MYSTERY: Ever since Morgan Partner Edward T. Stotesbury died in 1938, Whitemarsh Hall, his 145-room country house, north of Philadelphia's swank suburban Chestnut Hill, had stood empty and unlived in. In the winter of 1942 it became a place of mystery. Passers-by reported strange doings. Around the vast, Versailles-inspired mansion a high steel fence went up. By day armed guards patrolled the herbaceous borders. By night great floodlights on the parapets sometimes flashed on to light up Whitemarsh Hall's massive two-story limestone facade and Ionic columns. MAY 1

Rumors flew: Whitemarsh Hall was a fancy concentration camp for Axis diplomatic prisoners; it was an Army asylum for the insane.

Last week the mystery was dispelled. Whitemarsh Hall had been the hideaway for the priceless art treasures of Manhattan's Metropolitan Museum. In the feverish days after Pearl Harbor, when plane watchers on Manhattan's skyscrapers scanned the skies for the *Luftwaffe* (and sometimes thought they saw it), Metropolitan Museum officials feverishly sought some shelter where their millions of dollars' worth of art would be safe from Nazi bombs.

Into Whitemarsh Hall went 90 loads of crated, padded masterpieces and *objets d'art*. In case of accidents, no van carried more than a million-dollar load. But the secret, heavily guarded trips proved uneventful.

Soon some 450 great paintings were racked on scaffolds set up in the huge, thermostated hall where Financier Stotesbury once gave concerts for 1,000 guests. Among the hidden paintings were ten Rembrandts, El Greco's *View of Toledo*, Titian's

Venus and the Lute Player, Vermeer's *Lady with the Lute,* Raphael's *Virgin and Child Enthroned,* a spate of Italian primitives, twelve Sargents, twelve Winslow Homers. The priceless Sèvres porcelains were never unpacked.

JULY 24 **NUDES FOR HERMANN:** Allied and Papal officials in Rome rubbed their hands and prepared to break out the rescued Italian art from 45 crates turned over by the Nazis to the Vatican. Last week they rubbed their eyes. Missing from the crates were 13 of the Naples Museum's masterpieces, a scattering of lesser art works. Among the missing: a Raphael *Madonna,* Fra Filippo Lippi's *Annunciation,* Titian's *Lavinia* and *Danaë,* Peter Breughel's *The Blind Leading the Blind*—the only Breughel in Italy. Total estimated value of the missing art from two to three million dollars.

The 45 crates had been hauled from Monte Cassino, their first hiding place, by trucks of the Hermann Goering Division. Best guess was that the haul had disappeared into flesh-loving Hermann's gallery of high-class nudes. [After the war, the missing paintings were recovered and returned to Naples.]

AUG. 28 **CHARTRES:** The most celebrated Gothic monument in Christendom had survived four years of German conquest and, last week, the even greater dangers of liberation. After six German snipers had been driven from its north tower, Chartres Cathedral was found to be almost untouched by war.

Allied inspectors reported a gargoyle missing, one statue broken, one arch destroyed. The battle with the snipers had left little mark on the taller Gothic north tower, because the U.S. troops were careful to attack only with small arms. The plainer Romanesque south tower likewise showed only a little bullet chipping. Priests who ushered a correspondent around pointed out the slight damage to the interior—a few windows broken in the south transept, a few supports shattered behind the high altar. The glorious blue glass of Chartres was nowhere to be seen. But, said a priest: "At the start of the war we removed all the colored glass and stored it in the cellar."

SEPT. 11 **PAINTERS IN PARIS:** First art reports out of Paris:
  ¶ Pablo Picasso, 62, was well and busy in his Rue Saint Au-

gustin studio. Now almost white-haired, he had a new six-
months-old son. He had refused to sell to Germans personally. Because Hitler considers Picasso's work degenerate, Germans who had bought Picassos from dealers dared not do
so openly.

¶ Henri Matisse, now 74, and suffering from cancer, was at
Grasse. His recent works were bold, bright studies of young
girls.

¶ Georges Braque and Georges Rouault were working in
Paris as usual.

¶ Raoul Dufy, violently anti-Nazi, retired during the occupation to the Alps, was working occasionally but was plagued
by arthritis.

¶ Painters André Derain, Maurice de Vlaminck, Othon
Friesz, and Sculptor Charles Despiau were in disgrace as collaborationists.

MILESTONES

MARRIED: Sergeant Skeezix Allison
Wallet, 23, foundling son of Walt
Wallet, Frank O. King's comic-strip
character beloved by millions; and
Nina Clock, 22, his boyhood sweet-
heart; both for the first time; in Gasoline Alley.

KILLED IN ACTION: First Lieut. Peter
Gerald Lehman, 27, eldest son of
United Nations Relief and Rehabili-
tation Administration Director [and
former Governor of New York] Herbert Henry Lehman, in the crash of
his fighter plane; somewhere in England.

MARRIED: Cinemactress Paulette
Goddard, 33, lately labeled "Madame Cheesecake"; and Army Air
Forces Captain Oliver Burgess Mere-
dith, 36, homely peacetime sprite of
stage and cinema; each for the third
time; in Beverly Hills, Calif.

MISSING IN ACTION: Count Antoine
de Saint Exupéry, 44, best-selling

French aviator-novelist (*Wind, Sand
and Stars, Flight to Arras*); on a reconnaissance flight over Europe.
Saint Exupéry, veteran of over 13,-
000 flying hours, flew some 15 flak-
riddled missions in a P-38 before his
disappearance.

MISCELLANY

WILL RETURN: In Albany, Calif.,
Clarence Ford and George Craw-
ford escaped from jail, left a note:
"Please hold any mail because we
know we'll get caught sooner or
later."

HIS MASTER'S VOICE: In Lafayette,
Ind., Police Sergeant Cecil Baker,
acting on a complaint that a strange
dog would not get out of a car,
phoned his owner, Alvin Fay. Said
Mr. Fay: "Put the dog on the
phone and I'll talk to him." The
Sergeant put the dog on the phone,
overheard Fay say: "What are you
doing up there, Pat? Get right on
home." Pat went right on home.

$$\overbrace{\qquad\qquad \textbf{SCIENCE} \qquad\qquad}$$

JUNE 12 **DDT:** Censorship was lifted last week from one of the great scientific discoveries of World War II. It is an insecticide called DDT. DDT stopped a typhus epidemic in Naples. It promises to wipe out the mosquito and malaria, to liquidate the household fly, cockroach and bedbug, to control some of the most damaging insects that prey on the world's crops. An officer of the U.S. Surgeon General's office exclaimed last week: "DDT will be to preventive medicine what Lister's discovery of antiseptics was to surgery."

The use of DDT as a delousing agent against typhus has been an open secret for several months. But last week for the first time its manufacturers and Army, Agriculture and WPB officials joined in announcing some of its other amazing properties:

¶ Sprayed on a wall, it kills any fly that touches the wall for as long as three months afterward.

¶ Clothing dusted with it is safe from lice for a month, even after eight launderings.

¶ A few ounces dropped in a swamp kills all mosquito larvae.

¶ It is deadly to such common household pests as moths, roaches, termites, dogs' fleas.

¶ As a crop protector, it is deadlier and longer lasting than other insecticides, has been found effective against potato beetles, Japanese beetles, aphids, fruit worms, even corn borers.

So great are DDT's potentialities that no fewer than seven U.S. laboratories and hundreds of biochemists are concentrated on it. Production has multiplied 350-fold in the last year; four manufacturers are now turning out about 350,000 pounds a month—all for the Army.

Last week the developers of DDT, Geigy Co., Inc., an old dye firm with branches in Switzerland and New York, told reporters how the chemical was discovered. A complicated chemical (full name: dichloro-diphenyl-trichloroethane), whose chief ingredients are chlorine, alcohol and sulfuric acid, DDT was first synthesized in 1874 by a German student named Othmar Zeidler. But he had no idea of its possibilities as an insecticide.

On the eve of World War II a Geigy chemist, Paul Muller, rediscovered the formula and found that it killed bugs. Its first test came during a plague of potato beetles in Switzerland in 1939. DDT stopped the beetles dead. By 1942, the U.S. Department of Agriculture had begun to experiment with DDT, got such sensational results that other agencies launched a full-scale investigation, soon uncovered DDT's immense military possibilities.

DDT owes its deadliness partly to an almost unique property: on insects it acts as both a contact and stomach poison. It first paralyzes an insect's hind legs, then gives it a violent attack of the jitters, finally brings on complete paralysis and death.

GENIUS AT HOME: As a lordly dweller in the remote, cool, JULY 24 abstract world of mathematics, Albert Einstein inspires in ordinary earthlings something of the awe which would greet a visitor from Mars. But a new biography by a member of his household (*Einstein—An Intimate Study of a Great Man*) suggests that another secret of his fame may be his vast and simple humanity.

This family's-eye view of genius was written by Son-in-Law Dimitri Marianoff, who lived with the Einstein family for eight years. Einstein remains a fabulously simple modest human being. He rarely wears socks except in winter, at home usually dresses in slippers, baggy pants and a brown leather jacket, which he refuses to change even to receive distinguished visitors. His Spartan study at Princeton, from which even his family is sternly barred, is furnished only with an unpainted table, a few unpainted shelves, a pencil and paper for his mathematical calculations. Though his salary from the Institute for Advanced Study is $20,000 a year (four times the sum he suggested when the Institute asked him to name his own figure, according to Marianoff), he has never owned a car, fights off his family's efforts to make him buy a new suit, stops only at cheap hotels when he travels.

Einstein, whose love of music and sailing is well known,

also likes to visit 5-&-10¢ stores, admiring their glittering gadgets. When a friend gave him a zipper bag, Einstein delightedly zipped and unzipped it again & again. At home, he is almost unvaryingly gentle, even-tempered, meekly obedient —and impersonal. He has never tried to explain relativity to his family. His scientific life is strictly solitary. When, as often happens even at mealtimes, he falls into long mathematical reveries, his family is careful not to disturb him. This cool detachment extends even to his closest personal relationships. When his wife died eight years ago, Einstein turned stoically from her bedside, said quietly: "Bury her."

AUG. 14 **MATHEMATICAL ROBOT:** What Harvard University unblushingly described as "the world's greatest mathematical calculating machine" was last week shown to newsmen. The machine is a bewildering, 50-foot panel of knobs, wires, counters, gears and switches. It has 500 miles of wire, 3,000,000 electrical connections and, according to the University, will make any mathematical calculation suggested on earth, as well as a number posed by the celestial universe.

This colossal gadget was invented by Harvard's Associate Professor (now Navy Commander) Howard H. Aiken, with the assistance of engineers of International Business Machines Corp., which built the machine and presented it to Harvard last week.

The calculator adds or subtracts in a third of a second, multiplies in six seconds. It has solved in 19 hours a problem that took four operators three weeks on ordinary office calculators.

Commander Aiken predicts that after the war his machine will solve problems in star movements which have never been tackled because the computation was too laborious. [One section of the machine, which has been referred to as the "first true computer," is now on display in the Smithsonian Institution in Washington. Other parts of the computer were still in use after a quarter of a century.]

AUG. 21 **POINTLESS PEN:** News of a sensationally successful new fountain pen called Stratopen, which uses a ball bearing instead of a pen point, came from Argentina last week. One of its advantages: it does not leak at high altitudes. In the past three months Argentines have bought up the entire output of 20,000, and last week the U.S. Army was reported dickering for the pen's manufacture in the U.S.

Invented by a Hungarian newsman named L. J. Biro, the Stratopen works on the same principle as a printing press. Its inked ball bearing, fed by a fine coiled tube in the barrel, rolls (instead of pours) ink onto the paper. It uses a gelatinous, instant-drying ink. One filling lasts six months. [This was a forerunner of the ball-point pen.]

RESEARCH: From Switzerland came news that Nazi scientists SEPT. 11 have not neglected chances for biological research provided by Nazi executioners. German Radiologist A. Krebs, of Frankfurt, reported after extensive analysis that a normal human body contains about a hundred-millionth of a gram of radium. His research material: ashes from a crematory.

MILESTONES

KILLED IN ACTION: Lieut. Wells Lewis, 27, sandy-haired son of Sinclair Lewis—by his first wife—himself a novelist (*They Still Say No*); in France.

DIED: Claud Bowes-Lyon, 89, 14th Earl of Strathmore and Kinghorne, father of England's Queen Elizabeth; in Forfarshire, Scotland. Worried by taxes, the spare benign Earl once feared he would have to sell his Glamis Castle (pronounced Glarms), "the oldest inhabited house in Britain," long supposed the spot where Macbeth murdered Duncan.

MISCELLANY

NATURALIST: Near Camp McCoy, Wis., a Brooklyn G.I. returned to his company carrying a full-grown set of rattlesnake rattles, explained that he "got 'em off a big woim."

THOSE IRISH: In Manhattan, the Smiling Irishman, a German-American used-car dealer, lost a legal battle over trade-name violation to the Laughing Irishman, an Italian-American used-car dealer, launched a fresh complaint against an Irish-American used-car dealer, the Happy Irishman.

ERSATZ: In Washington, Assistant to the Director of Civilian Requirements Austin Grimshaw admitted that substitute fabrics for babies' waterproof pants were not working out too well, allotted some rubber to their makers.

RARITY: In Fort Worth, the only item reported missing after a three-day Army showing of several million dollars' worth of equipment was a pair of rayon WAC panties.

DREAMER: At Sedalia Field, Mo., a private first class sewed master-sergeant's stripes on his pajamas, said: "I can dream, can't I?"

```
╭─────────────────────────────────────╮
│               RADIO                  │
╰─────────────────────────────────────╯
```

JAN. 24 **JIMMY, THAT WELL-DRESSED MAN:** It is just 21 years this week since James ("Schnozzle") Durante, one of history's great clowns, first drew attention to his fine, foaming gifts at the old Club Durant off Broadway. The past year has been one of his best [he was appearing on the Camel cigarette radio program].

Jimmy is a free-wheeling satirist. He constantly kids the formalities of human discourse ("Dat's da conditions dat prevail!"). A great deal of his highest comedy is deeply rooted in his own past.

Jimmy was born in 1893, on Manhattan's swarming Lower East Side. His mother was a Neapolitan, and gave Jimmy her nose. His father, Barthelmeo, was a French-Italian barber. As his father's helper, Jimmy lathered the faces of many a Tammany politician. He quit school around the seventh grade, worked as a glasswasher, photoengraver, took piano lessons. At 17 Jimmy got his first professional job as a pianist—in Diamond Tony's saloon at "Cooney Island."

"Ragtime Jimmy" worked in a motley of joints. Around 1916 he got together a five-piece Dixieland combination for the Club Alamo in Harlem. There Jimmy met Eddie Jackson, a gentle, sentimental, one-time singing waiter.

At the beginning of the postwar boom a waiter named Frank Nolan told Jimmy that with a place of his own he could make "a million." On his own hook, Nolan rented a 20-by-70 ft. loft above a used-car salesroom on 58th Street, just east of Broadway. There the Club Durant was opened on the cold night of Jan. 22, 1923. Jackson was present. Lou Clayton, a magnificent soft-shoe dancer, popped in later. Clayton and Jackson joined in the fun, and the great team was in the making. One of their first and most obvious triple plays was the establishment of Durante's nose as a stage prop. Clayton, who always stood to his left, and Jackson, who strutted on the right, would grab at the nose or whack at it with their hats, as if it were something untamed and menacing.

Many of their routines are now remembered by Broadway's elder denizens with a nostalgia like their memories of Barrymore's *Hamlet* or Lillian Russell's corsetry. There was, for example, the team's greeting to customers who were also their personal friends:

> *"Here comes a friend of mine,*
> *Sit him down at table nine.*
> *See dat he don't buy no wine,*
> *Because he is a friend of mine.*
> *Skeet, skat, skat, skeet, skat, skoo."*

The "old friend" was then invited to strike a spotlighted pose. During one of these, Paul Whiteman overreached himself and his pants fell down.

One of the few truly modest men in show business, Jimmy spends almost nothing on himself and gives away about as much money as Clayton will let him get his hands on. He is superstitious (no hats on the bed). The nearest he ever comes to telling a dirty joke is his standard wheeze about the card from his girl telling him that she has a room with running water ("You better get rid of dat Indian!").

BY ANY OTHER NAME: Tokyo Rose is the darling of U.S. APRIL 10 sailors, G.I.s and Marines all over the Pacific. She is a Jap propagandist, but her broadcasts are popular among American listeners: she gives them humor, nostalgia, news, entertainment and good U.S. dance music. In a very feminine and friendly voice she murmurs:

"Good evening again to the all-forgetting and forgotten men, the American fighting men of the South Pacific. The *Zero Hour* to the rescue once again, taking up a few vacant moments you may have to kill. So here's our beginning number tonight. It is the Waltz King, Wayne King."

Tokyo Rose's voice is wafted over the Aleutians and the South Pacific on a stronger, clearer signal than any provided by U.S. radio. She can usually be heard around 8 p.m. daily, Australian time, on a 65-minute show designed for U.S. armed forces in the South Pacific.

Tokyo Rose is sometimes uncomfortably close to the truth: "Well, you boys in Moresby, how did you like that ack-ack last night over Rabaul? Your communiqué didn't say anything about losing those two Fortresses, did it? But you fellows know, don't you? You know what did not come back." [U.S.-born Tokyo Rose—her real name was Mrs. Iva Ikuko Toguri D'Aquino—was convicted of treason in 1949 in a U.S. court. She was sentenced to ten years and a $10,000 fine, was released after six years in prison.]

AUG. 7 **DOCTOR I.Q.:** Millions of U.S. radio listeners know Doctor I.Q. as the man who every week gives away about 850 silver dollars and hundreds of Milky Way candy bars. As "the mental banker" of the *Doctor I.Q.* quiz program he works from a stage in large auditoriums. Five assistants with portable microphones scattered through the house pick out contestants for the Doctor's questions. When he is ready, he cries for so-&-so "in the left balcony!" The assistant there cries back: "I have a lady in the balcony, Doctor!" The Doctor then intones: "Fifteen silver dollars to that lady if she can tell me whether the period between early June and early September is known as salad days!"

If the contestant misses, Doctor I.Q.'s voice drops to a consoling "Oh, I'm so sorry, but I think you'll find salad days are those of youthful inexperience. *But a box of Milky Way* candy bars to that lady!" A correct answer stirs the Doctor to the joyful cry: "Pay that lady 15 silver dollars!" One night he innocently asked a man to tell him the principal use of cowhide, expecting "shoe leather" for an answer. Said the contestant: "To keep the cow from falling apart." The nameless hero took the audience's heart and a pocketful of silver dollars.

NOV. 20 **CULTIVATED GROANER:** During the past seven years Edgar Bergen has made himself a national figure largely by talking to himself. He has done this with the aid of an apparatus called Charlie McCarthy, which has become an even more popular national figure, and probably more human to a larger number of people than any inanimate object in world history. So irresistible is McCarthy's personality—saucy, lethally precocious and irreverent—that it is all but impossible for listeners to remember that he is a ventriloquist's dummy. The instinct to forget it is natural.

Charlie was whittled out 25 years ago by a Chicago barkeep named Mack (price: $35). He was modeled on a sketch Bergen made of a redheaded Chicago newsboy. Bergen was then 16, the gawky, moody second son of a Swedish immigrant named Berggren who had run a retail dairy business in Chicago and a farm near Decatur, Mich.

At eleven, Edgar Bergen had found that he could throw his voice (his mother was forever answering the door in response to pleas of mysterious old men who begged to be let in). Charlie McCarthy was just what Bergen needed. The little dummy was such a social success (unlike Bergen alone) that he lured Bergen from his university premedical studies into vaudeville.

The turn in their luck came in Chicago. Out of work and deeply discouraged, Charlie and Bergen got a week's tryout at a nightclub. At 3 o'clock one morning they came on for their final performance. The club was almost empty. In the middle of their act, Charlie suddenly reared up, turned to Bergen and said: "Who the hell ever told you you were a good ventriloquist?"

Bergen blushed, fidgeted, tried to put his hand over Charlie's mouth. "Don't shush me," Charlie continued. "I'll mow-w-w-w- you down. You better go back to the farm and leave me alone. You're all through, brother, all through."

Charlie then turned on the customers and told them they were a disgrace to civilization. Bergen put him on a chair and backed away. Charlie went right on giving the customers a piece of Bergen's innermost thoughts. The management was getting nervous, but the patrons howled with laughter and pounded the tables. Backstage later Bergen was saying: "I just had to get that off my chest." But he was a hit.

RELIGION

JAN. 31 **THE WORD, RECORDED:** From the first word of Genesis to the last word of Revelation, the 774,000-word Bible (King James version) can now be heard as well as read. Manhattan's American Foundation for the Blind, Inc. last week completed Talking Book records of the entire Bible. Total playing time: 84½ hours.

MARCH 20 **FUNDAMENTALISTS:** One morning last week FBI agents broke into a house in Salt Lake City, carted seven people off to jail for living as man and wife. Similar posses in other cities swiftly followed suit. By nightfall State and Federal police had dragged from bedroom & parlor, and jailed 50 men and women in Utah, Idaho, Arizona. It was the biggest raid on polygamists since the orthodox Mormon Church officially outlawed plural marriage in 1890.

The jailees were members of a small (2,500 or so members), dissident sect of the Church of Jesus Christ of Latter-Day Saints. They are known as the "Fundamentalists." Their leader, 71-year-old Joseph W. Musser, did not deny that he had five wives, 20 children. Other Fundamentalists were said to have as many as six wives, 33 children.

The big (816,774 members), solidly respectable Mormon Church has learned that polygamy dies hard. Despite Mormon President Wilford Woodruff's 1890 revelation that the world was not yet ripe for plural marriage, there have been periodic polygamous scandals. Many polygamists went underground, kept their plural families in hideaways sometimes known as "lambing grounds." The Fundamentalists hotly reject President Woodruff's revelation, consider themselves the true disciples of the many-wived Mormon Founding Fathers, Joseph Smith and Brigham Young.

Cried Polygamist Rhea Allred Kunz, mother of eight: "Plural marriage cannot be stamped out. Regardless of wars and pestilence, there has always been a surplus of worthy women." Cried Polygamist Rulon C. Allred, husband of six: "Polygamy is a hard thing to live and anyone who thinks it is fun just ought to try it."

GREETING: Reported New York *Times* Correspondent Anne OCT. 9 O'Hare McCormick from Rome last week: "A story is going the rounds of a lanky, soft-voiced Texan in a large group of soldiers received by the Pope in a recent audience. First in line, he didn't quite know what to do when the Holy Father offered his ring to be kissed. So he shook the Pontiff's outstretched hand and said politely, as nice boys do in Texas, 'Hi yah, Mister Pope.' "

YOUNGEST ARCHBISHOP: As Archbishop of Boston, Pope Pius last week named Boston's Bishop Richard J. Cushing, who thus became the youngest Archbishop in the U.S. For the 1,133,075 Roman Catholics of the nation's second largest See, the Holy Father's choice could not have been happier.

Son of Irish immigrants (his father was a Boston Elevated blacksmith), tall, rugged, liberal Archbishop Cushing has spent all of his 49 years in Boston. Unlike his predecessor, the late, famed William, Cardinal O'Connell, who was aloof and often absent from Boston, the new Archbishop has always kept his latchstring out, always stuck close to his job. That job, since 1929, has been the direction of Boston's Society for the Propagation of the Faith, and Cushing is a name known & loved in the farthest Catholic missions. [Archbishop Cushing was named Cardinal in 1958.]

"THE STORY OF MY LIFE": In an Oakland, Calif. hotel room last week Aimee Semple McPherson, the most spectacular U.S. evangelist since Billy Sunday, died gasping in the arms of her son Rolf—a bottle of sleeping pills on the bed table beside her. Though tired and ill, she had come up from Los Angeles to conduct a series of four revival meetings and dedicate a new church of her Foursquare Gospel (which now has 400 branches and 195 missions). On the evening of the day she died, she was to have preached on "The Story of My Life."

That story began in the village of Salford, Ontario in 1890 when Minnie Pearce Kennedy, a Salvation Army girl turned farmer's wife, prayed for a child to carry on her missionary work. On October 9 her prayer was granted. Six weeks later she took the baby girl to prayer meeting and formally dedicated her to the work of the Lord.

At four little Aimee could name all the Books of the Bible. When other children were playing with dolls and hoops, she was teaching her dog Jip to pray, and preaching to the animals in her father's barnyard. Her faith began to waver as she grew older, and she was almost lost in agnosticism when in 1908 she attended a prayer meeting conducted by a handsome young Pentecostalist preacher named Robert Semple. She married him a few months later. Together they traveled to India and to China, Robert preaching and Aimee playing the piano. In Hong Kong, Robert Semple died of fever. One month later his daughter Roberta was born.

Aimee and her child returned to the U.S., where she soon married again. But Harold McPherson, her new husband, had small taste for evangelism. Soon after the birth of their son Rolf he decided to go back to his grocery business, and the marriage ended in divorce.

With her two children Aimee then began a long pilgrimage through the U.S. to preach her own brand of fundamentalist salvation, which she called the Foursquare Gospel. In 1918 she loaded her mother and her children into a broken-down jalopy and headed for Los Angeles.

California was fertile land for the Foursquare Gospel. Aimee was soon renting the largest auditorium in Los Angeles and finding it too small. What she needed was a church of her own. In 1922, with $1,250,000 donated by her followers, she built the huge (5,300 seats) Angelus Temple, provided it with crystal doors, a silver band, a $25,000 radio station. Clad in white flowing robes, her hair burnished gold in the glare of the arc lights, a Bible under one arm and a bunch of red roses in the other, she exhorted the Angelenos to come and be saved. They came in droves.

Like most missionaries, Sister Aimee's path was strewn with thorns. But in Aimee's case the thorns made excellent newspaper copy.

In 1926, after returning from a trip to Palestine, she went for a swim in the surf at Ocean Park near Los Angeles. No one saw her come out. For over a month the nation's front pages were frenzied. The Angelus Temple's faithful paraded the beaches mourning loud & long. A girl committed suicide and a diver was drowned. Then, 36 days later, Aimee reappeared in Agua Prieta, Mexico, just across the border from Douglas, Ariz. She had, she said, been kidnapped, but how or by whom nobody could find out. There were suggestions that Sister Aimee was the veiled woman who had been seen at Carmel, Calif. with one Kenneth Ormiston, the radio operator at Angelus Temple. The case was brought to court but dismissed for lack of evidence.

From that time on Aimee spent much time in the courts and in the papers. There was a series of well-publicized battles between her and her mother over the management of the Temple, during one of which the ex-Salvation Army lass claimed that her reverend daughter had punched her in the nose. But through all her trials Aimee kept her head high. Said she, "I only remember the hours when the sun shines, sister."

FOUR CHAPLAINS: Four chaplains were aboard the U.S. DEC. 11 troop transport *Dorchester* when it was torpedoed off Greenland last year. Two were Protestants, George L. Fox and Clark V. Poling, son of the *Christian Herald*'s famed Editor Daniel Poling; one a Roman Catholic, John P. Washington; one a Jew, Alexander D. Goode. Together they passed out lifejackets, encouraged panicky soldiers to jump. When all other lifejackets were gone, the four chaplains gave away their own. Survivors last saw them standing together on the deck, arms linked, praying, as the ship went down.

Last week the Army awarded each of the four a posthumous Distinguished Service Cross. Said Major General William R. Arnold, Army Chief of Chaplains: "Their example has inspired and strengthened men everywhere. Men of all faiths can be proud that these men of different faiths died together."

$$\boxed{\textbf{MEDICINE}}$$

JAN. 3   **INFLUENZA:** In the U.S. last week, everybody who had not yet had influenza either had it or thought he was getting it.

JAN. 10   **ADMIRABLE M & B:** The most important patient in the world was getting well last week, somewhere in the Middle East. A sulfa drug had again saved Prime Minister Winston Churchill from pneumonia (first time: last February). Before leaving for a good rest at an "unknown destination" Mr. Churchill issued what the New York *Times* called "one of the most poignant and personal communiqués ever issued from No. 10 Downing Street." It was the best advertising sulfa drugs ever had:

"On the 11th of December I felt so tired out that I had to ask General Eisenhower for a few days' rest before proceeding. This was accorded me in the most generous manner.

"The next day came the fever, and the day after, when the photographs showed that there was a shadow on one of my lungs, I found that everything had been foreseen. This admirable M & B (sulfa-pyridine was originally called May & Baker 693, after the firm which made it), from which I did not suffer any inconvenience, was used at the earliest moment and after a week's fever the intruders were repulsed. I did not feel so ill in this attack as I did last February. The M & B did the work most effectively. There is no doubt that pneumonia is a very different illness from what it was before this marvellous drug was discovered. I hope all our battles will be equally well conducted."

FEB. 28   **JEEP DISEASE:** Riding in Jeeps, touring in tanks and taking the bumps of basic training have caused such an increase in pilonidal cyst disorders that some doctors call them Jeep disease. Cause: an infection of a congenital cyst at the base of a man's spine.

Chief symptom: it hurts to sit down.

MASS DRILLING: Every day 94,000 Army men sit in dentists' MARCH 13 chairs. Major General Robert Hilliard Mills, head of the Army's dental division, reported that since Pearl Harbor the Dental Corps has: made 1,080,000 new jawfuls of false teeth, fixed 220,000 dentures, made 56,000 bridges, filled 31,142,000 cavities, given 3,235,000 gum treatments.

20TH CENTURY SEER: Medical news last week vied with news MAY 15 of the days before invasion. WPB announced that the wonder drug penicillin, for three years practically a monopoly of the Army & Navy, was now being manufactured in such quantity that it can be issued to civilians. Some 1,000 hospitals will be allowed to buy generous monthly quotas for distribution to patients and other hospitals.

For impatient sufferers (many of them dying), the good news came none too soon. Penicillin is the best treatment for all staphylococcic infections, all hemolytic streptococcic infections, clostridia infections, pneumococcic infections (of the lining of skull, spinal cord, lung and heart surfaces), pneumococcic pneumonia that sulfa drugs will not cure, all gonococcic infections (including all gonorrhea that sulfa drugs will not cure). Diseases against which penicillin is effective but not fully tested: syphilis, actinomycosis, bacterial endocarditis.

The man who made possible this incalculable alleviation of human suffering is Dr. Alexander Fleming, discoverer of the antibacterial effect of the mold from which penicillin is made. He is a short (5 ft. 7 in.), gentle, retiring Scot with somewhat dreamy blue eyes, fierce white hair and a mulling mind, which, when it moves, moves with the thrust of a cobra. Dr. Fleming is one of the great men of the 20th Century.

The story of his discovery is legendary. In 1928 Alexander Fleming taught bacteriology at St. Mary's Hospital Medical School, University of London. In his old-fashioned laboratory, he grew staphylococci in flat glass culture dishes. One day he found that mold had spoiled one of his cultures. Staphylococcus grew on only half of the plate. A blue-green mold spotted, but did not cover, the other half. He noticed that the mold had cleared a wide, bacteria-free area between itself and the staphylococci—perhaps had killed them.

Having made his great discovery, Dr. Fleming went on to other work. In the history of penicillin there ensued an eleven year hiatus. Then, in 1938 Dr. Howard Walter Florey, 45, an Australian-born professor of pathology, organized a research team at Oxford to study the practical extraction of capricious penicillin. Under Dr. Florey's dynamic supervision, the blue-green penicillium mold began to grow again. After heroic chemical cookery, the researchers accumulated enough penicillin to test the drug on living creatures. Eight mice were inoculated with a deadly strain of streptococci. Says Dr. Florey:

"We sat up through the night injecting penicillin every three hours into the treated group (four mice). I must confess that it was one of the more exciting moments when we found in the morning that all the untreated mice were dead and all the penicillin-treated ones alive."

During that historic night, Dr. Fleming's vision turned into a medical reality.

To Dr. Fleming's pioneer mind, penicillin is not an end, but a beginning. "It would be strange, indeed," says Dr. Fleming, who is hard at work on other antibiotics, "if the first one described remained the best." [Drs. Fleming and Florey were awarded the Nobel Prize for medicine and physiology in 1945.]

Battle casualties do exercises to build up their strength. Hospitals give the wounded "the first pampering they have had in the Army." Page 230.

AUTHORITY: As the proper climax for a hang-over cure, NOV. 20
the *British Medical Journal* last week threw its venerable
weight behind a small dose of the "hair of the dog."

The preliminaries: 1) a bottle of Vichy before retiring;
2) a teaspoonful of sodium bicarbonate upon rising; 3) a cold
bath; 4) breakfast, "no matter how revolting it may appear."

POLIO: Eleven weeks after the epidemic's peak, a belated re- DEC. 4
port—451 new cases of infantile paralysis for the week ending
Nov. 18—made it official that 1944 is the second worst polio
year in U.S. history. The 18,490 cases thus far reported exceed
1931's full-year total, but are mercifully short of 1916's 27,621.

THE WOUNDED: Thousands and thousands of the Army's DEC. 25
seriously wounded and sick are flowing back to the U.S. each
month. The Army's 60 general hospitals are filling up. What
can be done for them now—for the men with mutilated faces
and legs and minds?

A new arrival is usually tired, fed up with the war and the
Army. He thinks that no one, least of all a civilian, can understand what he has endured. He dreads civilian life.

In a ward with 29 other similarly wounded men, the newcomer is first allowed to do as he pleases: sleep, stare at the
ceiling, or think. As soon as he comes out of the medical and
surgical woods, pressure is gradually put on him to rouse his
interest in the Surgeon General's Reconditioning Program.
This program schedules every hour that a man is not eating,
sleeping or undergoing treatment. It aims to build up his
strength and keep him cheerful through physical and mental
exercises. Though few have much interest to start with, all
eventually take part with good grace. Asked to explain why,
one officer said: "They love it. The hospital gives a fellow
the first pampering he's had since he was in the Army."

MARCH 20 **THE PINCH:** Any U.S. citizen who is now down at heel can count up on his toes his chances of going barefoot. For the OPA's intent to keep shoe rationing "at about the current level" meant the civilian would get not more than two pairs of leather shoes a year. (In 1941 he used 3.7 pairs, and almost that much last year.)

Last week G-Man J. Edgar Hoover himself added a lurid footnote to the shoe shortage: shoes, he said, were the third biggest item in a mounting flood of hijacking. (The first two: liquor and rayon.)

APRIL 3 **ANNIVERSARY:** After one year's rationing of meat and processed foods, grocers last week took stock. Their findings:

¶ When the U.S. housewife sees "Fancy," "Choice," and "Standard" canned peas, she leaves the "Standard" on the shelf. With plenty of money and not many points, she buys the best.

¶ Macaroni moves slowly because tomato sauce and cheese are difficult to get; pancake-mix stays on the shelf when the butter supply is tight. Jello is in demand as a substitute for canned fruits. Unrationed relishes and pickles outsell rationed catsup. Since working women have less time and inclination to bake, sales of baking powder have slumped.

¶ Gas rationing and heedlessness of high prices have cut down the sales by chains and supermarkets, and have boosted the neighborhood grocer's business.

JUNE 19 **BY A DAMSITE:** High on Shasta Dam's vast concrete face last week a big steel gate opened. A mighty wall of water rushed down, exploded against the huge waiting turbine in the powerhouse below the dam.

To Bureau of Reclamation men and their boss, Interior Secretary Harold L. Ickes, that coming to life of the huge electric generator was the climax of the six-year job of building Shasta. But to strapping (205 lb., 6 ft. 3 in.), profane Francis Trenholm Crowe, general superintendent of construction for Pacific Constructors, Inc., the big moment had come four months before, when the Sacramento River began a regulated flow through outlet valves on the dam's broad, sloping downstream face. "That meant we had the river licked," said Crowe. "Pinned down, shoulders right on the mat. Hell, that's what we came up here for."

Builder Frank Crowe's 19th dam is the world's second biggest concrete structure (biggest: Grand Coulee Dam). Shasta is the highest overflow-type dam in the world (602 ft.). It is also California's tallest structure. When Shasta's reservoir fills (probably in 1946), water pouring over the center spillway will fall three times as far as Niagara. For California, Shasta Dam will:

¶ Prevent the wild "flash" floods which, through rain and melting snows from lofty Mount Shasta, have annually devastated the Central Valley.

¶ Regularly irrigate the vast, fertile, but often drought-parched San Joaquin Valley.

¶ Supply 1,500,000,000 kilowatt hours annually to northern California's power-hungry industry.

All this is Frank Crowe's work. Engineer Crowe, who finished Boulder Dam 26 months ahead of schedule, has changed the physical landscape perhaps more than any other individual in history. Lean, tough and bull-voiced, Engineer Crowe drives his men so hard that many quit. He hates carelessness. As a result Shasta has killed only twelve men. Once he bellowed at a worker: "Watch what the hell you're doing or you'll fall and break your neck." Retorted the worker: "Well, it's my neck." "Yes, it's your neck now," Crowe shot back, "but as soon as you break it, it's mine."

But when Shasta is dedicated, Frank Crowe's speech will probably be the same two sentences he spoke at Boulder Dam: "If you gentlemen want to see the fellow who really built this dam, go over to the mess hall. He wears a tin hat, his average age is thirty-one and he can do things."

EARLY BIRDS: A secret leaked last week from the Sikorsky Aircraft division of United Aircraft Corp. at Bridgeport, Conn. The secret: the company is now operating the first JUNE 26

OLDE SPUD

This is part of a shipment of potato whiskey put on sale in Manhattan. Thirsty crowds snapped it up at $3.32 a fifth. It was a blend of four-year-old rye and bourbon (20%), plus 80% neutral spirits distilled from waste potatoes and skins. The whiskey tasted like any popularly priced blend. The supply sold out quickly, but potato alcohol production was too small to relieve the great U.S. whiskey drought.

helicopter production line in the U.S., and probably in the world. In the last eight months, Sikorsky has produced 30 helicopters for the Army Air Force. The ships have been tested in Burma, evacuating wounded from the jungles; in patrol work along the Atlantic coast; in Alaska.

JULY 3 **THE DROUGHT BREAKS:** The great American whiskey drought was broken last week. WPB, which has long clouded up with plans to let U.S. distillers resume whiskey-making, finally promised a drizzle. During the month of August, distillers will be permitted to make whiskey or neutral spirits for blending—for the first time since the October 1942 ban.

JULY 17 **ROCK BOTTOM:** The U.S. is almost out of new automobiles. Since Feb. 1, 1942, when all production stopped, OPA has carefully doled out 500,000 precious new cars. Now there are only 30,000 left, a supply which in prewar years would have lasted only three days. To stretch them over the continuing production ban, OPA has thinned down the July quota to 7,000 cars, a drop of 22% from the June allotment.

1,300 MEN WITH A MISSION:

> *When the Great Chief of the White House*
> *Called the tribes of men together*
> *For a conference on wampum*
> *In the forest of New Hampshire,*
> *Came the prophets of the nations,*
> *Foremost in their craft and wisdom. . . .*
> *Keynes urged, "Be not slave to wampum,*
> *Throw away the truss of wampum,*
> *Start a fund for prudent lending,*
> *That all tribes of men may borrow,*
> *Each get credit from the other,*
> *Using anything for wampum,*
> *Sterling, beads or even fishbones."*
> *Morgenthau, the Chief of Wall Street,*
> *Tighter strapped the belt of wampum,*
> *"My world bank for reconstruction*
> *Must be on a wampum basis."*
> *So they reasoned as they wrestled,*
> *While they both exclaimed together—*
> *"Let us order world finances,*
> *Let us keep away inflation,*
> *Let us stabilize exchanges*
> *For the profit of the people. . . ."*

[So, in a parody of Longfellow's *Hiawatha,* wrote "Sagittarius" of London's *New Statesman & Nation* about the International Monetary Conference that opened in July at Bretton Woods, N.H., and led to the formation of the World Bank.]

THE HOT JOBS: The U.S. was in the grip of a war production JULY 31 slump last week that had the War Department thoroughly alarmed. Once again the brass hats considered asking Congress for a National Service Act to compel men to work in vital industries.

Lieut. General Brehon Somervell, chief of the Army Service Forces, said he was getting urgent requests from Generals

Eisenhower, Clark and MacArthur for more & more weapons and equipment. He said he could not begin to fill some of the orders. Some shortages:

¶ There was not a single bomber tire in the Army's inventory.

¶ There was a need for 300% more heavy shells than anticipated—due to the increasing use of massed firepower.

¶ General MacArthur needed tents badly, because the Pacific advance was so fast that wooden barracks were left behind.

¶ General Eisenhower needed big quantities of hospital tents, because the German scorched-earth policy was effectively wiping out billeting facilities.

With no law to back it up, the War Department can only make it plain that workers' failure to sweat it out in the toughest, most thankless war-production jobs may ultimately be measured in lost American lives.

17.9 BILLION OF HOPE: "I am greatly encouraged by the critical, skeptical and even carping spirit in which our proceedings have been watched in the outside world. How much better that our projects should begin in disillusion than that they should end in it."

With these words John Maynard Keynes last week moved the adoption of the completed plans for an $8,800,000,000 world stabilization fund and a world reconstruction bank whose capital will total $9,100,000,000. But the striking fact was that the delegates at the United Nations Monetary Conference at Bretton Woods felt very little skepticism about the value of their work. At no point did the conference break down into a fight between selfish interests. Throughout, the attitude of the delegates was: "If we can't agree on a thing like this, what hope is there for the postwar world?"

SHOCK ABSORBERS: Two institutions such as the world has never known before were completed—in plan—last week at Bretton Woods: an "International Monetary Fund" and an "International Bank for Reconstruction and Development."

The Fund is simply an $8.8 billion pot into which each member nation shoves a stack of its own chips. The purpose of the pot is to enable any player, who temporarily needs the chips of another, to shove in more of his own in order to borrow an equivalent value in the chips of the other. This is the whole function of the Fund—a reserve of foreign exchange from which to borrow when normal sources of exchange run short.

The Bank is merely a second pot in which the whole world puts chips to guarantee the lenders against loss. It also has power to take part of a loan too big for private markets, and to make direct loans on a relatively small scale if they cannot be floated privately.

The Bank will lend only for specific projects which promise to increase the productivity of the borrower and his ability to pay off the loan. The loans will be paid out only as work is completed (like progress payments on a mortgage), so the Bank can be assured the loans are not being misused.

THE FIRST 2,000,000: Russia tried to buy 2,000,000 artificial legs OCT. 9 on the American market last week. The small U.S. factories, already far behind on domestic orders, could not help out— none of them produces more than 5,000 artificial limbs a year. The Soviets, who must step up their own small output, are already studying American methods. For 2,000,000 false legs was only a starting estimate; after three and a half years of fighting, the number of war cripples in Russia is unknown.

THE MAN'S GLOSSARY: The smooth, smart advertising copy- DEC. 11 writers at Manhattan's R. H. Macy & Co. last week had their little annual joke on themselves and all other writers of smooth, smart department-store Christmas advertising. Macy's bought a six-column ad in the New York *Times* and printed "The Man's Glossary (revised 1944 edition) of Unfamiliar Words & Phrases—As Used by Advertising Writers to Describe Female Apparel and Appurtenances." Samples:

gossamer: the nearest thing to nothing—and better in black.

mink: when a woman turns around to look at another woman—that's mink!

sable: when a woman in mink turns around to look at another woman.

chichi: the bow on the bird cage.

lush: anything softer than stone.

glamorous: anything plus a sequin.

fabulous: we haven't seen anything like it for an hour.

CINEMA

JAN. 3 **"HIGHER AND HIGHER"**—One of the most remarkable events since the Flood took place on New Year's Eve in some 50 U.S. cinegogues. On a screen wispy with angelic clouds, a clinching pair of lovers receded to a vanishing point and were replaced by a speck which grew & grew into the huge image of a gaunt, sad-eyed, solitary young man. His posture suggested St. Francis preaching to the birds, and the hysterical twittering of the audience sustained the illusion. The young man was, in fact, in his own peculiar way, delivering a benediction. He was singing, rather hoarsely and with incredible effectiveness, a little popular tune.

This scene is the climax of Frank Sinatra's screen debut. The curious magic of Frank Sinatra's voice was described once & for all by Ludwig Bemelmans when he wrote of another popular voice (Richard Tauber's) that it made you feel the way you do when a waiter reaches under your overcoat to settle your clothing. Sinatra's voice has become a national feature comparable to Yosemite Valley.

FEB. 7 **"THE SONG OF BERNADETTE"** lacks the razor-edged realism, the urgent poetry, the freshet-like creative vitality of great cinema or great religious vision. But within its limits, most of *The Song of Bernadette* is reverent, spiritually forthright, dignified.

As Bernadette, Newcomer Jennifer Jones makes one of the most impressive screen debuts in many years. If she can do other roles as well, Hollywood should watch and guard Miss Jones as sedulously as the Church watched over Bernadette.

APRIL 10 **"COVER GIRL"** begins by undressing eight superb Technicolored chorines within an inch of the law, sets them to dancing as if they were trying to kick your chin and singing as if they were enjoying themselves too much to talk. The scene is a small Brooklyn nightclub full of whistling sailors. The 97-

"Cover Girl" begins by undressing these superb chorines within an inch of the law, sets them to dancing as if they are trying to kick your chin. Page 237.

minute picture that unfolds from this frolicsome beginning is the best cinemusical the year has produced, and one of the best in years. Rita Hayworth's and Gene Kelly's amatory ups-&-downs have a warmth and poignancy which is unprecedented in a cinemusical. When they cue into a song—especially the sentimental bull's-eye *Long Ago*—they do not step out of character for the number. Their dance duets are the best since Astaire and Rogers split.

"GOING MY WAY" is one of the year's top surprises. It presents Bing Crosby as a Catholic priest, and gets away with it so gracefully that Crosby, the priesthood and the audience are equal gainers. It offers, in the performance of nutcracker-faced, 56-year-old Barry Fitzgerald, the finest, funniest and most touching portrayal of old age that has yet reached the screen.

Going My Way is a sort of friendly contest between two diametrically different kinds of acting: Fitzgerald's, the immensely experienced, stage-wise sort which leaves mere virtuosity miles behind, and Crosby's, which is hardly acting at all, but merely the unaffected exploitation of an amiable personality. The picture shows that neither kind, at its best, can possibly be beat, and that together, they bring just about the last word in teamwork.

MAY 1

JULY 10 **"DOUBLE INDEMNITY"** is the season's nattiest, nastiest, most satisfying melodrama. James M. Cain's novelette was carnal and criminal well beyond screen convention. Director Billy Wilder's casting is just as unconventional. Naturals for their parts are Fred MacMurray as an insurance salesman capable of murder; Barbara Stanwyck as the unprintable blonde (for the occasion) who exploits his capabilities; Edward G. Robinson as the insurance-claims sleuth who sniffs out the flaws in their all-but-perfect crime.

DEC. 11 **"TOGETHER AGAIN"** is a title which presumably refers to the fact that Irene Dunne and Charles Boyer once made a successful romance called *Love Affair* (1939), and are now at it once more. It can hardly refer to the present picture.

DEC. 25 **"NATIONAL VELVET"** combines some of the most attractive elements of *The Song of Bernadette* and of *Lassie Come Home.* It is almost a children's classic.

Twelve-year-old Elizabeth Taylor, a beautiful little girl who has hitherto had minor roles, is probably the only person in Hollywood who could bring to this curious role its unusual combination of earthiness and ecstasy. Mickey Rooney proves once for all that he can be a sincere, capable actor when the role calls for it.

MILESTONES

DIED: Mrs. Julia Columbo, 78, mother of the late famed Bing Crosby-style crooner, Russ Columbo; in Los Angeles. When Russ Columbo was killed in 1934 by the accidental discharge of an antique dueling pistol, his mother was too ill with heart trouble to be told of his death, soon after began losing her eyesight. For ten years the family kept Russ's death secret from her, explained he was having great success in England, read her affectionate weekly letters signed "Russ."

MARRIED: The Aga Khan, 67, melon-faced Mohammedan multimillionaire; and Yvette La Brousse, 38, "Miss France" of 1932; he for the fourth time; in Vevey, Switzerland.

MISCELLANY

ACCOMPANIST: In Springfield, Ill., Sheriff Walter Hagler listened carefully, then broke up a prisoners' quartet and took away the discordant saw with which one of the singers was cutting through the bars.

COPPED: In Los Angeles, Reporter Chick Felton arrived with the police at the scene of a murder, noted the corpse, sidled up to the victim's landlady, asked: "Can I rent this apartment?" Said she: "I already rented it to that police sergeant."

THE PRESS

UN-DIGEST-ED: The small, smart *New Yorker* (circ. 205,- FEB. 21 000) last week cast a stone at the famed, fabulously successful *Reader's Digest* (domestic circ. 8,000,000). The missile at once set up widening ripples in the U.S. publishing pond. The *New Yorker's* irascible, bristle-topped Editor Harold W. Ross sent a bristling letter to contributors, told them that the *New Yorker* would no longer allow the *Digest* to reprint any *New Yorker* material. Reasons:

"The *Digest* started out as a reprint magazine, but grew into something quite different. Nowadays a large proportion of its contents is frankly original with the *Digest* and not presented as reprint material; and of the stuff that is present- ed as reprint material, much actually originates in the office of the *Digest* and then gets farmed out to some other maga- zine for first publication.

"The effect of this (apart from spreading a lot of money around) is that the *Digest* is beginning to generate a con- siderable fraction of the contents of American magazines. This gives us the creeps, as does any centralization of Genius. We were willing to be digested, but we are not willing to be first supplied, then digested.

"The *New Yorker,* furthermore, has never been particu- larly impressed with the *Digest's* capsule theory of life and its assumption that any piece of writing can be improved by extracting every seventh word, like a tooth. We have occa- sionally been embarrassed to see our stuff after it has under- gone alterations.

"Mostly, however, we object to the *Digest's* indirect creative function, which is a threat to the free flow of ideas and to the independent spirit."

The *New Yorker's* departure was not a new experience for the *Digest*. The Curtis Publishing Co. (*Saturday Evening Post, Ladies' Home Journal, Country Gentleman*) had once dropped out, then returned. So had others.

JULY 3 **STORMY:** Captain Joseph M. Patterson's battery of headline writers for the huge New York *Daily News* took Cherbourg six times last week. Their banner communiqués:

Wednesday:
> STORM CHERBOURG,
> CITY ABLAZE

Thursday:
> YANKS HIT CHERBOURG
> IN FLAMING FINALE

Friday:
> YANKS STORM CHERBOURG
> FROM THREE SIDES

Saturday:
> YANK BAYONETS SLASH
> PATH INTO CHERBOURG

Sunday:
> YANKS STORM CHERBOURG'S
> LAST HEIGHTS

Monday:
> CHERBOURG IS OURS

JULY 17 **ERNIE PYLE'S WAR:** Ernie Pyle is well on his way toward becoming a living legend. Four years ago he was an obscure roving reporter whose syndicated column of trivial travelogues appeared in an unimpressive total of 40 newspapers. Aged 40, small and skinny (5 ft. 8 in., 155 lbs.), perpetually sick or worrying that he was about to be, agonizingly shy, he was completely lacking in the brash and dash of the Richard Harding Davis tradition. Neat in his habits, he hated dirt, disorder and discomfort. Above all, he hated and feared war. He stood in awe of professional war correspondents and firmly believed himself incompetent to become one.

Yet now, four years later, he is the most popular of them all. His column appears six days a week in 310 newspapers with a total circulation of 12,255,000. Millions of people at home read it avidly, write letters to him, pray for him, telephone their newspapers to ask about his health and safety. Abroad, G.I.s and generals recognize him wherever he goes, seek him out, confide in him. The War Department and the high command in the field, rating him a top morale-builder,

scan his column for hints. Fellow citizens and fellow newsmen have heaped honors on him.

What happened to Ernie Pyle was that the war suddenly
made the kind of unimportant small people and small things
he was accustomed to write about enormously important. As
John Steinbeck has explained it:

"There are really two wars and they haven't much to do
with each other. There is the war of maps and logistics, of
campaigns, of ballistics, armies, divisions and regiments—
and that is General Marshall's war.

"Then there is the war of homesick, weary, funny, violent,
common men who wash their socks in their helmets, com-
plain about the food, whistle at Arab girls, or any girls for
that matter, and lug themselves through as dirty a business
as the world has ever seen and do it with humor and dignity
and courage—and that is Ernie Pyle's war. He knows it as
well as anyone and writes about it better than anyone."

One reason that Ernie Pyle has been able to report this
little man's war so successfully is that he loves people and for
all his quirks and foibles is a very average little man himself.
He understands G.I. hopes and fears and gripes and duty-born
courage because he shares them as no exceptionally fearless
or exceptionally brilliant man ever could. But what chiefly
distinguishes him from other average men is the fact that he
is a seasoned, expert newsman. Ernie himself was a little slow
to recognize the nature of the new assignment. At first he
tried to be a more or less conventional war correspondent,
covering the news as others did. The change began one day
in Africa when the press corps was invited to meet Admiral
Darlan. Scripps-Howard cabled him to be sure to attend. He
was hurrying across an airfield to the interview when a swarm
of *Stukas* swooped down, began splattering bullets around
him. He dived into a ditch just behind a G.I. When the
strafing was over he tapped his companion on the shoulder
and said, "Whew, that was close, eh?" There was no answer.
The soldier was dead.

Pyle sat through the interview in a daze, went back to his
tent and brooded for hours. Finally he cabled his New York
office that he could not write the Darlan story. Instead he
wrote about the stranger who had died in the ditch beside
him. For days he talked of giving up and going home. But

when the shock wore off, he knew for sure that his job was not with the generals and their strategems but with the little onetime drugstore cowboys, clerks and mechanics who had no one else to tell their stories.

Last week, after a breather at a Normandy press camp in the rear, Ernie Pyle—who will be 44 on Aug. 3—was preparing to go up to the battle line again. He dreaded it more than ever. To a fellow correspondent he confided: "The thought of it gives me the willies. Instead of getting used to it, I become less used to it as the years go by. With me it seems to have had a cumulative effect. I am much more afraid of a plane overhead now than I was during the London blitz, or even during our early dive-bombing days in Africa. With those four narrow squeaks at Anzio [in one a bomb blew in two walls of a room where he was sleeping] coming after a year and a half of sporadic squeaks, I have begun to feel I have about used up my chances." [On April 18, 1945, on the tiny Pacific island of Ie Jima, Ernie Pyle was killed by a Japanese machine gun.]

AUG. 21 **TESTIMONIAL:** In the lower left corner of page 17 of the Cleveland *News* appeared a two-column patent medicine testimonial from a Mr. Alexander Kellough, of 2508 Morris Black Place, who rejoiced to find himself now rid of backache, insomnia, sour stomach and gas pains, and enthusiastically concluded:

"Giljan is a wonderful medicine. Any person with trouble such as mine should lose no time in taking it."

In column seven of the same page appeared a briefer notice:

"Kellough, Alexander, passed away at late residence, 2508 Morris Black Place, Wednesday morning."

NOV. 6 **GENUINE G.I.:** Sergeant George Baker's "Sad Sack" is a hilarious caricature. But Sergeant Bill Mauldin's weary, grimy, unshaven "Joe," the "Old Bill" of World War II, is by G.I. testimony grimly true to life. Quiet, baby-faced, 23-year-old Cartoonist Mauldin can draw the infantryman truthfully because he has been one himself since he was 18. He has fought and drawn his way through the campaign in Sicily, wears the Purple Heart for wounds received in Italy. "Joe" is beside, behind and ahead of him right now on the southern front in France.

Farm-born in New Mexico's Sacramento Mountains, Bill Mauldin started drawing when he was three. He left high school without graduating, went to Chicago, worked variously as a truck driver, dishwasher and menu designer to pay for his studies at the Art Institute of Chicago. He entered the Army in 1940.

"Joe" has kept pace with his creator in the process of becoming a soldier. From an average, homely rookie, surprised at being jolted out of his civilian rights, he has slowly hardened into the seemingly resigned, latently hopeful man he is. In battle his hatred for MPs has softened, because MPs also die.

"GOOD HEVVENS!": Military censors got a new kind of kick NOV. 20 in their chair-worn pinks. The kicker was the author of "Marmaduke's Colum (The Journal of a London Sub-Editor's Youthful Son)" which appears weekly in London's *World's Press News.* Fortnight ago Marmaduke tried to imagine what would happen if Alfred, Lord Tennyson had had to get his *Charge of the Light Brigade* cleared through the Censorship Division of the British Ministry of Information.

" 'Good hevvens!' a shocked officiel would cry. 'You can't mension the Light Brigade—it's not officielly released that they're out there at all yet. That'll have to come out.' (Slash.)"

" 'Half a league, half a league . . . good lord! This is serious. You must cut that, though you can say we made small advances in that sector.' (Slash.)"

" 'Into the valley of Death . . . no, no, no! You'll have to wait for the official communique before you mension where the fighting is takeing place. You could mension there was patrol activity in certain areas, but you're not allowed to state the actual place.' (Slash.)"

"And so," mused Marmaduke, "the epic peice would be wittled down to a few lines which dident even scan, and would be handed back to the noble poet with the embargo: 'Not for publication before 00.30 hours B.S.T.' And the noble poet would probely give up poetry alltogether and get a job writing hand-outs for the Ministry."

BOOKS

FEB. 21 **"A BELL FOR ADANO"**—John Hersey. This is a first novel. Angry and intense, it is half sharp-eyed, unsparing war reporting and half fast-moving, self-consciously hard-boiled fiction. It is the story of what happens behind the lines of a typical Italian town in the confused interlude between war and reconstruction—when the Germans have been driven out and the Allies have come in, when the fascists are out of office but the civilian governments have not yet been set up, and when the high aims for which the war was fought disappear before the realities of incompetence, brutality, red tape, swollen eyes, dead bodies, ruined buildings, ruined lives, cynicism, contempt, and the starved inertia of purposeless living.

The mood of *A Bell for Adano* is bitter. Its humor is raucous and wild. At its worst, it descends to college humorous magazine slapstick. At its best it is a superb piece of reporting.

FEB. 28 **"THE LOST WEEKEND"** by Charles Jackson is a world inhabited by only one soul, and that one damned. The story tells of five days in the life of Don Birnam, a clever coward who is drinking himself to death.

If Don Birnam were more purely tragic he would be Hamlet. What makes him such an Ancient Mariner for the unwilling but fascinated reader is that he epitomizes the quiet desperation that many an ordinary American occasionally feels in himself.

MARCH 20 **"STRANGE FRUIT"** by Lillian Smith is a story of racial conflict in a small Southern town (called Maxwell, Ga.), in which the dramatic action is the love affair of a white man and a Negro girl, the climax is his murder by her brother, and the end is a lynching.

The town of Maxwell in the windless heat of Georgia midsummer, with a revival meeting in full swing, with nice girls (white) also discovering they are pregnant, sins being sweatingly confessed while the old Methodist hymns roll out over the darkened houses, has the quality that explorers attribute to native villages in Africa. People are fever-stricken, enervated and blinded by headaches. And after the first unexpected actions that start them on the way to tragedy, Miss Smith's characters move less like struggling human beings than like prisoners on whom literary sentence has been passed, torpid, dazed, well-nigh speechless, and locked in the confines of her narrow plot like Georgia chain-gang prisoners.

"THE RAZOR'S EDGE"—W. Somerset Maugham, always a APRIL 24 discreet man, has been so imprudent as to live to a ripe age (70) when novelists are usually far past their prime. But, unlike some of his other books, *The Razor's Edge* is not a potboiler. Nor is it a mess of dotage. It deserves to rank after *Of Human Bondage* (1915) and *The Moon and Sixpence* (1919) as one of his three major novels.

Maugham disarmingly calls attention to the fact that he is making his first attempt to write a novel about Americans: "I don't think one can ever really know any but one's own countrymen. I do not pretend that the characters are American as Americans see themselves; they are American seen through an English eye."

"JOSEPH THE PROVIDER"—Last week Thomas Mann pub- JULY 3 lished the final volume of his major work. Few novelists in the history of literature have planned a work of such scope and significance, and made their plans come true.

Joseph the Provider finishes a masterpiece. It is a masterpiece in the way that Tolstoy's novels are—*i.e.,* it is deliberate, sustained, careful (often tiresomely so), rather than spontaneous and overflowing with its own imaginative energy. The final volume's 606 pages bring the epic of Joseph to its end (Bible version, 21 pages; Mann's version, 2,005 pages).

When the first volumes of the Joseph series were published, Novelist Willa Cather brilliantly characterized their "dreamy indefiniteness . . . the story has almost the movement of grazing sheep." The deliberateness, digression and slow tempo are more marked in *Joseph the Provider* than in the previous volumes. It is the most difficult reading of all the Joseph books.

SEPT. 25 **"THE LEANING TOWER AND OTHER STORIES"**—Katherine Anne Porter. Six of the nine short stories are crumbs from the cake of childhood—gentle, affectionate epitaphs for a dead world, which read more like a continuous record of nostalgic memories than like separate stories. They spring from the grass roots as clearly as their author does. Katherine Anne Porter has lived in most of the intelligentsia's favorite prewar haunts: Paris, Majorca, Berlin, Vienna and Mexico. But she was born in Texas and schooled in Louisiana convents.

Some readers may be more impressed by *The Leaning Tower*'s long (100 pages) title story, set in the Berlin of 1931, than by its vignettes of Texas. The elements of this story are a few dingy streets, a beerhouse, a room filled with "the winter day like dirty water," and five principal characters: a gawky young Texas artist; an aristocratic student from Heidelberg with a freshly gashed dueling scar on his cheek; a wolfish but pathetic landlady; a Polish pianist; a browbeaten, impecunious professor of mathematics. Out of these Author Porter has carefully built a somber, horrifying picture of a country on the verge of tragedy—a leaning tower ready to fall at the touch of a strong hand.

OCT. 23 **"FOREVER AMBER"**—Kathleen Winsor had always wanted to write something more impressive than the stuff she was

John Hersey. His "A Bell for Adano" is sharp-eyed, hard-boiled. Page 245.   *Kathleen Winsor. Her "Forever Amber" is sexy to excess.*

paid to write—football stories ("from the woman's point of view") for the Oakland, Calif. *Tribune*. Not long after her husband, Robert John Herwig, an All-America footballer, brought home a book on King Charles II, she decided to write a novel about the reign of Britain's gamiest monarch.

She began by reading some 400 books on the period (1660-1685), filled four fat notebooks with data, made scores of water-color sketches of period houses, furniture, costumes. The actual writing, which ran to six complete drafts for a total of nearly two and a half million words, took in a lot of territory; after her husband joined the Marines, Kathleen followed him from camp to camp, lugging her swelling manuscript. Finally, after five years' labor of love, she sent *Forever Amber* to Macmillan's.

The book will stagger most readers. It is not only bulky but sexy, and both to excess. A 971-page exploitation of the bawdiest phases of the bawdy Restoration, it weighs two pounds even. And every ounce sizzles—with seductions, abortions, childbirths, miscarriages, bedroom raptures. Its characters wallow in pox, perversion, impotence, pregnancy. For sheer voluptuousness, the book's heroine, honey-haired Courtesan Amber St. Clare, makes Scarlett O'Hara look like a schoolmarm.

MILESTONES

MARRIED: Army Air Forces Lieut. Thomas Dudley Harmon, 24, twice All-America Michigan halfback, twice reported lost on duty; and Hollywood starlet Elyse Knox, 26, dressed in a gown made from his bullet-riddled silk parachute; in Ann Arbor, Mich.

KILLED IN ACTION: Marine Corps Sergeant Peter Brook Saltonstall, 23, son of Massachusetts' Governor Leverett Saltonstall; while leading a patrol in the jungles of Guam.

MISCELLANY

MAN'S CASTLE: In Portland, Ore., Zoo Director Arthur Greenhall moved six alligators to a new tank at the Zoo, had his bathtub all to himself for the first time in ten months.

WRONG NIGHT: In Bryn Mawr, Pa., George Baird, returning from a party at 5 a.m., banged at the back door, was greeted with gunfire. Hospitalized, he learned that he had returned to the wrong house in the wrong town.

MEXICANA: In Mexico City, *Gráfico* reported that the Health Department was about to clamp down on "The Last Supper," a popular rat poison.

Numerals in italics indicate an illustration of subject mentioned.

PICTURE CREDITS

XX

PRODUCTION STAFF FOR TIME INCORPORATED
John L. Hallenbeck (Vice President and Director of Production),
Robert E. Foy and Caroline Ferri
Text photocomposed under the direction of Albert J. Dunn and Arthur J. Dunn

QUOTES OF THE YEAR

Comedian Bob Hope *(commenting on speculation that President Franklin Roosevelt would run for a fourth term—p. 11):* "I've always voted for Roosevelt as President. My father always voted for Roosevelt as President."

Senator Kenneth McKellar of Tennessee *(answering Columnist Drew Pearson, who had criticized him in print—p. 27):* "Pearson is an ignorant liar, a peewee liar, a congenital liar, a liar by profession, a liar in the daytime, a liar in the nighttime."

Harry S. Truman *(after being nominated for Vice President—p. 49):* "A statesman is only a dead politician. I never want to be a statesman."

The London Express *(after U.S. forces have captured the French port of Cherbourg—p. 81):* "Americans have proved themselves to be a race of great fighters."

General MacArthur *(on his return to the Philippines—p. 115):* "Rally to me. Let every arm be steeled. The guidance of Divine God points the way. Follow in His name to the Holy Grail of righteous victory."

H. G. Wells *(on fellow Englishman Winston Churchill—p. 152):* "His ideology is a pitiful jumble of nonsense. He has served his purpose and it is high time he be retired upon his laurels."

ANSWERS TO PICTURE QUIZ—1: General George C. Marshall, U.S. Army Chief of Staff; 2: Earl Warren, Governor of California; 3: Colonel Oveta Culp Hobby, Director of the WACs; 4: War Reporter Ernie Pyle; 5: Britain's King George VI; 6: Marshal Tito of Yugoslavia; 7: France's General Charles de Gaulle; 8: Comedian Jimmy Durante; 9: Presidential Candidate Thomas E. Dewey; 10: General Joseph Stilwell; 11: Argentina's Juan Perón; 12: Edward R. Stettinius, Secretary of State; 13: General Omar Bradley; 14: The city of Paris; 15: TV performers Edgar Bergen and Charlie McCarthy; 16: British Field Marshal Sir Bernard Montgomery.